CITYSCAPES OF VIOLENCE IN KARACHI

CW00820707

NICHOLA KHAN

(*Editor*)

Cityscapes of Violence in Karachi

Publics and Counterpublics

HURST & COMPANY, LONDON

First published in the United Kingdom in 2017 by
C. Hurst & Co. (Publishers) Ltd.,
41 Great Russell Street, London, WC1B 3PL
© Nichola Khan and the Contributors, 2017
All rights reserved.
Printed in India

A Cataloguing-in-Publication data record for this book
is available from the British Library.

ISBN: 9781849047265

This book is printed using paper from registered sustainable and managed sources.

www.hurstpublishers.com

CONTENTS

CONTENTS

LIST OF IMAGES

ACKNOWLEDGEMENTS

This book evolved out of a wish to formalise conversations that occur between academics, journalists, writers, and activists in Karachi, but which rarely populate the same pages. It juxtaposes some diverse perspectives in order to add complementarity and depth to the slow scholarship, rapid investigative ethnographies, and fierce and lyrical insights that such writers often provide. In seeking to provoke alternative ways of talking about violence, it is an edited volume with a certain agenda.

A book is an accumulation of relationships and indebtedness. I gratefully acknowledge the support, labour, and infinite patience of all the contributors to this project. I thank the World Sindhi Congress, especially Rubina Greenwood and Saghir Shaikh, for hosting me at their 2010 annual meeting in London. This conference was invaluable in enriching my appreciation of the international reach of Sindhi intellectuals and activists, and the manifold forms of violence facing Sindhis in Sindh. Amongst those others, not in these pages, who helped me refine my thinking I thank Naseer Dashti, Aamir Ghauri, Kadir Jatoi, Mahim Maher, Abbas Nasir, Raza Rumi, and my interlocutors in Karachi. I thank the *Dawn* newspaper for permission to print images. My thanks to Michael Dwyer at Hurst and Co. for taking on this project, and to Jon de Peyer for work on the production of the book. The School of Applied Social Science at the University of Brighton provided me time and resources to write, and my students unfailingly ignited questions about violence in the classroom. This book is not the outcome of any singular labour, or mere professional arrangement between editor and contributors, but of multi-authored collaboration,

ACKNOWLEDGEMENTS

long engagements, and conversations only partially reflected in its pages. Last, given my decisions, events in Karachi, and the erratic path that brought me to this wonderful, troubled city in the first place all affected those closest to me, my heartfelt thanks go to S, S, and H.

Nichola Khan   East Sussex, 28 October 2016

CONTRIBUTORS

Kamran Asdar Ali is Associate Professor of anthropology and the Director of the South Asia Institute at the University of Texas, Austin. He is also the serving President of the American Institute of Pakistan Studies. He has previously taught at the University of Rochester and has been a member of the Institute for Advanced Study at Princeton, a senior fellow at the Institute for the Study of Islam in the Modern World (ISIM) in Leiden, The Netherlands, and a fellow at the Wissenschaftskolleg at Berlin. He has published several articles on issues of health and gender in Egypt and on urban issues, labour history, gender, and popular culture in Pakistan. He is the author of *Planning the Family in Egypt: New Bodies, New Selves* (UT Press, 2002) and the co-editor of *Gendering Urban Space in the Middle East, South Asia, and Africa* (Palgrave, 2008) and *Comparing Cities: Middle East and South Asia* (OUP, 2009). His co-edited volume *Gender, Politics, and Performance in South Asia* was published recently (OUP, 2015) as was his book, *Communism in Pakistan: Politics and Class Activism 1947–1972* (IB Tauris, 2015).

Asif Aslam Farrukhi is a fiction-writer, critic, and translator. For his distinguished work, he was awarded the Prime Minister's Literary Award by the Pakistan Academy of Letters in 1997, and the Tamgha-i-Imtiaz by the Government of Pakistan. A public health physician by training, he was educated at the Dow Medical College, Karachi and Harvard University. Known for short stories and essays, he has published seven collections of short fiction, two collections of critical essays, and translations of prose and poetry from modern and classical writers. His publications include a collection of new critical essays on

Manto and *Look At The City From Here*, an anthology of writings about Karachi, published by Oxford University Press. Asif Farrukhi contributes regularly to the English-language press. Two of his adaptations have been staged in Karachi. He is the editor of *Duniyazad*, a literary journal of new writing and contemporary issues in Urdu. Asif Farrukhi has presented papers and participated in literary events at home as well as abroad. He is a founder member of the Karachi Literary Festival. Asif Farrukhi lives and writes in Karachi.

Laurent Gayer earned his PhD in political science from Sciences Po in Paris in 2004. He specialises in the Indian sub-continent, and more particularly the study of urban dynamics and violent mobilisations in India and Pakistan. Through his research on the violent transformation of South Asian cities, he also became interested in the role of poetry in the manufacturing of consensus and dissent among South Asian Muslims. Laurent taught at Sciences Po (1999–2002) and INALCO (2003–2005) before joining the Centre Universitaire de Recherches sur l'Action Publique et le politique (CURAPP) in Amiens in 2008, and the New Delhi based Centre de Sciences Humaine (CSH), and then the Center for International Studies and Research (CERI) in Paris in 2013. His book *Karachi. Ordered Disorder and the Struggle for the City* was published by Hurst (London), HarperCollins (Delhi), and Oxford University Press (New York and Karachi) in 2014.

Arif Hasan is a Pakistani architect, planner, teacher, social researcher, and writer. He is a recipient of Hilal-i-Imtiaz, the country's highest award for its citizens. Since 1982 he has been involved with the Orangi Pilot Project, a non-governmental organisation which works to provide low-cost housing, sanitation, healthcare, and microfinance in Karachi. In 1989, he founded the Urban Resource Centre (URC). He is the author of many articles and books including *Participatory Development* (2010, OUP), *The Unplanned Revolution* (2002, Oxford University Press), *Understanding Karachi* (2000, City Press), *Planning and Development Options for Karachi* (2009, Sheher Saaz), *Hijrat Aur Pakistan Mein Chotey Shehr* (2009, Ushba Publishing International, with Raza Mansoor), and *The Hawkers of Saddar Bazaar* (2008, Ushba Publishing International, with Asiya Sadiq Polak and Christophe Polak).

CONTRIBUTORS

Kausar S. Khan is an activist for women's rights, and minorities and disenfranchised groups vulnerable to violence in Pakistan. Trained in philosophy, she became a development worker, then subsequently joined the department of Community Health Sciences at Aga Khan University, Karachi where she is an Associate Professor and Head of the Division of Behavioural and Social Sciences. Her research encompasses primary healthcare and health systems, gender, rights, equity, structural political and gender-based violence, civil society movements, participation and participatory approaches, bioethics, nutrition, and the structural determinants of health and rights in urban and rural poor settings. She is a regular contributor to the Karachi press, and to academic journals. She is on the board of several Karachi based non-governmental organisations. These include the Institute of Development Studies and Practice (IDSP), the Health Education and Literacy Program (HELP), Shirkat Gah, and the Omar Asghar Khan Foundation. She is a founding member of the Karachi-based Women's Action Forum (WAF).

Nichola Khan is a social anthropologist and Principal Lecturer in the School of Applied Social Science at the University of Brighton, UK. She completed her PhD at the University of Sussex in 2008. She has published a number of articles on violence, war, and migration drawing on fieldwork in Karachi. She is the author of *Mohajir Militancy in Pakistan* (2010, paperback edition 2012, Routledge). Her subsequent research and publications analyse migration, mobilities, transnational labour, and kinship networks amongst Afghan migrants in the UK, Peshawar, and Afghanistan. She is also a Chartered Psychologist and the author of *Mental Disorder: Anthropological Insights* (2017, University of Toronto Press).

Nida Kirmani is Assistant Professor of sociology in the School of Humanities and Social Sciences at the Lahore University of Management Sciences. She has published widely on issues related to gender, Islam, women's movements, development, and urban studies in South Asia. Her book, *Questioning 'the Muslim Woman': Identity and Insecurity in an Urban Indian Locality*, was published in 2013 by Routledge. Her current research focuses on urban violence, gender, and insecurity in Karachi.

CONTRIBUTORS

Nadeem F. Paracha is a cultural critic, satirist, and columnist with Pakistan's largest English-language daily, *Dawn*. Born and educated in Karachi, he was active as a student leader against the dictatorship of General Zia-ul-Haq in the 1980s before becoming a journalist in 1991. He has written extensively on the political dynamics of the media and popular culture in Pakistan, and the rise of religious conservatism amongst the nation's urban middle classes. Apart from being one of the most read English columnists in Pakistan, he enjoys a large readership in India, and among the South Asian diaspora in Europe and the United States.

Zia Ur Rehman is a journalist and development researcher whose work primarily focuses on issues of conflict, human rights, and democratic development in Pakistan. He has published in several international and national publications, including the *New York Times*, Central Asia Online, *The Friday Times*, *CTC Sentinel*, *Terrorism Monitor*, *The News*, *Herald*, *The National* and *Pique*. He has worked with various research and development organisations including the Open Society Foundation, Amnesty International, the Sustainable Development Policy Institute, and the Labour Education Foundation. In 2013 he published a book entitled *Karachi in Turmoil* (Narratives Press).

Razeshta Sethna is a journalist who has worked with the Dawn Media Group. She was senior assistant editor at *The Herald* (2010–14). She has anchored current affairs for Dawn News Television and Geo Television and interviewed world leaders, including Pervez Musharraf and Benazir Bhutto. She writes on democracy, violations against women, children and minorities, human rights, culture, media freedoms and terrorism. She was a Thomas Reuters Fellow (2015) at the Reuters Institute for the Study of Journalism (University of Oxford), Chevening South Asia Journalism Fellow (2013) at the University of Westminster, and was awarded the first Women in Media Awards by the Uks Research Centre and the All Pakistan Newspaper Society Award (APNS) in 2013.

Farzana Shaikh is an Associate Fellow of the Asia Programme and Co-convenor of the Pakistan Study Group at the Royal Institute of International Affairs, Chatham House, in London. She is a specialist on Pakistan and the regional politics of South Asia. Born in Pakistan, she has a PhD from Columbia University, New York and is a former research fellow of Clare Hall, University of Cambridge. Her work has been published widely on Pakistan and South Asian Islam and she has held university lectureships in the UK, the US, and Europe. She has been a visitor at the Institute for Advanced Study in Princeton, and in 2013 was elected to a fellowship at the Institut d'Etudes Avancées in Paris. She is a frequent commentator at international events on Pakistan and has testified to the House of Commons Foreign Affairs Committee. Her book *Making Sense of Pakistan*, published in 2009 by Hurst (London), was selected by the *Guardian* as one of four 'essential books' for Prime Minister Cameron's government. Her current project explores the relationship between the state and the language of Sufi Islam in Pakistan.

Oskar Verkaaik is an Associate Professor of anthropology at the University of Amsterdam. He has worked on Mohajir politics and political identity in both Karachi and Hyderabad. Apart from a large number of articles and book chapters on politics and violence in urban Sindh, he has published a monograph on the Mohajir Qaumi Movement, entitled *Migrants and Militants: 'Fun' and Urban Violence in Pakistan* (2004, Princeton University Press). He has also co-edited (with Thomas Blom Hansen) a special issue of *Critique of Anthropology* on urban ethnography in South Asia and Southern Africa (2009). He currently works on a research project on contemporary religious architecture, including mosques, synagogues, and churches.

PREFACE

A TRANSFORMED LANDSCAPE

Nichola Khan

We might begin with the Indus, Darya Shah, or 'Syndhu' which runs through Sindh and meets the Arabian Sea near Karachi (Khan 2010b). Enfolding the diverse languages, religions, and cultures of those who peopled the Indus Valley, its appellations are as eclectic—'Darya Shah' (Great River), 'Plurali' (capricious wanderer), 'Samander' (Ocean), 'Nilab' (blue water), 'Sher Darya' (Lion River), and 'Abbasin' (Father of Rivers) (Albinia 2009). The British East India Company acknowledged ambitions for the Indus in the early seventeenth century. Although the British eventually commanded great swathes of India, Sindh eluded them. Finally, in 1843 Charles Napier, conqueror and first Governor of Sind, dispatched the apocryphal message in Latin—'*Peccavi*': 'I have Sind (sinned)'.

West of the Indus Delta lies Karachi, whose appellations have included Krokola, Kolachi, Koratchey, Kurrachee, Currachee, Crotchey, Krotchey Bay, and Karáchí (Baillie 1890). Under Napier, Kurrachee leapt from a 'miserable native fortress into a civil town of considerable size' (Ibid.), forcing the ancient capital Hydrabād to abdicate. Kurrachee grew from a sleepy town of around 8,000 in 1839 to a world leading port and trading centre for fruit and vegetables by the late nineteenth century, to its present status as a megacity housing over 23 million. By Independence, the city's growth had outpaced the ability of civil amenities to cope. The Indus Delta dried out, and became flooded with industrial and household waste and raw sewage. Ever since, Karachi's fermenting waterways have been a conduit for the violent confrontation of communities, not around foreign colonials and invaders, but around internal grievances of immigration, urbanisation, language, ethnicity, and confession.

During the 1947 British Partition of India up to half a million people died and fourteen million were displaced in two directions. Between 1.6 and 2 million Muslim refugees arrived in Sindh. Census data record Karachi's exponential growth from around 450,000 in 1947 to 1.137 million in 1951; the promise of economic opportunity led to perceptions of an 'immigration explosion' (Malik 1997, 201); Karachi's Hindu population dropped from 96 to 2 per cent in ten years. Massive internal migration to Karachi followed. Pashtun migrants opened 'hotels', worked in transport or as military men and police; Balochis worked as dockworkers, shipbreakers, gravediggers, and in the tanneries and salt works (Hasan 2005). During the 1971 Bangladesh Independence war around half a million East Bengal Biharis migrated to Pakistan, and 'back-door' Bihari migration continued into the 1980s.

The migrants transformed Karachi's geography. Hasan (2005, 131–2) describes how many migrants settled along the Lyari River running North to South through Karachi. Most Indian migrants settled properties vacated by around a million Sikhs and Hindus, and occupied much available open land. In the 1950s, Punjabi migrants who provided transport for port cargo settled near these areas. In the 1960s displaced communities from the North-West Frontier Province (NWFP) settled Tarbela Colony on the river. From 1980 to 1995, Pashtuns, Hazrawals and Afghans flooded the *katchi abadis* (squatter settlements), settling in Sorabh Goth or 'workers' colonies' in Orangi or Lyari. The 1998 census records more Balochis residing in Karachi than Balochistan, more Pashtuns than in Peshawar, and only 9 per cent Sindhis. Political affiliations followed suit. Baloch communities voted for the Pakistan People's Party (PPP) and Baloch nationalist parties.

Pashtuns supported the Awami National Party (ANP), and before the emergence of the MQM Mohajir (and Punjabi) communities supported the Jamaat e Islami (JI), Jamiat-ul-Ulema-i-Islam (JUI), Jamiat-i-Ulema-i-Pakistan (JUP), and Pakistan Muslim League (PML).

The 1940s and 1950s consolidated the Mohajirs as an elite, and officialised Urdu as the national language, precipitating fatal violence over refugee issues (Ansari 2005). In 1948 Karachi was declared the federal capital. Sindhi nationalism, which had campaigned for Sindh's separation from the British Bombay Presidency, claimed a 'cultural genocide', and resurrected anti-British slogans such as '*murvesoon, Sindh na desoon*' (we will die but not give up Sindh) (Ahmed 1999, 65). Sindh's separation from Karachi was expressed in a unique connection to the 'soil'—as in the saying a Sindhi might utter to a Mohajir: 'My ancestors' graves are in Khairo Daro, yours are in Uttar Pradesh'. The 1955 One Unit bill brought Karachi under central government control. When Pakistan's first military ruler Ayub Khan (1958–65) moved the capital from Karachi to Islamabad in 1959, the Sindhis became increasingly antagonistic towards the Urdu-speaking 'refugees' who, in turn, began identifying as 'Mohajirs'. They stressed the precepts of migration and homeland within a *hijra* paradigm and their ancestry in the *ashraf*, the ruling aristocracy of Imperial Muslim India.

Prime Minister Zulfiqar Ali Bhutto (1973–77) replaced the Mohajirs in national institutions, transforming the Punjabis into a majority, and elevated Sindhi to a provincial language. Emboldened, the Sindhis furiously advocated for Sindh's secession, a separate Sindhudesh, and the expulsion of non-Sindhis from Sindhi land. Bhutto's 1973 quota system caused Mohajirs losses of position. In 1979 General Zia-ul-Haq staged a military coup, and executed Bhutto, a Sindhi, the same year. Zia instrumentalised Islam as a tool of political legitimacy, spearheaded in Sindh by JI, JUI and JUP, and promoted Pak-US alliances in the Soviet-Afghan War (1979–89). Opposition to Zia mounted. In 1983 a protest by the multi-party Movement for Restoration of Democracy in rural Sindh was brutally suppressed.

The opening up of political space that preceded the end of martial law in 1985 ignited student conflicts on Karachi's campuses. In 1984 Altaf Hussain formed the Mohajir Qaumi Movement (MQM) (the Muttahida Quami Movement after 1998) to achieve Mohajir rights and

PREFACE

recognition. Following a meteoric rise, in the first post-Zia elections of 1988 the MQM formed a coalition government with the PPP. Mohajir-Sindhi confrontations in Sindh soon followed (Verkaaik 2004). Mohajir grievances consolidated around unemployment, refugees from Afghanistan, and Pashtun incursions into Karachi's narcotics, weapons, land, and transport economies. This narrative virtually effaces the hardships Karachi's working-class Pashtuns faced, the unforgiving exploitation of young Pashtun men in Karachi's transport sector, and their sacrifices for the city. It is challenged by Kamran Asdar Ali who points out that the lives of many transport workers resembled the lumpen of Marxian dimensions: navigating pot-holed roads, corrupt traffic police, pollution, and Karachi's immense crowds for up to eighteen hours each day, they slept in their minivans or buses, or in make-shift hostels in unhygienic conditions in order to meet the demands of fixed rents levied on their vehicles (2012).

The eventual catalyst for Mohajir-Pashtun violence was the accidental killing of Bushra Zaidi, a Mohajir girl travelling to attend Sir Syed College in Liaquatabad in April 1985, by a Pashtun truck driver racing another driver in the busy commercial area of Orangi. Angry student protests met with brutal police repression. The following morning Pashtuns, mobilised by transport owners, attacked a Bihari settlement in West Karachi. Scores of deaths ensued. In 1986 further Mohajir-Pashtun rioting transmuted into ferocious violence, described as 'both in scale and sheer brutality, unprecedented since the partition of the subcontinent' (Hussain 1990, 105).

The MQM subsequently attempted to force their demands in a total 'war' (*jang*) against the state. Violence became integrally bound up with political processes. Deadly confrontations between the MQM, Pashtuns, all ethnic parties, and the state ensued, in parallel with landslide electoral victories for the MQM in Sindh in all the elections of 1988, 1990, 1993, and 1997. The state conducted military operations against the MQM in 1986, 1990, 1992, 1995, and 1998. Thousands of Mohajirs were displaced, MQM workers 'disappeared' from state custody, and death sentences were enforced. Altaf Hussain fled to London in 1992 and claimed asylum, joined by prominent MQM figures and many workers. After 1992, the MQM split into two factions. The violence intensified. The MQM's organised tactics of extortion, strikes, and shutdowns severely impacted Karachi's economy. Violence worked. For communities the MQM offered security and protection, including from Karachi's politicised, corrupt and violent police force. Local militants gained power and local respect (Khan 2010a).

In 2002 the MQM assumed office in provincial government. By 2005 Karachi newspapers were accusing the MQM of eliminating opponents with impunity. In 2006 and 2008 the MQM was elected to city government amidst the violent, unchecked expansion of land and real estate development. After the deregulation of the economy in 2004, 'entrepreneurs' speculated in illegally or violently occupied land and real estate driven by major, questionable land-use conversions, and powerful political patrons (Hasan 2015)—interests blamed for the devastating burning of Karachi's historic Bolton Market in 2009 (Hasan 2010) and the murder of the Orangi Pilot Project Director Perween Rehman in 2013.

These intense struggles over the urban economy, unchecked by the authoritarian military state, culminated on 12 May 2007. A multi-party demonstration protesting against President Musharraf's autocratic rule, exemplified by his dismissal of Chief Justice Iftikhar Mohammed Chaudhry, clashed fatally with a MQM-organised pro-government rally, resulting in around fifty killings at sites of the 1980s Mohajir-Pashtun riots. Violence surrounding the 2008 general elections led to the imposition of emergency rule in November 2007. Benazir Bhutto was assassinated in Karachi in December, and Musharraf resigned as Chief of Army Staff. 2008 and 2009 saw the Pakistani army engaged against the Pakistani Taliban in the Federally Administered Tribal Areas (FATA) while the US conducted drone attacks along the border with Afghanistan. This resulted in massive civilian displacements, support for Taliban alliances across FATA and NWFP, and deep incursions of radical Islamist groups into Karachi's Pashtun settlements. As a consequence of the safe haven Karachi provided many fighters, the Pakistan Taliban's power expanded. In summer 2010, deadly violence re-erupted between Mohajirs and Pashtuns, the two key groups involved in land development. Escalating factional violence gave way to the Taliban's rising power.

In September 2010 the MQM founder Imran Farooq was murdered in London. Speculation circulated about an intended leadership bid.

Farooq's murder followed the monsoon rains, when the Indus burst its banks the length of the country (Khan 2010b). According to Pakistan's National Disaster Management Authority, the 2010 floods constituted the worst natural disaster in the country's history, and the worst global humanitarian disaster in a decade, with 12 million in need of urgent humanitarian assistance, 6 million homeless, and 7 million affected people in Sindh. The perceived 'profitability' of the floods for provincial governments was mooted by angry citizens as a reason for the delay in the humanitarian response.

The situation further intensified during the PPP government of 2008–13, when the People's Aman Committee (PAC) was founded in Lyari in 2008 by Rehman Dakait. The Baloch 'bandits' led by Dakait became involved in gang wars, and bitter conflicts with the MQM, PPP, and Taliban groups around the lucrative profits available from organised crime. Shifts in power now meant that protection racketeering remained the province of the MQM's *bhatta-khori* system, kidnapping for ransom that of the Taliban, and drug trafficking the PAC's specialty. Dakait was killed in 2009 and succeeded by his cousin Uzair Jan Baloch. Spiralling gang wars led the Sindh government to ban the PAC in 2011. This was largely ineffective in curbing violence, but led Uzair Baloch to turn against PPP politicians. In 2012 PM Gilani started Operation Lyari to destroy the gangs. The operation continued into 2015.

The May 2013 general elections returned Nawaz Sharif as PM. In Karachi the Pakistan Tehreek e Taliban (TTP) claimed responsibility for bomb-blasts. MQM workers threatened voters, intimidated polling officers, and attacked other parties' offices. After Zahra Shahid, a senior member of Imran Khan's Pakistan Tehreek-e-Insaf (PTI) party was killed, Imran Khan accused Altaf Hussain of ordering her murder, and the UK government of harbouring him. Whilst the PTI make significant inroads, the MQM commanded a mandate. This pattern of voting according to ethnic and provincial loyalties was echoed countrywide.

By 2014 the ground was shifting. After a Taliban attack on Karachi airport, the army launched operation 'Zarb e Azb' against the Taliban in Karachi, and received special powers to try 'terrorists', a move towards 'soft' martial law. On Independence Day, 14 August, Imran Khan organised a sit-in outside parliament in Islamabad, accusing PM Sharif of election rigging. Khan won popularity with the army whose General, Pervez Musharraf, was under house arrest pending trial for the 1999 military coup in which he ousted Sharif. Meanwhile, in the Karachi operation dozens of MQM workers were also killed, actions not unfavourable to the PTI's ambitions.

In developments viewed as a barometer for the MQM's demise, in March 2015 state security forces raided the MQM headquarters, one day after the MQM committed to the (anti-army) PPP in the upcoming Senate election. That day, Saulat Mirza, imprisoned since 1999 for killing the Karachi Electric Supply Corporation (KESC) chief Shahid Hamid, received notice he would hang. At the twelfth hour, Mirza broadcast a video from prison stating he had killed on direct orders from MQM chiefs, with the extraordinary outcome that the Federal Government postponed his hanging. A furore ensued concerning the media acting in place of the judiciary, and the processes which could turn a murderer into a national hero. The eye-witness testimony that convicted Mirza was subsequently cast into doubt. Meanwhile operations intensified alongside a by-election for the Nine-Zero constituency, home to the headquarters of the MQM. MQM supporters rallied. Alongside wider concerns about Altaf Hussain's health and the future of the party's command, irrevocable transformations in Pakistan's most multi-ethnic, politically diverse city meant Hussain's power was undeniably dented. These developments show us cities are far from totalising or impervious, but highly dynamic spaces—and changes in political consciousness may be imagined from within even the most intractable political impasses. 2015 closed with a landslide victory for the MQM in Karachi's local elections, and a mandate to appoint the city's next mayor. 2016 brought new speculation around a leadership bid and the bizarre spectacle of Rangers visibly engaging in politics by removing posters of Altaf Hussain across the city, and replacing them with those of the former mayor, Mustafa Kamal. Last, decisive events at the end of August led the MQM leadership in Karachi, fronted by Farooq Sattar, to publicly disavow Hussain and the UK branch. With the future of Karachi's Urdu-speaking politics arguably more uncertain than ever, this seems as good a moment as any to begin.

References

Albinia, Alice, *Empires of the Indus*, London: John Murray, 2009.
Asdar Ali, Kamran, 'Women, Work and Public Spaces: Conflict and

PREFACE

Co-existence in Karachi's poor neighborhoods', *International Journal of Urban and Regional Research*, May (2012), pp. 585–605.

Baillie, Alexander, *Kurrachee, Past, Present and Future*, Rarebooksclub.com, 2013 (1839).

Hasan, Arif, 'The political and institutional blockages to good governance: the case of the Lyari Expressway in Karachi', *Environment and Urbanisation*, 2, 2005, pp. 127–141.

Hasan, Arif, 'Land and the Politics of Ethnicity,' *Dawn*, Karachi, 16 June, 2010.

Hasan, Arif, Karachi: *The Land Issue*, Karachi: Oxford University Press, 2015.

Hussain, Akmal, 'The Karachi riots of December 1986: crisis of state and civil society in Pakistan', in Das, Veena (ed.), *Mirrors of Violence. Communities, Riots and Survivors in South Asia*, New Delhi, Oxford University Press, 1990, pp. 185–93.

Khan, Nichola a, *Mohajir Militancy in Pakistan. Violence and Practices of Transformation in the Karachi Conflict*, London and New York: Routledge 2010.

Khan, Nichola b, '*Naturalising Politics; Politicising Nature: Ethnicity, Violence and the Indus in Sindh*'. Keynote Address, 22nd Annual Conference of World Sindhi Congress, London, 9 October, 2010.

Verkaaik, Oskar, *Migrants and Militants. 'Fun' and Urban Violence in Pakistan*, Princeton: Princeton University Press, 2004.

INTRODUCTION

Nichola Khan

Why Karachi? Karachi is Pakistan's largest city, its commercial centre, and former capital. Colloquially named 'City of Lights' during the 1960s for its vibrant cosmopolitan nightlife, Karachi also houses Pakistan's largest and oldest stock exchange, many public and private universities, medical and research institutions, a world-class cricket stadium, hundreds of bazaars, and the headquarters of most of Pakistan's national television and media channels. Located on the Arabian Sea, the city is a major fisheries nucleus, accommodates Pakistan's largest bridge, and has picturesque beaches at Seaview, Paradise Point, Manora Island, Sandspit, and Hawke's Bay. The architecture of its historic palaces and old quarters evoke the city's rich Indian past, the British colonial administration, and the European styles of Art Nouveau and the Belle Époque. Karachi's shipping ports and major international airport are vital to its status as Pakistan's financial capital, and the nerve centre for Pakistan's banking and financial services.

With a population of over 23 million Karachi is also the world's largest Muslim city, the world's seventh largest conurbation, the third largest city in the world by population within city limits, and it is projected to become the world's largest city by 2030 (World Population

1

Review 2015). Studies by the McKinsey Institute, the World Bank, Mercer and PricewaterhouseCoopers *inter alia* calculate that Karachi contributes around 25 per cent of Pakistan's total GDP—$78 billion in 2009, with projections of around $193 billion in 2025. The city's economy comprises 90 per cent of Pakistan's international trade, 30 per cent of its manufacturing sector, and the largest share of national tax revenues. After 2005, Karachi's city mayor Mustafa Kamal inaugurated many development, transport and recreational projects, parks and gardens, seeking to transform Karachi into a global city proudly 'owned' by its citizens. This beatific image of the harmonisation of tradition and modernity amidst flourishing economic growth is conspicuously misleading. Karachi also holds the dubious title of the 'world's most dangerous city' (Gayer 2014, 4). Beneath the surface of the sparkling city 'that never sleeps' also lurk the nervous currents of an 'insomniac metropolis' (Paracha 2013), and anxieties around uncontrolled expansion. City life more commonly pulsates with frustrations around air pollution, chronic traffic problems, extreme wealth inequality, housing and water shortages, prolonged power cuts, unmitigated heat, waste and sanitation problems, a lumbering antiquated state bureaucracy, the reckless destruction of heritage, legal and illegal real estate expansion, the unbridled arrogation of multiplex opportunities for bribery, corruption and illegality, and the intrusive patina of fear. These examples undoubtedly describe assorted scenes of violence.

More commonly associated with Pakistan are forms of violence which describe a well-rehearsed narrative of political events beginning with the bloody scenes of Partition in 1947. The success of Mohammed Ali Jinnah in negotiating Independence for a new Islamic republic resulted in the arrival of almost 2 million migrants from India, and violent upheavals related to demographic destabilisation and refugee settlement in Karachi. Pakistan subsequently faced decades of military rule, three wars with India, contentious problems of internal independence and secession movements, a militarised nexus of radical Islamism and external interference, and crossfire from international wars.

The dominant interpretive framework for understanding politics and violence in Pakistan has historically largely been situated in the neo-Marxist tradition, which prioritises crises of state power in the ethnic fragmentation of civil society. Theorists in this tradition are Ayesha Jalal,

Hamza Alavi, Feroz Ahmed, Tariq Rahman, Tariq Ali, amongst others. Detailed historiograpical works by Sarah Ansari and Iftikhar Malik inter *alia* have enriched these explanations. This approach emphasises Pakistan's longstanding failures in democratic political legitimacy, the military as the ultimate arbiter of political power, the plundering of state resources by those in power, and the collapse of the taxation system. Powerful syncretic forms of ethnic class protest emerge from the state's failure to accommodate provincial interests, grant civil rights, and remedy class divisions. Further, dependence on US aid and foreign capital contribute to the militarisation of domestic affairs, and clientelism and elitism at the state level. Siddiqua additionally singles out powerful business interests run by Pakistan's military personnel (2007). These perpetuate a predatory style deriving from a feudal, authoritarian, non-democratic, political system which allows the military to nourish a symbiotic relationship with political power, create strong patron-client relationships, and a state apparatus that perpetuates inequity, and dependent, authoritarian social systems (Ibid., pp.1–4).

Taking a different approach, Farzana Shaikh views Pakistan's problems with military dictatorships, its relations with India, economic development, ethnic fragmentation, regionalism, foreign policies, and the military's financial support from external powers not as 'causes' of the nation's fragility, but 'symptoms of the underlying uncertainty about its identity' stemming from the lack of consensus over Islam and state-nationalism (2009, 9). She locates the roots of Pakistani state-militarism and its alliance with the US as a 'strategic partner' in a quest for military parity with India not in national security interests, but in a national identity-crisis born out of the pre-Independence origins of opposition, not to British colonial rule but to the Indian nationalist movement—and the legacy of a dis-unified Pakistani identity as 'not India' (180). The unreliability of Pakistan's political system paradoxically renders the army's presence more necessary, leading it to simultaneously cause and solve crises. In this situation, both ethno-nationalist and Islamist movements flourish. For Shaikh, Pakistan's troubled relationship between Islam and nationalism is its most salient source of ideological and violent conflict (2). She criticises the argument that the state's 'dsyfunctionality' originates in contestations around multiple interests that describe an 'enduring problem to be solved' (3). Instead, we should take 'the prism of Pakistan's fragile identity' as a positive way to deconstruct the history of disjunctural interests that have 'unified' so uneasily around a singular interpretation of shared religion and national identity—and strengthen consensus and stability around the value of pluralism (13). Similarly critical of evaluations of Pakistan in crisis is Naveeda Khan, who proposes we should examine instead what seems undeserving of urgent reporting (2012, 1). Herein we can find a sense of belongingness (what Shaikh calls identity) premised not on any common sense of origin, language or territory, but on a shared feeling of alienation, and acts of disclaiming the nation (1). Similar such attempts to upturn dominant narratives (or analytic tendencies to look in the 'wrong place') mark several of the chapters that follow.

These national political events and crises are inevitably and idiosyncratically textured within progressive decades of escalating violence in Karachi. Enfolding the ethnicised, criminalised, urban geography of lethal politics, Karachi furls circuitously on the dynamics and drivers of its own violent axis. Far from the image of Pakistan's megacity serene in the process of beautification, the city appears caught in a veritable maelstrom. Unfolding a different cartography of collective vantage-points on violence and Karachi is the purpose of this book.

The project

While perennial global, national, and city crises precipitate new waves of violence in Karachi, these have occurred alongside an increase in critical voices and commentary, and a greater willingness on the part of publishers to take on the controversies these phenomena entail. This collection brings into conversation some prominent figures, each of whom has been engaged with issues related to violence in Karachi for at least a decade, some for much longer. The approach is experimental insofar as it combines in one volume the diverse specialist insights, generated over time, of key academics, publishers, journalists, activists, and writers. Therefore it differs from the usual academic 'study' of a 'type' of violence, group, or political party in the city. A second key focus of the book is one of personal and professional engagement, and thinking through the ways each dimension has informed the other. Hence, it comprises a collection of reflective essays that captures the contributors' mix of specialisms in a focus that is analytical rather than scholarly, and that can appeal to a wide readership. Third, the book brings these aspects to a public engagement focus which encourages a shift outwards from the purely academic realm towards the creation of wider publics and counterpublics engaged in cultural and political commentary, and collective collaborations for change.

Unpacking Karachi's violence encompasses a wide brief. The authors in these pages combine academic contributions, creative non-fiction, literary works, journalistic analyses, social movement texts, and auto-ethnographies. They investigate the structural, political-economic, cultural, and geographic shaping of Karachi's violence, and make comparative, synchronic, and diachronic connections in their particular case studies, biographical analyses, studies of particular localities, and analyses of the city as a whole. The subject span covers many diverse topics. These include the contingency of institutional power entanglements on militarism and state violence; narratives of Partition; migration and settlement; environmental displacement and land and water politics; cultures of relocation, indigenous societies, and multiethnic and cosmopolitan communities; student movements; gender politics and sexual violence; representations of violence in media, film, and literature; the impact of violence on communities, especially the socially marginalised; political and peace activism within communities; the ways violence shapes subjectivity and selfhood; and instances of the silenced 'Other' within the postcolonial nation-state.

The book's focus on violence and Karachi implies neither that violence is an all-subsuming condition, nor that practical and analytic opportunities for peace cannot emerge. Instead, its multi-dimensional approach is designed, at least initially, to provoke questions concerning taken-for-granted assumptions about approach and definition. The anthropologists Scheper-Hughes and Bourgois (2004, 1) argue for analysing a 'continuum' of multiple interrelated kinds of violence, and for blurring distinctions between categories of violence in war and peace. Correspondingly, this book eschews critiques that conceptualise types of violence (political, institutional, criminal, domestic, gendered, interpersonal etc.) as paradigmatically distinctive. It recognises the interplay of structural and symbolic violence (Bourdieu 1977, 192) inherent in the institutional legacy of colonialism, the fearful instability of Karachi's violent urban geography, the disdain in the city's elite enclaves for the city's poor, peripheralised, and marginalised, in the invisible desperation of people's struggles for daily survival, their shortened life-spans, social exclusion, the city's corrupt and ineffective police force and judiciary, and the mundane refractions of everyday racism. Whilst violence is produced in the micro-exchanges of everyday life, at the other extreme of the 'continuum' individuals and groups assault, mutilate, torture, and kill without compunction, and with regularity. Drawing false distinctions between peace and conflict and 'political' and 'everyday' violence may be a typical artefact of political engineering or policy-making, but this book begins with the premise that is an error nonetheless.

Accordingly, the topic also involves a consideration of the ethics of researching and reporting on violence. These contributing authors, and many others, enjoy frontline access to public audiences. Therefore they occupy a unique position to critique, trouble, or resist the political establishment and the capital forces that allow violence to flourish. As writers they must navigate paths through highly sensitive and politicised contexts, and positionings between analysis and activism, distance and proximity, voice and silence, and security and endangerment. These questions about position concern the ways research itself becomes enfolded into processes of violence, the extent to which researching violence can be a public exercise in 'empathy' with oppressed communities, or a form of advocacy.

Karachi's highly politicised public is fully aware that no 'news' or analysis is not already a product of interpretation that may bear little similitude with actual events. Bearing on the affective and imaginary dimensions of violence, each new crisis or prominent killing instantiates a frenetic labyrinth of guesswork, rumour-mongering, and conspiracy theories about 'hidden hands', international states, intelligence agencies, and double-dealing. This is no surprise given Karachi's strategic importance as a military arsenal and supply corridor since the nineteenth century for British interests in Afghanistan, through to the years of jihad sponsored by General Zia-ul-Haq to fight the US war on Soviet communism in Afghanistan (1979–89), to the twenty-first-century US-led wars in Afghanistan (2001–14) and on Al Qaeda in Pakistan, to controversies over Chinese investments in Karachi's infrastructure, and ways that Chinese interests in Balochistan's rich natural resources collide with the brutal state repression of a regional insurgency.

The idea that any singular instrumental motive can 'order' Karachi's conditions of dislocation and disarray is thoroughly debunked in Laurent Gayer's book *Karachi* (2014). Gayer meticulously tracks 'patterns and routines of ordered disorder' (14) across the city as a whole in order to reject 'static' explanations that equate 'social order with the control of violence and its gradual monopolisation by the state' (12). Instead, he favours a processual analysis that views violence as unplanned, self-generative, emerging from human interdependencies, configured historically, and inscribed into the city's very sociality. He points to relationships between powerful political-economic and state entities, geographies of fear, and 'disordered' social states which underscore a series of orderly disordered dilemmas and lead violence to endlessly reproduce itself, whilst evading full-scale eruption.

This is a sophisticated perspective which can add contingency and complexity, for example, to Bourdieu's (1977) concepts of *habitus* and *doxa* that point to the deep internalised unconscious structures and modes of understanding and perception that position individuals, in a kind of 'circular relation', as both the product and (re)producers of the dominant arrangements of the social world. Bourdieu's idea of a 'circular relation' places limitations on possibilities for social change, and on alternatives to the normalisation and demoralised acceptance surrounding a situation in which violence appears never-ending. Karachi's situation is degenerate, and it may be entirely correct to claim that violence will continue, although power shifts between different actors. Yet do not theories and arguments about the circularity of violence minimise possibilities for change, for thinking about change, as well as those efforts of many civil society activist groups who work tirelessly to oppose violence (Khan 2014)? Instead, is it possible—and if so, how so—to exit the deterministic struggle of claims to representation, disrupt oppositions constructed around movement and stasis, the city and its parts, violence and peace? Next, to highlight ways that change to established orders can occur from inside, and seem like the radical interference of an external force? Last, to tap the undefined potential residing in new creative patterns being actively constituted by writers on Karachi—and fully take advantage of new possibilities that may emerge from a public conversation on violence?

The politics of publicking

Academics, including founding anthropologists, have been trained to gather multiple observations from fieldwork, and interpret these as manifold kinds of written reflection on self and other. Whilst publication typically marks the end of the research process, the dissemination of published research through public debates has received less attention. Such discussions might be achieved through analysing the practice of publicking itself, in a study of 'public' research—alongside its reception in the media, the academy, and by governments and politicians. Didier Fassin proposes this practice involve an examination of first, 'politicisation', whereby (certain kinds of) findings or stories enter the realm of public, political, and legal debate; second, 'popularisation', whereby particular findings or writers become popular (the rockstars of conflict zones) and widely taken up in public conversation; and third, 'mediation', requiring an examination of ways stories are distorted, blocked or controlled (Fassin 2013).

Publicking thus, loosely theorised, reveals interests in relationships between newspapers, television, political actors and activists, academics and the state. Strong social and cultural processes at play also reflect strong critiques of normativity, ideas about outlaw groups, culpability, economic and human impacts, and profoundly shape the direction of public conversation. These additionally highlight the emotional work in ways media commentators repeat readers' anxieties, in a double-layered kind of para-ethnography. Whilst media publics used to primarily concern newspapers, this is no longer so. All authors now form part of a diversity of counterpublics that are continually recruited and mobilised, textually and practically. Alongside, and sometimes instead of the slow labour of writing books, academics pursuing increasing demands for relevance and public impact publish in the press, on blogs, and other media—and journalists write books. Thus there is ripe ground for academics, journalists, and activists to usefully confer. This ideally means their correspondence can be less about policing professional boundaries, and more about transforming the conditions of public understanding, so that new social worlds can become thinkable.

In his compelling work on violence, Walter Benjamin critiques the notion of the media as the script of the city. He reminds us of the necessity to subject to public scrutiny the indiscriminate use of media sources as a window onto 'reality'. The uncritical use of media sources by analysts to narrativise Karachi's violence as 'Talibanisation', 'MQM terrorism', 'orchestration by dark forces', 'a city on the edge' *etcetera* is highly problematic. Equally distorting are academic theories that root Karachi's violence in macro-level variables such as institutional failures in democracy, ethnicised forms of exclusion and class protest against the state, ideological battles, the instrumentalism of political leaders, or the military-authoritarian state. Such all-subsuming explanations sketch out a political biography that fails to address the complexity, uncertainty, and fragility of unfolding relations and experience that living within such 'conditions' ordinarily entails.

Further to contestations and conflicts over representation, writers and researchers are continually asked to engage with a cacophony of explanations of collective violence and politics; to plough through the complex, contradictory discourses surrounding these, and a fearful situation where the control of information is restricted, licensed, censored, and flagrantly manipulated. In this environment, challenging repression with counter hegemonic discourse is a form of counterpublicking. It bears on Warner's concept of counterpublics which he views, like publics, as forms of publicness and privacy that are damaged by the distortions of dominant cultural norms and contexts (2002, 63). Correspondingly, it is important to subject to examine the question of what happens when research that is deeply committed to its subjects becomes used, because of its ethnographic specificity, to unsettle or support dominant understandings? When research that is received by many publics goes beyond (and even against) writers' original intentions? What happens to its meanings when it travels across fractured global publics, or becomes caught in the crossfire of counterpublics?

It is important to acknowledge the many struggles that writers about violence in Karachi face to publish at all. Authors and their publishers are frequently subject to online abuse, threatened, intimidated, censored, and even killed. Many authors (including in this volume) have had work refused by publishers cautious of the potential for its content to incite, or of retaliation. They have adopted a careful conservatism that may not reflect an ethical or political stance so much as a more straightforward response to conditions of fear. I too have had work rejected by Karachi-based book publishers and newspapers. In 2008 no Karachi press I approached would publish my book on Mohajir militancy. In another case, I gave an interview that was published without my knowledge in the 'Jewish Journal'—politically hijacked by a readership with an interest in an anti 'Muslim', pro-Israeli, anti-Pakistan agenda in the only news journal that would publish it at that time. Although freedoms have improved, once research is published it may nonetheless be used to illuminate the political stakes of an issue, revive debates about truth and lies, be praised by activists for 'combatting stereotypes', be criticised for misrepresenting communities, circulate through discourses of dishonesty and truth, and reviews may take a personal and emotional tone.

How to address the question of scholarship's contested role in social change? Concerning 'ugliness': should the voices of killers and bandits be highlighted (see Khan 2014)? The anthropologist Elliott Leyton conducted a study of multiple murderers; he argued that 'the eradication of a disease requires the intensive study of all the pus and blood and deformed tissue'. This striking metaphor resonates with many disturbing images and portrayals of Karachi's political landscape as 'deformed tissue'. Whilst political groups terrorise the media, and use the media to terrorise the public, closed doors should be opened. This invites risk, and endless pitfalls for exoticising or rationalising violence. While I do not agree that the entirety of gory details need public exposure, analysts should tackle what seems unfathomable, to better confront the ugliness that surrounds us. Erving Goffmann wrote in his 1961 book *Asylums* that 'to describe the patient's situation faithfully, it is necessary to present a partisan view' (p. x). In thinking through violence in Karachi, the metaphor of a political asylum does not seem inapt.

'Foreigners' writing about Karachi are moreover easy targets for their 'parachute' research style, ignorance, and reiteration of exoticised notions of barbarism—often with good reason. Yet locals also reproduce dominant media frames and representations of the 'primitive' and 'barbaric', and position themselves as guardians of the modern grotesque. Shocking news sells. To cite one example, while conducting fieldwork in Karachi in 2000 I vividly remember reading multiple reports about Pakistan's 'first reported suicide attack' on the newspaper offices of *Nawaiwaqt*. These detailed the gothic image of the female attacker's blasted hand, found beside the Quaid-e-Azam mausoleum across the road.

Violence in Karachi is a topic to which many writers are contributing through scholarship, journalism, activism, film, and at literary, poetry, music, and performing arts festivals. These include the newly international Karachi Literature Festival, the Kara Film Festival, the Pakistan Music Conference, and exhibitions and events at the National Arts Council, art galleries, museums, cultural centres, and at the grassroots events in communities. Certainly a book is not the culmination of expertise, nor the last word, nor the whole story. Perhaps its afterlife may conceivably contribute to a broader 'culture change' that can contest and articulate a pressing issue. For example, large-scale public mobilisations and loud cries of outrage accompanied the murders of activists such as Perween Rahman in 2013 and Sabeen Mahmud in 2015, and they circulated globally across the internet and news media—in the style of 'citizen journalism' (Yusuf 2012). Without underestimating the entrenched nature of Karachi's violence, or being naively optimistic, we need alternatives to silence, indifference, and resignation. Social change need not always entail social action. Tania Ahmed argues that 'socialities of indignation' constitute new Karachi publics around the high moral stance of non-political participation (2014). This book locates itself in many such efforts to create alternatives. At the same time, with all this emphasis on words, their possibilities and limitations, let us not neglect the power of the image, and how producers of Karachi's rich visual culture (documentary and filmmakers, photojournalists, artists, graffiti artists) are also a source of narration and renarration of the city.

This book fundamentally concerns the relation of violence and language. We are working through difficult questions. For example: how does an 'explanation' find, free, constrain, and define people? What use are sophisticated writings about violence and suffering if they do not improve people's lives? If conflict reconfigures relations and identities, how can public culture help constitute conflict and post-conflict publics? This collective endeavour offers us a way to scale out from state and nation, to the international, global, and back—and to rewrite, rethink, and cajole the public landscape into critical forms and questions regarding how to live with, write, and talk about violence.

Words that move

How do words move us? Some reflection follows on what this lexical mobility and lexical mobilisation entail. The question organises the approach to counterpublicking around three overlapping schema. First is social science and ethnography, involving a critique of the ability of social science language to capture violence. This means questioning the relation of suffering to institutional power and language, the potential in different orders of explanation for 'misreading' the ways people inhabit worlds of violence, and finding ways to work with theory and to complicate categories based on caste, confession—or conspicuously, 'class and state' (Alavi 1983). What ethnographic processes and ethnographic writing can offer this task is a way to interweave the language of social science alongside the words of people in communities, and individual stories. This means showing, rather than classifying, how feelings of rage and despair become actualised as acts of killing; how truth claims practically institute violence into political power processes; and how local communities become connected and also alienated from national crises of territory, polity, and terror.

Methodologically, gathering words is also a way to connect Karachi with worlds outside the city, spectacular events and everyday life, the fieldsite and office, and the academy with non-academic voices. Ethnography intrinsically implicates ways in which the repeated narration of violence on different scales, and other linguistic forms, inscribe violence as a truth that permeates through the city. This focus concerns Tambiah's study of the 1985–6 Mohajir-Pashtun Karachi riots (1996). Tambiah maps on incremental movements of scale, from the local outwards to the nation. He highlights ways that information about local disputes materialises as rumours, cumulatively escalates into larger ethnic clashes denuded of their local particulars, and assimilates to larger causes around notions of irreconcilable community difference (192). His study tracks how words spread like wildfire, as if with centrifugal force, and transform episodic riots in Orangi, Benares Chowk and Nazimabad into a 'virtual civil war' (221).

A Foucauldian position would also see words as lethal. Here, discourses of violence become their own battlefield for power. Words carry the power of hatreds, the ruling political class, state terror, and violent intention. This approach concerns the violence inherent in categorisation, wherein rhetorical battles over terms like 'riot', 'genocide', or 'pogrom', for example, directly influence the extent to which power is available to social actors. Certainly classifications and propaganda are often used instrumentally by politicians to incite violence, and linked to the critical timing of elections (Brass 2003). Furthermore, when politicians and legal actors refuse to apply classifications such as 'murder' or 'state terrorism' to explain systematic killings and torture, silence becomes an act of power, and of interpretive violence. And when communities are terrorised into silence, silence points towards the dangers inherent in voicing what people are prohibited to voice and remember (whether this be rape, massacres, or disappearances), or an individual's inability to express an interior state.

Aside from power, we need also to attend to passionate elements of violence. This means uncovering how powerful emotions of rage, grief, and despair may be transformed into bloodlust, revenge, and killing, and yet simultaneously serve party or state interests. It means trying to understand events that push people to the edges of their existence, that untie, distort, and rend people often irreparably from the bonds that attach them to the everyday world, in what Scarry calls 'unmaking and remaking worlds' (1985)—and the extent to which such suffering is officially recognised. It is a supremely decadent or brutalised society that can normalise numbers of people murdered daily in its midst. As Cavell writes tellingly in the foreword to Das' book *Life and Words*, 'to know a society is to know its capacity to inflict suffering upon itself' (2007, xi).

Das' book links fine-grained ethnographic work with the philosophy of Ludwig Wittgenstein and Stanley Cavell in order to query the relation between language and the everyday, the problem of recovering violence in the repression of voice, of linking the subject to the world, and the limits of language to express suffering (2007, 5). Taking as her problem the ways people find to go on living within devastation, she proposes we might recover 'life' not through any grand metaphysical gestures, but through 'a descent into the ordinary' (7). Herein she argues for uncovering the gap between what is communicated in words and what is revealed non-verbally in everyday gestures or silences. The ethnographic task is to give survivors of violence not speech, but 'voice': to explore 'how feelings of skepticism come to be embedded within a frayed everyday life so that guarantees of belonging to larger entities such as communities or state are not capable of erasing the hurts or providing means of repairing this sense of being betrayed by the everyday' (9).

Das' focus on how the past insinuates ordinarily into present relations of public and interior states is an approach reflected in several chapters that follow. It bears on the second schema of transition, or historical or epochal change. Transition here involves shifts, *inter alia*, from cosmopolitanism to Islamism, communalism to communism, and the transformation of feudal power structures in communities into the power structures of gangs. It begs attention to ways national, cultural, and personal histories are intimately bound in experience, and evoke motifs of ressentiment, repetition and historical return. As Naveeda Khan argues, much 'intellectual soul-searching' invoked by critical events recursively extends to the origins of Pakistan, rather than events themselves (2012, 5). I additionally draw attention to ways that revolutionaries of history have become the state's collaborators and apparatus, and distinctions have apparently collapsed between those who resist the state and those who embody it. To what extent might we view the army as a militant group? This question points to the site of duplicitous stories where killers and the state employ the same lethal, unlawful tactics. Their mirror practices force violence into the future. Regarding the past, the language of social science often struggles to capture the complicated incoherence of remembering terrible violence. Here we may be assisted by literary examples, for example Bilal Tanweer's novel *The Scatter Here is too Great* which poignantly interlaces fragments of remembered violence in Karachi with rich ethnographic detail (2014).

To paraphrase Walter Benjamin, perhaps the real 'emergency' will arrive when we can introduce the conditions to improve our struggles against violence:

> The tradition of the oppressed teaches us that the 'emergency situation' in which we live is the rule. We must arrive at a concept of history which corresponds to this. Then it will become clear that the task before us is the introduction of a real state of emergency; and our position in the struggle against [Fascism] will thereby improve (1968, 257).

Following Benjamin, if transforming violence requires looking backwards to find revolutionary energy and possibilities from history, a study of violence requires modes of historicisation. Because this book regrettably leaves many communities and voices unrepresented, it comprises an inevitably partial historiography. Benjamin also cautions that history itself may construct a state of siege: insofar as we accept chronic states of emergency as a public reality, 'terror talk' risks becoming as much a paranoiac convention of co-ordinating power as that it seeks to eliminate (Taussig 1989, 4).

The third schema is oral history and personal memoir. Personal histories can effectively destabilise the language of political theory which obliterates life from violence. Individual memoirs illuminate the social and deeply personal, literal struggle to match words to life. Writing on urban Brazil, for Biehl they evince pain and an ordinary life force seeking to break through forms and foreclosures, and define a subjectivity and a 'human' critique of the machines of social death in which places, poor households and families are caught, struggle through words to survive, and connect with a wider humanity (2005, 367). Reflected in several chapters that follow, Biehl's approach is to use subjectivity, words, and the single life story as a powerful channel to uncover how layers of bureaucracy, public institutions, unaccountability, and patronising hierarchies affect the course of social abandonment, and of dying (8).

In connecting the language of deep experience to the wordy interests of counterpublicking, we might return to Das who sees the public role of anthropology as one which can:

> act on the double register in which we offer evidence that contests the official amnesia and systematic acts of making violence disappear, but also witnessing the descent into the everyday through which victims and survivors affirm the possibility of life by removing it from the circulation of words gone wild—leading words home, so to speak (2007, 221).

In 'leading words home' we should be mindful of claiming the expert position. All sites of authorial knowledge are difficult to sustain in a world where critique is increasingly 'democratised' and with ordinary people who have no lack of information. Our problem is not a lack of knowledge but deciding which kinds of knowledge are useful, and for whom. The task requires more than a single unified mode of inquiry. Nonetheless, when our deep perceptions of life and endurance become embedded into our words, they lay the rich ground for engagement and advocacy—for enlisting an 'ordinary ethics' of speech, reasoning, and action to question social life (Lambek 2010). Here I draw optimism from Wilkinson and Kleinman who combine approaches from sociology and anthropology to argue that the role of structural violence in conditioning distress and the social distribution of mental illness demands fierce moral and critical scrutiny (2016). Rather than develop critique purely for the sake of sophisticated critique (a criticism they level at Fassin), critique should be used to advocate for an intellectually grounded, more humane social science that forges 'more adequate responses to suffering' (15). These authors invite us to turn unpredictability, interruption, and violent loss into new opportunities for reflection, and to view critique as a positive, if practically flawed, modality to reimagine and transform hegemonic orders of social science practice (160).

Finally, addressed to pain, words as therapeutic tools are a way to hold corroded words, lives, and worlds together. Much work concerns the healing potential of writing, and writing as resistance and re-representation (Abu-Lughod 1991, Bakhtin 1986) and recovery (Bollas 2002), especially where prevailing models hold that a condition is chronic and life-long, and locate the therapeutic value in creativity. Notably, I mean something more here than the kind of 'healing through creativity' (fiction, poetry, photography, art) that is often endorsed by governmental bodies, wrapped in power relations, or concerned to reinforce 'official' narratives. Finally, in attempting a more ordinary public 'working through' (rather than healing, which seems to overstate what might be possible) of a deeper relation between violence, hurt, and different writing experiments, I offer Das' words to stand for something of we are striving for:

> I propose that looking at fragmentary and unreliable knowledge that is secreted in the everyday and that renders it unstable; poisonous knowledge that is digested, eaten, swallowed, contained, but still needs attention so that it does not become a curse on the world; the loss of voice and its appearance as simulacrum in the proliferation of words that circulate (2015, 386).

Book Outline

This volume absorbed substantial time and spirit. As editor, I was not interested to produce a traditional set of studies, or a reiteration of dominant opinions. Instead, contributors were encouraged to reflect on how violence is central to the structuring of many people's lives, and their myriad unequal positionings in relation to governance, political mobilisation, cultural regimes, the accumulation of various kinds of capital, and social connections and networks. Whilst the authors were given the flexibility, over several revisions, to persuade their chapters into various directions, each chapter contains an in-depth analysis of Karachi's violence, and first-hand examples illustrating the issues at hand. In sum, this collaboration decidedly enhances the central debates, and ways their genealogies, contradictory uses, contestations and conflicts, are embedded in different contexts. It is distinct in its aim to unpack the constitutive relation of violence to contributors' personal views. Some chapters address this exclusively, others less so. All reflect, although not always explicitly or optimistically, a common aim to 'write against' violence—and to provoke the shattering and remaking of worlds of violence. Whilst the precise shaping of these collective ethics is as yet unclear, it is dynamic and being worked out in public. As the contributors included anthropologists, political scientists, ethnographers, journalists, and activists from inside and outside Pakistan, the project was soon challenged with diverse genealogical traditions and approaches. Thus, it was a provocative but fertile exercise in broadening our understandings of the discourses, ideological formations, and contestations surrounding violence in Karachi.

Opening the book with the theme of transition, Asif Farrukhi pays tribute to the Karachi-based poet Azra Abbas, whose work he has engaged with for over thirty years as a reader, critic, translator, and publisher. Through the motif of the 'ordinary', he traces the shadows and appearance of violence in the weave of everyday life. In this chapter Farrukhi presents a poignant selection of eleven of Abbas' poems. These poems variously address experiences of fear, loneliness, grief, death, and shock, in ways that political and random acts of violence insinuate themselves into domestic, commonplace experiences of daily life in Karachi. Farrukhi shows how, in moving away from the traditional *ghazal* form of Urdu poetry, Abbas carved out a distinctive, unconventional style of gritty resistance. He charts a parallel personal response to her work which transformed from initial scepticism to deep admiration. His relationship to Abbas' work, and the poems themselves, raise broader questions around how to articulate suffering in words, what languages are appropriate to capture pain, and how poetic forms may capture a fiery expression of outrage and resistance to violence.

The following five chapters draw on ethnographic fieldwork, and various social science traditions. My own chapter revisits a complicated relationship I formed with a key interlocutor and self-identified MQM mercenary whom I call 'Arshad'. Reflecting on one year, 1994, from a longer period I spent living in Liaquatabad in the 1990s, it challenges the metaphor of madness to query the ways violence raises existential questions about humanity; question ways writers channel their own feelings into analyses of violence; and examine the inevitable partiality and incompleteness of these framings. It also highlights ways commentaries of violence produce a frenzy of fascination and collusion around atrocities they supposedly protest against. The single life story is provocative insofar as it does not require cultural interpretation to render experience sensible. It reminds us as human beings to resist violence, whilst raising dilemmas concerning how to represent those who have committed atrocious acts, and about whether even the 'worst' cases offer possibilities for positive change.

Zia Ur Rehman problematises a view of Karachi as a predominantly Mohajir city under the control of the MQM. This chapter thoroughly documents transformations Karachi has experienced in regard to historical Pashtun migrations and settlement, and the subsequent entrance of the Taliban into Karachi's Pashtun neighbourhoods. These developments reveal how Karachi's Pashtun geography and demographic patternings involve far from monolithic political mobilisations of Pashtuns from all classes, neighbourhoods, and originary regions of Pakistan and Afghanistan. Rooted in decades of Rehman's field research as an award-winning Karachi journalist, the chapter comprises a richly detailed reflection of the controversial question of whether Karachi is fast becoming a Pashtun-dominated city.

Laurent Gayer examines one part-time fighter or 'intermittent combatant' in the MQM in 2013. The case of 'Iqbal' both updates existing accounts of an older vanguard of MQM militants and offers a window onto ways violence may serve as a form of labour exchange in Karachi neighbourhoods. Gayer characterises militancy as a type of 'dirty work' that includes collecting extortion, land grabbing, creating public disturbances, and fighting enemy groups when necessary. Whilst Iqbal joined the MQM to access opportunities for labour and reward, as a non-Mohajir he was relegated to the least appealing tasks of MQM militancy. Iqbal strategises to avoid rather than embrace becoming a killer. Gayer elaborates on ways violence is intrinsic to and regulates political conduct in a compelling account of how one young man gains a sense of purpose and agency in a (real and imagined) battlefield, by living life on the edge—but not too far.

Next, Nida Kirmani offers a rare academic study on Lyari. She historicises Lyari's development as a (contradictory) no-go site of resistance, protest and gang war, organised around its two notorious protagonists, Rehman Dakait and Uzair Baloch. Drawing on narratives of fear that comprise everyday life in Lyari, she analyses the persistent question of the extent to which gang war *is* politics, rather than separate from and an obstacle to politics. Through the figure of Rehman as 'Robin Hood', Kirmani's analysis describes a geographic mapping of the paradox of 'military-humanitarianism' at the level of local gang warfare. This mirrors and provokes original perspectives on the ways these projects are inextricably linked in national and international politics.

Oskar Verkaaik explores a neglected comparison between Mohajir support for the MQM and Mohajir membership in the Dawat-i-Islami proselytising movement in the 1990s. Initially Verkaaik outlines some superficial differences that mark this comparison. Whereas the MQM comprises a political party and ethnic movement, the Dawat-i-Islami condemns politics and promotes Islam as an antidote to ethnic strife. Although the two movements are therefore partial adversaries, both depart from a singular notion of Mohajir religiosity that is rooted in the modernist condemnation of popular religion, and exacerbated by ethnic stereotyping. Unfolding motifs of physical and spiritual migration and journeys (for example, from Mecca to Medina, India to Pakistan, Pakistan to countries abroad), Verkaaik argues that both movements distinctly appeal to young Karachiites' aspirations and anxieties about the future—and tap into popular religious traditions that bind and separate Mohajirs from other segments of the Pakistani population.

The following four chapters bring oral history and memoir to the fore. Nadeem Farooq Paracha interweaves national, social, and personal histories in an extraordinary analysis of how alcohol, its sale and consumption, became intrinsic to Karachi's leftist political culture in the euphoria of the post-Zia years; how political rebellion involving alcohol fuelled violence on Karachi's student campuses, and shaped Paracha's personal nemesis and life trajectory into journalism rather than militancy. The adage that the 'personal is political' acquires enriched meaning in these unfoldings of a simultaneously painful, exhilarating, and destructive era that shaped one radical element of the city's political commentariat. The politics surrounding alcohol from 1970–1990 offer a perfect lens, Paracha shows us, onto transformations of religion, morality, and revolution within student support for the PPP in a saturnalian urban setting.

Razeshta Sethna examines her experiences as a print journalist for the Dawn Media Group, and presenter for Geo TV and Dawn TV. She reveals professional tensions between levels of editorial control, the failure of newspaper owners and editors to protect journalists, and the fear which prevents journalists from protesting against the murder of colleagues. She explores connections between violent politics, state violence, and the media. These involve the MQM party, whose militants have burnt the city's newspaper offices and threatened journalists—and the military and Inter-Services Intelligence (ISI) agencies which pressure senior editors to censor views considered too liberal, keep silence around the state's repression of democratic freedoms and human rights, and the 'disappearances' of activists in Balochistan. Notwithstanding, the proliferation of Karachi's television media since 2007 positioned journalists at the forefront of open criticism against violence.

Arif Hasan's careful, nuanced account begins before Partition and progresses through General Zia-ul-Haq's era of Islamisation to the present. This chapter describes a rich public entertainment culture in Karachi that was thoroughly multi-classed, multi-ethnic, and cosmopolitan. Hasan debunks any nostalgic distortions that suggest that the city's golden past was 'golden' only for a few elites. Karachi's good times were available to all, although stratified by class. Whilst the Europeanised classes patronised gymkhanas, clubs, and commercial hotels, Karachi's working, merchant, and middle classes frequented their own bars, clubs, and cinemas. Around Saddar, a thoroughly mixed clientele enjoyed music halls, stage shows, food establishments, and discotheques. Hasan points to Karachi's new emerging liberal performing arts, film and literary culture, and asks if it might assist the development of a more unified, progressive public culture, and a transition from the painful present to a more humane society.

Kausar S. Khan draws continuities between her early research in Orangi's *katchi abadis*, her activism in the Karachi's Women's Action Forum, and her academic research into the effects of structural, gendered, and political violence on women and marginalised communities. This is a moving account of the deaths of four friends in 2013. Khan writes using the first person pronoun, with the effect of forcing the reader into an intimate, uncomfortable relation with the text, and the emotional landscape she engages. This compelling auto-ethnographic piece highlights the contradiction in experiences of loss and grief which are deeply unfathomable, compared with the need to crystallise their articulation in activist agendas. Thereby it comprises a view into violence's lasting effects, the ways research and activism co-constitute spaces of mourning, and the basis of a hardening desire to oppose violence by the means available.

Two afterwords close the book. With delicate incisiveness Farzana Shaikh enriches some issues pertaining to local and national, historical and global, transformations, and religion, in relation to five of the chapters. She elaborates on the possibilities of a pluralistic rethinking of the term 'Mohajir' proposed by Zia Ur Rehman; she affirms Hasan's efforts to not reiterate an elitist nostalgia; and her reading of Verkaaik's chapter reflects on how ideas of 'popular', 'modern', and 'secular' do and do not easily co-exist as discourses of difference. Certainly Kausar S. Khan will appreciate her highlighting the insistence on peace as a right that must be fought for, even if the way is unclear. 'Secularism' as a solution to sectarianism is woefully limited, and Shaikh rightfully adds a note of realism. It is also the case that this book will only reach a small minority of English-speaking readers, being restricted in its aims by its own peculiar elitism. I enormously regret it was not possible for a Sindhi writer, or writer on Sindh, to contribute. The omission and its symbolism feel uncomfortable. Likewise, any project concerned with violence ought ideally to represent the views of those who function to enforce or control violence. Therefore I also regret the absence of the voices of the state apparatus in this volume.

Second, Kamran Asdar Ali returns us to the city, and to the lives of Karachi's working women and working classes. He draws on women's poems, diaries, and memoirs to capture some more ephemeral qualities of everyday living and dying. These contrast with the violent suppression of an underclass of trade unionists and labour activists by a coalition of the state, military courts, and industrialists since the 1950s. Given the long, progressive erosion of peace in Karachi how, he asks, might we imagine a therapeutic process of social, economic, and cultural healing? Through an image of citizens 'at work' creating citywide networks and connections, we are offered finally some possibilities of dreaming. Specifically, through increased understandings, not of conflict, but of each others' intimate everyday lives, the dream emerges of a new political space or public where even intractable disagreements *can* be managed through gestures of kindness, compromise, and fresh vocabularies of how to carry on and get by.

This comprises the hard work and modest contribution of the authors in these pages.

References

Abu-Lughod, Lila, 'Writing Against Culture', in Richard Fox (ed.), *Recapturing Anthropology:Working in the Present*, Santa Fe: School of American Research Press, 1991, pp. 137–62.

Ahmad, Tania, 'Socialities of Indignation: Denouncing Party Politics in Pakistan', *Cultural Anthropology*, 29, 2, May (2014), pp. 411–32.

Ahmed, Feroz, *Ethnicity and Politics in Pakistan*, Karachi: Oxford University Press, 1999.

Alavi, Hamza, 'Class and State', in Hassan Gardezi and Jamil Rashid (eds), *Pakistan: The Roots of Dictatorship. The Political Economy of a Praetorian State*, London and Delhi: Zed Press, Oxford University Pess, 1983, pp. 40–93.

Ansari, Sarah, *Life After Partition. Migration, Community and Strife in Sindh, 1947–1962*, Oxford: University Press, 2005.

Bakhtin, Mikhail, *Speech Genres and Other Late Essays*, Austin: University of Texas Press, 1986, trans. Vern McGee.

Benjamin, Walter, 'Theses on the Philosophy of History', in *Illuminations*, trans. Harry Kohn, New York: Schocken Books, 1968 (1937), pp. 253–64.

Biehl, João, *Vita. Life in a Zone of Social Abandonment*, Berkeley: University of California Press, 2005.

Bollas, Christopher, *Free Association*, Birmingham: Ikon Books, 2002.

Bourdieu, Pierre, *Outline of a Theory of Practice*, Cambridge University Press, 1977.

Brass, Paul, *The Production of Hindu-Muslim Violence in Contemporary India*, Washington: University of Washington Press, 2003.

Das, Veena, *Life and Words. Violence and the Descent into the Ordinary*, Berkeley: University of California Press, 2007.

Das, Veena, 'Adjacent Thinking: A Postscript', in Roma Chatterji (ed.), *Wording the World. Veena Das and Scenes of Inheritance*, New York: Fordham University Press, 2015, pp. 372–99.

Fassin, Didier, 'Why Ethnography Matters. On Anthropology and its Publics', *Cultural Anthropology*, 28, 4, November (2013), pp. 621–46.

Gayer, Laurent, *Karachi. Ordered Disorder and the Struggle for the City*, London and New York: Hurst & Co., 2014.

Khan, Naveeda (ed.), *Beyond Crisis. Re-evaluating Pakistan*, London, New York, Delhi: Routledge, 2012.

Khan, Nichola, *Mohajir Militancy in Pakistan. Violence and Practices of Transformation in the Karachi Conflict*, London and New York: Routledge, 2010 (paperback, 2012).

Khan, Nichola, 'The poetics of violence', Book Review *of Karachi: Ordered Disorder and the Struggle for the City* by Laurent Gayer (Hurst and Co.), *The Herald*, November 2014, pp. 87–9.

Lambek, Michael, *Ordinary Ethics. Anthropology, Language, and Action*, New York: Fordham University Press, 2010.

Paracha, Nadeem Farooq, 'Visual Karachi: from Paris of Asia, to city of lights, to hell on earth', *Dawn*, 27 September 2014, http://www.dawn.com/news/1134284/visual-karachi-from-paris-of-asia-to-city-of-lights-to-hell-on-earth, last accessed 2 May 2015.

Scheper-Hughes, Nancy and Phillipe Bourgois (eds), *Violence in War and Peace. An Anthology*, Oxford: Blackwell Publishing, 2004.

Shaikh, Farzana, *Making Sense of Pakistan*, London: Hurst & Co., 2009.

Siddiqa, Ayesha, *Military Inc. Inside Pakistan's Military Economy*, London: Pluto Press, 2007.

Tambiah, Stanley, *Leveling Crowds. Ethnonationalist Conflicts and Collective Violence in South Asia*, Berkeley: University of California Press, 1996.

Tanweer, Bilal, *The Scatter Here is Too Great*, New York: HarperCollins, 2014.

Taussig, Mick, 'Terror as usual: Walter Benjamin's Theory of History as a State of Siege', *Social Text*, 23, Autumn-Winter (1989), pp. 3–20.

Verkaaik, Oskar, *Migrants and Militants. 'Fun' and Urban Violence in Pakistan*, Princeton University Press, 2004.

Oskar Verkaaik, 'At Home in Karachi: Quasi-Domesticity as a Way to Know the City', *Critique of Anthropology*, 29, March (2009), pp. 65–80.

23

Warner, Michael, *Publics and Counterpublics*, New York: Zed Books, 2002.

Wilkinson, Iain and Arthur Kleinman, *A Passion for Society. How We Think about Human Suffering*, Berkeley: University of California Press, 2016.

World Population Review, *Karachi Population 2015*, http://www.worldpopulationreview.com/world-cities/karachi-population/, last accessed 6 May 2015.

Yusuf, Huma, 'The Convergence of Old and New Media during the Pakistan Emergency', in Meg McLagan and Yates McKee (eds), *Sensible Politics. The Visual Culture of Nongovernmental Activism*, New York: Zone Books, 2012, pp. 183–211.

1

PEOPLE ALL AROUND YOU

LOCATING KARACHI IN THE POETRY OF AZRA ABBAS

Asif Farrukhi

A city emerges from the shadows and becomes an essential component of a poet's story, an entirely ordinary story. Insignificant details
coalesce to become parts of a larger whole, nonetheless fragmented
and inchoate. Such is the view of Karachi presented through the writings of the Urdu poet Azra Abbas. As a metropolitan centre soliciting
both controversy and global attention in the twenty-first century,
Karachi has transformed from its barely discernible beginnings in
folklore, through concerns with the legacy of British colonialism, to
what now more commonly describes a nerve centre of international
terror. This transformation is remarkable, not least because of the
rapidity with which changes have occurred. Yet these transformations
tend not to have found literary representation in the works of
Karachi's writers, or certainly none that adequately do justice to the

city's population or its politico-cultural importance. The shadow of this absence lies heavy on Karachi.

Through its chequered years, Karachi has embodied several literary voices and forms. In my introduction to *Look At The City From Here* (Farrukhi 2010), an anthology of Karachi writings, I complained about Karachi's under-representation as a literary location. Even as I wrote, changes were on the horizon. There subsequently issued a spate of books on Karachi, especially works of fiction in English which became accessible to large international audiences. While perspectives on Karachi in the writings of contemporary Urdu writers and poets are less well-known, nonetheless a number of writers have become occupied with the city's descent into chaos. There is no dearth of sentimental poems lamenting the *qismat* (fate) of Karachi. However, the poetry of Azra Abbas is distinct. She is repeatedly drawn to the urban experience, and political violence appears in her poetry, as it does in civic life. Rather than taking political violence as a discrete 'subject', she concerns herself with ways violence is embedded into overall everyday experience. Abbas' territory largely concerns the daily routines of ordinary household life, onto which she stamps the imprint of violence. In this chapter I have translated a selection of eleven poems. They are distinctive insofar as they reveal the presence of violence in both smaller and larger configurations of urban life, amidst people's continuous struggles for daily survival.

Following Pakistan's independence in 1947, a significant number of poets and writers moved to Karachi as a part of the large-scale migrations from India. As one of those who grew up with the new state, Azra Abbas was born in Karachi and lived in Karachi for most of her life. She received her education there, completed a Masters degree at the University of Karachi, and subsequently taught Urdu literature in a government college. In 1976 she married the novelist, poet and journalist Anwer Sen Roy, an important writer in his own right. Azra Abbas became prominent in literary circles after the publication in 1981 of her long prose poem 'Neend Ki Musafatain' (Voyages of Sleep). In her foreword to the poem, she wrote:

> Spread over a period of three years this poem unfolded to me the mystery called poetry. I had taken a tedious path. This poem gave me strength for the journey. Even today it is my companion. It watches me silently as I spend the days and nights it had predicted for me (iv).

This poem represents an important benchmark for Abbas, whose poetry subsequently matured and developed in different directions, and a less abstract manner.

Abbas' reputation was further consolidated with her collections *Maiz Par Rakhay Haath* (Hands Lying On the Table) (1988) and *Main Linain Khenchti Hoon* (I Draw Lines) (1996). However she is considered neither a popular nor a mainstream poet. The critic Salim Akhtar's rather patronising overview of women poets writing in Pakistan fails to comment on her work altogether (2008). One possible reason could be Abbas' rather jagged style, which Rahman notes gives the impression of the writer being 'hasty, even careless', and her work 'breathless, rushed' (1996). More disturbing for many is her choice of themes, especially 'the fearless venturing into the relatively uncharted domain of female sexuality' (Ibid.), a taboo subject for many in Pakistan today. On the other hand, the critic Abdus Sami devoted a chapter to her work in his study of Urdu prose poetry, and praised her ability to capture expressions of human helplessness in the face of oppressive realities (2014). Otherwise, an extract from 'Neend Ki Musafatain' is included in *Hoops of Fire* by Aamer Hussein (1999), and Hameed includes two poems by Azra Abbas in his *Pakistani Urdu Verse: An Anthology* (2010). In his introduction to that volume, Hameed comments that 'the content and style of her later poems is different', and makes the point that: 'She is still striving to find herself but knows more about the world around her and is sure of her observations and perceptions. She unmasks the crude realities of life and at times comes down hard on the pretentiousness of moral standards and values of the system which we have created' (345). Here is another indication of why Abbas makes some critics uncomfortable, and her poetic observations are so remarkable.

Abbas has published a number of books in prose, primarily memoirs and fiction. Her best known is the short memoir entitled *Mera Bachpan* which describes her early days in a lower middle-class Karachi locality. Contextualising this volume with similar works which describe the spaces available to young women, and small acts of rebelliousness in Karachi's lower middle-class neighbourhoods, Ali writes that Abbas' 'narrative is filled with small rebellious acts by a young girl growing up in the city in the late 1950s who is trying to understand the world around her with all its ironies and contradictions. Told in short passages with sometimes dream-like sequences, the way memory works when recalled many years later, *Bachpan* shows us a world through a female child's eyes and emotions' (2014, 3). In her introduction to *Kicking Up Dust*, the English translation of this book, Rahman regards these reminiscences as 'shaped fragments' animated by the spirit of 'irrepressible curiosity' (1996, ii). Abbas also published a novel, entitled *Main Aur Moosa* (Moses and I) and a collection of short fiction, *Raastay Mujhay Bulatay Hain* (Roads Call Out to Me). In 2001 she moved to London with her husband who took a post with the BBC Urdu Service. Her poems about London were published in the collection *Hairat Kay Us Paar* (The Far Side of Wonder) in 2009. After eleven years she returned to Karachi. Her renewed contact with the changed city emerges in her later poems which were published in literary journals, but not collected in book form to date.

Abbas has developed a remarkable perspective on her experience of Karachi, and on violence as continuously menacing presence. Her clarity of vision lacks the sentimentality and disconnection from the past characterising much Urdu poetry written around these themes. A point worth noting is that the city is hardly ever named in these poems. Similarly the localities in which the poet spent her childhood are unnamed in her memoir. Her later poems mark a reconnection with Karachi but they are more complicated than her earlier work. She intersperses more than one voice, not easily separable, between observations and descriptions which constitute the poem. The last three poems translated here come from this group of poems.

I first came across Azra Abbas' poetry over thirty years ago. Since then, my involvement with her work has undergone many changes. In my salad days as a student and aspiring writer keen to explore Karachi's vibrant cultural and literary scene, Azra Abbas was already a well-known name among the younger poets who were experimenting with form and diction, breaking away from the strong conventions of metre and poetic language which still largely govern Urdu poetry. She was making a mark for herself among the younger, rebellious poets who wrote prose poems. Unlike Afzaal Ahmed Syed and Sarwat Hussain, two of the finest poets on the literary scene in the 1980s, she avoided writing *ghazal*, the traditional Indo-Persian form which continues to dominate Urdu poetry. I was rather baffled with her first book, and my comments rather guarded. Over time, my response to her poetry evolved and deepened. I have been involved with it as a reader, reviewer, critic, translator, editor, and publisher. I visited the open house she and her husband maintained, and heard her recitations. In this creative space, I thrillingly recited my early work. Gradually she developed her unconventional and gritty distinct style, in her second and third books particularly. As I explored these poems, I recognised her as an outstanding contemporary Urdu poet. She represented a new trend in Urdu poetry. Remarkably she used language close to the experience of the ordinary, and responded to historical events with irony, and a sense of bewilderment and dispossession. I translated some of her poems for *An Evening of Caged Beasts*, an anthology of contemporary post-modernist Urdu poets I edited with Frances Pritchett (1999). I noted her seemingly 'prosaic awkwardness' and commented:

> Azra Abbas is unconventional, deliberately un-poetical in her choice of themes and style of expression. She writes the poetry of life's prose. Her realm is that of the commonplace, the ordinary. She writes about the hackneyed routines, the dull emptiness, and boredom of life. Her deadpan style seems all the more glaring when she writes about her tribulations as a woman (xvi).

Stories and story-telling are important for Azra Abbas. In her collection *Main Lineain Khenchti Hoon* she experimented with short stories and poetic stories. Fascinated with the combination of the short poem and the short story, I translated three of these stories in *New Writings From India and Pakistan* (Rakshanda 2013). Another level of involvement with this poetry opened for me when in 1999 I founded the literary journal *Duniyazad* in order to showcase contemporary writing from Karachi, and to establish a meaningful dialogue with international writing in a rapidly changing scenario. Azra Abbas became a frequent contributor. Later, I published her collection of short stories, novel, and her collection *Hairat Kay Us Paar*. Azra Abbas still lives in Karachi and writes regularly. In my tribute to her work, which is highly relevant for people's experiences with violence in the city, below I present some works I have translated from her collections '*Maiz Par Rakhay Haath*' and '*Main Linain Khenchti Hoon*'.

Eye-witness
A man
  shot dead

In front of
    your eyes,
Then what?

You are just like the wall
    or dust-bin,
Or that tree,
A few inches away
    from the one who was killed.

    You are immobile, inert.
You are not even scared.
You stand still,
You do
    nothing

    Not even turn back
To take a look.

And later
When your wifesistermother
Is serving you dinner,
You tell her
    you have something
Eye-witnessed
    hot and fresh
For tonight's dinner.

When you want to write a story
When you want to write a story
You can
    write a story.
Suppose you do want to write
    a story,
Then you can go ahead
    and write
    a story.

A story is written about living people
Who are all round you,
Going about,

Running here and there,
Who leave their bed early in the morning
And go home at the end of the day
When their wives, mothers, sisters, children
Wait for them,
Or when they quarrel with each other
In the neighborhood,
   or on the road,
Over some petty matter,
Or happily
   embrace each other.

   A story can be about young girls and boys,
It can be about any one of them.
Write in any which way you want.

A living person can do anything,
Can fall in love,
Go for a swim,
Fall ill,
Take care of somebody who is ill,
Or anything.
Keeping life in mind,
A story too
Can begin.
That person is crossing a road
With a shopping bag in one hand,
Holding a child's hand with the other,
The child has a flower in its hands
And a butterfly.

As you turn to look
An explosion
   Like death
Cuts into him from one side
   and comes out of the other,
The other side
Where
A finger is separated from others

And a butterfly is trying to move its wings,
But without any
    action.

What happened?
The story has come to a stop.
Obviously,
How can a story be written
About that ambulance
Carrying dead bodies,
Or a flower
Plucked before its time?

Darkness
In the dark
    all this
Is born.
Many unknown hands,
Somebody in a dark room
Whose throat can be slit
Or arms
Or legs
Twisted,
    broken
    and thrown out
In a dustbin.

But all this has to be seen,
All this
Which can be scratched out from the eyes
With a sharp instrument.
Who is the one thriving
Through means fair or otherwise
    And who gets dumped in the dustbin?

The light of a hundred watt bulb
Is not enough.

On one side there is music
And on the other, the face of darkness.

The hocus pocus is spread all round,
Here and there.
Like the screams of a pregnant woman
Everybody is in labour,
What finally remains
Is the dustbin with its mouth wide open.
It can be seen clearly
Even in the dark.
Nothing will remain.
It is coming from all around,
This darkness,
The whole game is of darkness—
He too who is caught
Also the one who is killed,
Also the one who is born,
Even the one who went into a dark alley,
They are playing hide and seek in the darkness.

Late at night
When the night begins to drip drop,
The drumbeat can be heard from far off
And the watchman's call of 'Keep awake!'
And close by the chirping of a cricket,
One—two—three—
The sound of the clock-tower
Comes off and on,
On looking outside from the window
What can one see?
A tree—two trees—
The library's boundary wall
And many birds
And the sky in the distance,
Clothes fluttering in the wind
Hanging in the air
As if on the verge of suicide
And the sounds—
Children
Poring over books,

Watching grown-ups spinning like tops,
Is it possible for them
To go beyond darkness
    Towards light?

Lone liness
Loneliness can catch hold of anybody.
It is not necessary
That it has to be you
Or me
Who get selected each time.

It can be anybody.

Even him
Who was taking a nap on a chair
Just before his death

Almost unconscious in an empty corridor
And remembering those
Whom he always liked to remember
But all that was left
Is this walking down deserted streets
And thinking
Who can it be,
    walking down the streets?

One can be all a lone
One can be lonely at any place in the world

Suddenly
While standing
As if he was on a deck
With music behind him
Played by his companions
For a festive occasion
And the dance

As he
    bends down on the deck railing
Thinking

34

Where is he
One can be cut off any place in the world

Instead of being close to the heart
Be far off
Far from the balcony in his home
Where he used to look at people
   as they come and go
Waving at them, saying goodbye
   and welcome.

A fear
A fear
   Runs along the railway track
Is entwined
   Around a machine's wheel

The ship's crew
Can see it on the surface of the sea
It coils
   like the branches of a tree
Around a man walking

It is visible in any eye
   at any given time

When it rains for long
When the sun begins to melt iron
When roofs no longer
   make you think of shadows
A fear gets up from some place
And fills the heart
   with strange premonitions

It is fear
Which snatches away
   bread from the hungry
   water from the sun
   raindrops from the cloud

A fear which enters

From my nostrils
   to the pit of my stomach
And causes
   my death.

The final victory
A fear
Creeps out of some corner
And begins to dance
In front of my eyes
Like an expert
Showing off his movements
Or telling
   a great secret of life and death.

The curtain falls
Nobody knows when
The fear climbs up
   and sits on my chest
I scream
In sleep and in waking hours
I keep fighting

Who will win
This war?

Thinking
Is it not enough to think
That cleaning the house is necessary
And is it not enough to think
That the dishes have to be done
Food has to be prepared
The children would soon be coming back from school

Or is it important to think
What is happening in the Third World,
Inflation, poverty and injustice

No running water in the home
How will I do the laundry
   Think about this

Why are you thinking
That the riots must stop
Why are people being killed

Not enough money
How will I pay the children's school fees
Only this—think about this only
And not that
Your sister was killed in the language riots
As if the responsibilities of this home are not enough
So what if your currency came down in the international market
Why do you have to worry
There are so many others
To think about all this

If your home did not have a meal one day
Then the children will turn against you
And if you did not have the money for fees
They will be thrown out of school
How will I do the dishes
Why is there a sound
    of people crying in the streets

A sound of gunshot
Why? Who was hurt?
Thinking about all this
Is not necessary
For you to be alive.

Who are they?
Remorse is spread out on the streets
Trees are shedding their leaves out of embarrassment
Flowing water has added its tears
The inside of their cheeks are filled with a bitter taste
They are throwing out mouthfuls of sorrow
With rich bits stuck between their teeth,
Buffalo dung is ready to be smeared on their faces.
They say
Those who died are martyrs

And those who are still alive
Put their heads together
   in anticipation of such a martyrdom
Wondering when it will be their turn.
Don't say such things in a roundabout manner,
Spell it out clearly,
The child says to its mother.
   Who are those people who want to kill us, Ma?
The mother wraps her *chador* around the child.
   This I will ask from our protectors
If they come to look at us without the company
   of those who are assigned to protect them,
But I am hungry, Ma!
   Don't you even step out
They will kill you otherwise.
   But then I will be left hungry forever
I have heard that hungry crows
Have picked the food clean from their teeth.

Naked
A poem stands over there making a face
I ask her:
   What happened?
She stares back at me with fiery eyes
   The same which happens everyday
Meaning what?

Killed

Those who carried bundles of dreams
And those who brought death for them
Were half-naked themselves
Upper portion or down below?
The poem started sobbing uncontrollably
But who?
Millions and millions were mis-appropriated
Searching out for them.
But by whom?
Those who say they will seek out death

And defile its honour.
They say that the money needed
To drive away hunger and death
Was washed away

So they are in tears
They cry and tell the audience
We have been hurt
Our peace destroyed.
Then with music playing in their ears
    And drunk with this,
They go back to sleep.

The poem sits down on a rock
And tells me
Don't you even try to touch me,
I will spend this night on these rocks
Marked by the blood of those
    Who were put to death.

Banner
How to write a poem of love?
How to write that the weather is picture perfect
How to tell everybody
    To turn off their TV sets
Each channel is repeating the same
    tale of dead bodies
But windows are open everywhere
The carts for picking
    the dead bodies make such a din
I can hardly hear anything.

And what the poem wanted me to write

There she stands crouching in a corner
Look, she is probably trembling with fear
She can constantly see and hear
The coming and going of dead bodies.
The dead bodies being shovelled inside the grave
And dead bodies which are living,

And some wrapped like mummies

Yes, people were in a great hurry
To throw them in the grave
They have a contract to bring in more dead bodies.
Look, over there's my poem
With the wailing women
Standing with a banner in her hands
On that scorching summer noon.

References

Abbas, Azra, *Neend Ki Musafatain*, Karachi: Jadeed Classic Publishers, 1981.

————, *Maiz Par Rakhay Haath*, Karachi: Jadeed Classic Publishers, 1988.

————, *Mera Bachpan*, Karachi: Aaj Ki Kitabain, 1995.

————, *Main Linain Khenchti Hoon*, Karachi: Jadeed Classic Publishers, 1996.

————, *Mera Bachpan*, Karachi: Aaj Publications, 1997.

————, *Kicking Up Dust*, Lahore: ASR Publications, 1996 (1981), trans. Samina Rahman.

————, *Voyages of Sleep*, Karachi: Pakistan Association for Women's Studies, 1998 (1981), trans. Yasmeen Hameed.

————, *Raastay Mujhay Bulatay Hain*, Karachi: Scheherzade, 2001.

————, *Hairat Kay Us Paar*, Karachi: Scheherzade, 2006.

————, 'Seven Poems From the Far Side of Wonder', *Annual of Urdu Studies* 22, 2007, pp. 271–4, trans. Muhammed Umar.

Akhtar, Saleem, *Pakistani Shairaat: Takhleeqi Khado-o-Khal*, Lahore: Sang e Meel Publications, 2008.

Ali, Kamran Asdar, 'The freedom to fly kites and play marbles: women and public space', *Dawn*, 1 June 2014, Karachi, p. 3.

Farrukhi, Asif and Frances Pritchett, *An Evening of Caged Beasts. Seven Postmodernist Urdu Poets*, Karachi: Oxford University Press, 1999.

Farrukhi, Asif, *Look at the city From Here. Karachi Writings*, Karachi: Oxford University Press, 2010.

Hameed, Yasmeen, *Pakistani Urdu Verse. An Anthology*, Karachi: Oxford University Press, 2010.

Hussein, Aamer, *Hoops of Fire. Fifty Years of Fiction by Pakistani Women*, London: Saqi Books, 1999.

Jalil, Rakhshanda, *New Writings from India and Pakistan*, New Delhi: Tranquebar, 2013.

Sami, Abdus, *Urdu Mein Nasri Nazm*, New Delhi: Idara Tehqeeq, 2014.

2

1994

POLITICAL MADNESS, ETHICS, AND STORY-MAKING IN LIAQUATABAD DISTRICT IN KARACHI

Nichola Khan

From 1993–5 I lived in a community in Central Karachi where many residents consisted of Indian Muslim migrant 'Mohajirs' who moved to Pakistan following Partition in 1947. I lived in Liaquatabad district, a historical theatre of intermittent conflict dating back to anti-government riots in the 1960s, ethnic conflicts between Mohajirs and Pashtuns in the 1980s, and where in the 1990s the security forces raided houses, arrested, terrorised, and fought armed battles with residents. Many residents, but not all, supported the Muttahida Qaumi Movement (MQM) party, formed in 1984 to represent the Urdu-speaking Mohajirs' concerns. Since 1985, intense violence involving the MQM, the state, and all political and ethnic groups dominated Karachi. At the same time, the MQM won all elections in Karachi. The party's political dominance in Karachi has been dented by malaise amongst Karachi's Mohajirs themselves after three decades of violence,

41

by large-scale changes in Karachi's demography, by political interference and interests of the state (see Rehman, this volume), and new liberal reforms to the media (Sethna, this volume).

Between 2000 and 2006 I conducted periods of anthropological fieldwork with supporters of the MQM, and Jamaat e Islami in Karachi. In 2004 I returned to Liaquatabad in order to record interviews with men who became mercenaries in the MQM throughout some intense early phases of the conflict. This chapter draws primarily on my time in Liaquatabad in 1994, which served effectively as my introduction to Karachi, and the basis for my subsequent research on violence. It does so via a focus on a single case, that of 'Arshad', which I have discussed in detail elsewhere (Khan 2010a; 2014). I use pseudonyms for all my informants who have since moved from Liaquatabad, died, or left Pakistan.

I want to reflect here on questions of 'madness'—as a psychic and political metaphor, rather than absolute category—that have preoccupied me over several years. Here I seek company with writers such as Begona Aretxaga, Byron Good, and Thomas Blom Hansen (see Verkaaik, this volume), who have reflected on violence and political madness in diverse contexts, or otherwise sought to link individual and political disorders without collapsing individual political or cultural factors into one another. Likewise, with the presence of what cannot easily be grasped in an ethos of surviving violence that disrupts practices rooted in territorial modes of historicism and grand theories (Singh 2015), in favour of dreams, stories, and retaining the ineffable 'inscrutability of suffering' (Das 2015, 212).

My concern derives from a more existential question about the limits of humanity and human action, as well as my personal difficulty to assimilate the details of much of what I heard, and my work as a social and psychological anthropologist. There are many 'types' of people who have killed—those who work at steady jobs during the week, have killed once, several times, and those 'intermittent fighters' who avoid doing so (Gayer, this volume). Men like Arshad approached killing with all the seriousness of a military career, and they occupy a different category. Their violence, which certainly constitutes what Gayer discusses in this volume as a form of labour seemed to go far beyond any 'call of duty', and prompts my questions about the ways political and individual aspects of extreme violence are related in ideas of madness. I also consider some ethical questions regarding the role researchers, journalists, and communities play in the representation of violence. Violence was not a totalising condition in Liaquatabad. Indeed, the majority of my neighbours were not involved in violence, certainly did not condone killings, and had small knowledge of their local militants' activities which mostly occurred outside the neighbourhood.

Academic accounts have characterised the Mohajirs' condition as deeply intertwined with their position in Muslim India, Pakistan's bloody inception, and their marginalisation from Pakistan's social and political power structures. They provoke questions regarding why theorisations of state power inevitably revert towards explanations of corruption, state failure, or disappointed political aspirations. Alternatives include Gayer's analysis of the unifying potential of Karachi's violent topography wherein a complicated palimpsest of actors are at the root of a series of orderly disordered dilemmas which pattern crises of violent transition (2014). Some interesting perspectives developed by anthropologists include Veena Das who refers to the 'illegibility' internal to the modern state, Talal Asad who describes the 'margins of uncertainty' alongside legal-bureaucratic legitimation, and Brighupati Singh whose focus on the natural waxing and waning of forces across 'thresholds of life' de-emphasises the moralised struggle between 'freedom-fighting heroes' and 'colonising villains' in favour of 'more ordinary necessities and desires' (2015, 123). These works critically open up a more complex view and set of problems where 'normality' may not be the opposite of 'madness', weakness of strength, or democratic politics a logical salvific solution for the problem of violence.

To the extent only a small minority became killers such as I describe, this chapter's centre of gravity concerns individual dimensions of violence. Previously I elaborated an (arguably controversial) moral-political position to reveal these men's humanity, and show how their actions developed 'normally' within the specific contexts of political mobilisation, discrimination, and military repression in Karachi, and Liaquatabad particularly, in which they grew up. I drew on neo-Marxist critiques, South Asian anthropology, and psychodynamic arguments, drawing on intersections of national, cultural, and biographical histories. I argued that violence is destructive but also generative insofar as it restores or intensifies the self. At the same time, it produces a stubborn fascination with tales of extraordinary terror that are also very ordinary. This shapes the experience of being unable to move on—and reproduces radical violence as a conventional means of conducting politics.

Since then, I have felt uneasy about this analysis. I wonder if I was too close, too influenced by, or defensive of these men (my former neighbours) to consider more deeply questions of pathology and accountability, or to shine a light on my own complicity and fascination. Following what Kapferer terms the 'aporia of the exotic' (2013, 822), here I ask how we can represent violence neither as radically other, nor as the minor discourse, in the sense of giving voice to sane individuals in insane situations—that is, as neither madness nor sanity? One way to avoid the question of either/or is through the problem: to question the concord between metaphors of normality and madness, societal and individual violence. Let us be clear. Case study analysis can reveal features of madness in an individual. However, it would be quite erroneous (even mad) to claim all killers are mad, or to impose a model of psychosis on all forms of violent political practice. At the same time, it is important not to leave individual dimensions, the psyche and the psychoanalytic, out of analyses of violence (Good, 2012). Likewise, while Veena Das argues it may be entirely correct to view the subject of madness as an ensemble of relations and conditions, 'in no case does this conception authorise us to put aside the separateness of the individual or the fact of his or her suffering on the grounds the subject is not simply the individual. Such is the complexity of the situation that madness brings into existence' (Das 2015, 84). Thus my aim is to highlight ways 'madness' creates differing modes of attachment and detachment, agonistics and aesthetics, for people who commit and live amidst extreme violence. Correspondingly, I aim to examine how lives are 'really' ruined by realities of a collective enthralment with atrocities, but also to take seriously the safety imagined in a situation which fosters individual and political continuities between normative and floridly pathological modes of violence.

Those men I wrote about spoke in graphic and varyingly personal and impersonal detail of whom, how, and why they killed. Each case raised questions that still trouble me. What are the moral limits of sympathy for the suffering of a killer? Why are tales of fantastic violence, even if racked with terror, torment, and exaggeration, often perversely enthralling? What does it mean for Arshad to 'confess', with a look simultaneously proud, defiant, and strangely blank, that he was named on eighty-six murder charges? Is telling such stories an exercise in 'empathy' with oppressed communities and actors, or an 'exoticisation' of violence? In a highly charged situation where stories of violence are distorted for political gain, should they even be told at all? And who will publish them? Individuals like Arshad are certainly accountable for their actions. Yet politicians, communities, and commentators are also responsible, albeit to differing degrees, for the thrall in which violence can hold them, even while they produce excoriating accounts that fiercely oppose it. That is, is 'commentary' a distancing tactic that fails to foster a relation of respect with the populace it engages—one which might lead such stories to become a site of refusal and a way to write against, rather than more superficially abhor, violence?

1994

For all of 1994 I lived in Liaquatabad, an area known interchangeably as Lalukhet. Lalukhet ('Lalu's farm') was the pre-Independence name given to the neighbourhood, changed in honour of the first Prime Minister Liaquat Ali Khan after 1947. Since the 1950s it has been an almost exclusively, low-to-middle income Mohajir settlement. I had been living in South-East Asia, and I came to Liaquatabad for the first time with my former Mohajir husband.

We lived in a three-storey building that backed onto the Lyari river, between the 'old' *sabzi mandi* (vegetable market) and the *Teen Hatti* bridge, following S. M. Taufiq Road. The attenuated river separated our area from the largely Pashtun areas *sabzi mandi* and PIB Colony, and a bridge divided it from the squatter settlement *Nishtar basti*. Here migrants from Afghanistan, Peshawar, and the tribal agencies lived in severer conditions and, until its closure in 2002, many worked as hawkers and lorry-loaders at *sabzimandi*. Half the ground floor was let to a garment factory; some small apartments upstairs were rented to Mohajir tenants. Several Kashmiri migrants rented cot-beds on the roof. I lived behind *Akhri* stop, last stop for the no. 7H bus. My days passed mostly in the narrow '*gullies*' (lanes) and homes between the river and the main road. That is, between five bus-stops: Akhri, Sindhi Hotel,

45

Image 1: Liaquatabad district, A Area, 1994 (Nichola Khan).

Image 2: Liaquatabad district, 1994 (Nichola Khan).

Nursery, Sheesh Mahal and, passing the mechanics' workshops, lastly Dakhana (the Post Office), where the road met the roar of city traffic.

By 1994, military operations against the MQM in Karachi had continued for almost two continuous years. Earlier, in the 1960s, Lalukhet had become a site of anti-government riots, and in the 1990s a 'no-go' area for non-residents and the police. My arrival in Liaquatabad coincided with the aftermath of 'Operation Clean-Up', a severe military repression in the 1992 operations on Karachi's 'kalashnikov culture', in which Liaquatabad was targeted by the security forces as a major MQM stronghold. Whilst the curfews, strikes, and armed Rangers patrolling the streets in trucks all signalled the danger, they also shut down possibilities of movement—to work, school, onto the main road—enforcing a claustrophobic idleness and oppressive sense of boredom, confinement, suspense, and waiting—for the curfew to end, for something to happen. Many MQM workers did not go to work for fear of being arrested, or because their salaries were paid in any case. Some spent time leafleting and chalking MQM slogans on the walls. Others had murder charges or militancy-related First Information Reports (FIRs) registered against them. They were officially 'underground', living between relatives and friends.

People eagerly greeted the tempo change around 4pm when the *Jang* newspaper was released with its usual numeric headline: 17, 9, 12 *et cetera*, referring to the numbers killed across the city that day. This was the time to venture into the gullies to sit, gather, talk about the news and how Mohajirs finally had a hope in the MQM who would crush the army and honour the sacrifices they had made and were making for Pakistan. Small shops and foodstalls also opened now. The local men hung around near Hakim's shop, savouring *pan parag* (betel nut mix), smoking, joking. Perhaps I'd join them to chat, or be pulled by their giggling children into their homes to drink tea, sit with their mothers, and be teasingly questioned about my life. Shahjah, white-haired now, would fry potato chips on his small portable cooker; one, two, or five rupees a portion. The mood in the gullies was relaxed in contrast to the main road which was tense, and patrolled by Rangers who largely did not enter.

When there was no curfew, in the mornings, the Kashmiris left for work as labourers, porters at *sabzimandi*, or in the garment factory.

Rabia, who lived upstairs, set off to sell *baryan* (dried cooked pulses) and hair-removal powder door to door. Her mother might drop in, a locally famed 'princess' from Uttar Pradesh in India who had lost 'all' her money and jewellery when she migrated to Pakistan during Partition, this being her sacrifice to build the new Pakistan. Most days Rashid, Rabia's brother, worked on the buses. In the evenings he sold packets of heroin to local addicts. Occasionally his estranged wife and children visited, and he would parade his sons about, though more often sit outside on the *chabouter* (stone ledge), too drugged to sit upright. I might climb to the rooftop and chatter with the women opposite. Or gaze over the river, the cows grazing on the scrubby grass, the washing laid out to dry, the remnants discarded from the garment factory, the accumulating rubbish. Once I fired a kalashnikov here, recoiling at the deafening sound, surprised at the physical effort required. Yasmin, who lived in the building, turned up her nose— someone had to disapprove. But another day she laughed and we took photographs of each other with the gun. Another neighbour proudly demonstrated he could take a Kalashnikov apart and rebuild it in one minute. His weapon bore the inscription 'Made in China by Muslimer'. He also had two TT pistols stuffed behind a sofa in his room. During army raids after I left, many weapons were buried by the riverbed. Many of those first-generation Mohajirs I knew have died, or moved away; the building I lived in has long been empty. Now that the river-bank is being dug up and many houses there are scheduled for demolition in order to finish construction on the Lyari Expressway, the unsuspecting ground-workers will no doubt uncover the cache.

Liaquatabad's fearsome reputation largely protected the area from strangers and the 'agencies' who might venture inside. A symbolic space of Mohajir pride and of MQM power, it was also an 'inside' space for its residents to pursue everyday life; to pass time, perhaps invite one's friends, or rent a film from Kashif Video Store. Not every house had a television then. If visitors came, I found it was only a short walk to Mohammadi Sweets to buy biscuits and snacks, *naan khatai*, or *namak parai*; or sweets such as *ladoo*, *jalebi*, *gulab jamun*, or *ras malai*. Sometimes, eager for a change of scene, I walked to the 8A bus stop in PIB Colony where the stalls sold second-hand English books and novels. Or perhaps cross the riverbank to the poorer

Nishtar basti and visit a family whose father and young daughter, Salma, made money performing magic and card tricks on the street, she a queen of marvellous prestidigitation.

To borrow a motorbike felt like a passage to freedom. Sometimes I caught a ride out to visit Mr Nadeem at Sindhi Hotel who kept a fancy of pigeons on his roof. Or, past the lengths of dyed cloth drying in the breeze, where Sindhi Hotel gave way to Liaquatabad Areas 6, 7, 8, 9 and 10, to visit Irfan. Here, in a row of old houses painted jade blue, Irfan lived in two rooms with his twelve children. His wife invariably sat beatifically in the centre of the room, while her daughters busied around her. Or perhaps the bike would bump past the armed police at the checkpost at Akhri and continue over the crossing, past the butchers and teashops in Mohammadi Colony, past Gulberg School where vendors mixed powdered glass with coloured paint for the most cutthroat kite-strings in all Karachi; kite fighting was a popular past-time, in Ramadan especially, on the rooftops in the cooling hour before breaking the fast (*iftar*). On through Sooka Bagh and Azam Nagar where children played on the dusty ground; past Baloch hotel, across the main road into Azizabad, and on to Aisha Manzil for fresh juice.

Near Sooka Bagh in Sikander Abad was the infamous '*Peeli Kothi*' (Yellow house) dwelling. One interlocutor and self-defined MQM mercenary, Arshad, told me he had been a member of an elite 'militant wing' of seven 'bodyguards' who lived here in 1988–9. These 'bodyguards' were chiefly charged with conducting killings and kidnappings, providing armed assistance, firing on opposition rallies or raising funds through robberies and violence. They operated under secrecy. Arshad described a haunted house which before 1947 was occupied by Hindus, who were killed during Partition by Muslims who ransacked the dwelling. He described a cloying eeriness which intensified in the room where political opponents and wealthy businessmen 'died under torture' (notably he did not say 'were murdered'). The room felt terrible and cold; none of the 'boys' wanted to enter there. As the bodies piled up, they took them away and dumped them in the Nazimabad or Gulshan-e-Iqbal areas. By 1990, the dwelling had become too notorious. It was abandoned and converted into a party sector office. Later the sector office moved to Liaquatabad No. 4 and the house reverted to more ordinary, pedestrian uses.

During 1994 many rumours of killings circulated. Sometimes violence occurred in our neighbourhood. Or perhaps local Unit leaders would dispatch 'boys' to attend clashes outside—although not Arshad and his comrades, who considered themselves 'above' such lesser tasks. The Rangers would patrol the main road at night, and sometimes enter and conduct dawn raids. In other neighbourhoods if there was a strike-call or protest, someone would burn a government building or bank, fire at the police station, or set a bus alight—not at Akhri because the local drivers lived nearby. One day the still curfew was broken when someone set fire to the Habib bank at Sindhi hotel. Hundreds of people poured onto the road, furiously decrying the army, calling for violence. Someone shouted to me that I should publicise the atrocities being perpetrated against Mohajirs to the world outside. Someone else pushed me back inside; for my safety, in case of reprisals, or if matters deteriorated.

Word often spread that there would be a strike the next day. In Liaquatabad the shopkeepers, MQM loyalists, always closed without hesitation. Elsewhere MQM workers would pass by on motorbikes, banging shutters with sticks. During the stultifying heat, endless power

Image 3: Burnt vehicles, A Area Liaquatabad district, 1994 (Nichola Khan).

cuts, and the utter boredom of daytime curfew, many workers would sleep. Because of the cover and ease of movement afforded by the night, these became the hours the 'boys' went out; to spy on Rangers, build makeshift lookouts from where to fire into the road, burn buses, or just whisper excitedly and plot. One night, amidst a noisy secrecy, some young men received a delivery of weapons; they decided to go out to fire at the Rangers. One, Shabbir, shot his leg by accident. I watched as they carried him, a shaken unwieldy bundle barely out of childhood, across the water to PIB Colony and called the ambulance there, mindful of alerting the Rangers into our area.

Another such night, I watched some workers block the bridge to *sabzi mandi*; they would ensure no traffic passed here. About 4 am they ventured in silence onto the road. One jumped aboard a bus and manoeuvred it into the road. The others fortified the blockade by placing tyres across the road; then home to sleep through the long daylight hours of strike.

One *mohallydar* (local neighbour), too 'important' for such low-scale activities, was Javaid. Lumbering and typically taciturn, Javaid was a prominent local militant. Little educated, he had trained as an electrician; his father bred pigeons and derived a small family income by betting on pigeon racing. One afternoon amidst a flurry of activity I saw Javaid and a friend step out from the gully into a waiting rickshaw, with covered faces. Later the news spread a Haqiqi 'spy' had been shot dead at the *paan* stand opposite Akhri. Had Javaid hurried to 'protect' the area? I tentatively ventured to look. The ground had been doused clean with water. People said the blood was everywhere; a sense of trepidation, and a foreboding fear of reprisals hung in the air. I asked Javaid directly if he was responsible. He smiled but said nothing.

Unravelling

In mid-1995 I left Karachi. Our building and the entire area were subsequently raided by the Rangers, three times. Many residents fled. Two young brothers from one family, one studying for his matriculation exam, spent long weeks in police custody, then jail. Their mother, a widow, scraped around for the bail money. When the youngest was released his eye was damaged, his leg fractured. One evening, amidst

51

another raid on the area, she gathered her four younger children and fled in a rickshaw to a relative. They spent three years moving between relatives until, finally, they were able to rent a house elsewhere in the city. She never saw the building again.

I did, when I returned in 1998. Trying to pick up the pieces, to find and understand what had become of those I lived with was the beginning of my fieldwork. Arshad had been jailed, I heard. Now released, he complained shakily that Altaf Hussain had sold his efforts; he was a murderer, not a revolutionary. He had nightmares about the people he killed, one woman in particular. He saw her face at night, in the trees, he awoke at night crushed by her ghost. The same year, in October, another former neighbour, Aamirullah, was jailed in a high profile case for the murder of Hakim Said, the Governor of Sindh. Everyone talked about it. 'Stupid boy', they said. 'He didn't do it. He just wanted to be famous, to emulate the bigger guys.'

In summer 2001 I returned to conduct a study on the MQM and Jamaat e Islami in Karachi, and to make a trip to Afghanistan. By September, preparations were under way for Aamirullah's release; a group of friends from Liaquatabad would join an official party at Central jail to welcome him. I hoped to speak with him about his experiences but his release was delayed and I returned to the UK. A week later, the 9/11 attacks happened in New York. The next weeks were overshadowed by the bombing of Afghanistan which I watched, stricken, on British television. Given President Bush's threatening rhetoric about Pakistan harbouring terrorists, Karachi again seemed too close to violence, too dangerously vulnerable.

In 2004 and 2006 I returned to conduct fieldwork in Liaquatabad and met many old neighbours. It will be difficult to talk to Aamirullah, I was told. He is scared of being seen, talked about, rearrested. He is hiding, paranoid, 'underground' in his mind. You can ask Arshad for an interview instead. Javaid, I was told, had been jailed for multiple murders. He had given up politics and now worked as an electrician. Others whispered he was involved in robberies, pimping, 'doing violence' for money. When I saw him, I asked him about the murders he was jailed for. Had he committed them? He cocked his head with an enigmatic grin and asked me, 'What do you think?'

How should we interpret Javaid's smile? How can we understand why Aamirullah might claim a murder he may not have committed?

How can we understand Arshad's disclosure, in a gesture simultane-ously intimate but also detached, that he cut bodies into pieces? Let me return here to violence's irrational quality. This is where attention to the details of an individual case come into play. Despite the 'normality' of killings in Karachi, Arshad's actions might certainly fall under what psychiatrists and other professionals of the mind would consider patho-logical. I am not a clinician and cannot comment, save speculatively. What I do find interesting is how these men's activities find normal expression within the 'double-bind' madness of a political culture (that must be historicised), wherein killings and reports of killings in part relished the brutalities they deplored. That is, what can violence reveal about the frontiers and limits a culture or a self is open to?

Classical psychiatry is less concerned with the symptomology of classifications as with the underlying logic of symptoms, which may take 'normal' or pathological form. Darian Leader argues that many people have 'ordinary psychosis' and live perfectly normal lives: that is, they are 'mad' without going mad (2012,11). Psychosis is often trig-gered via revelatory moments involving the crystallisation of a delu-sional idea. This provides the logic for the person's conviction that something is wrong with the world (paranoiac), or themselves (melan-cholic). Psychosis, Karl Jaspers argued, concerns less the content of a delusional idea which may be quite reasonable (for example that politi-cal realities are not what they seem; that they are engineered by invis-ible forces), than the person's belief that it expresses an undiluted truth (1913). Ronald Laing later attributed psychosis with cathartic and transformative potential (1960). He argued (as did Freud, Jung, Lacan, and Winnicott) that psychosis and delusions are not constitutive of madness. Rather, they express people's attempts to communicate their distress, and recover their natural state. Psychosis may not be apparent in people who have strong support structures or ways of coping with everyday life: it is only if the paranoid area is touched upon, for exam-ple in an increased distrust in a person's environment (which may reflect real circumstances), that it may trigger and they go and kill someone (Leader 2012, 94).

Psychosis may originate in childhood trauma; traumatic events may precipitate psychosis (for a short variation on this argument see Khan (2014)). Arshad's clear realisation, amidst deadly attacks on Mohajir areas in the mid 1980s, that killing would be necessary precisely 'because a war was happening' may have brought to the fore the repetitive homology of these conflicts with earlier violences of his childhood. Arshad was the first child born into an impoverished family in Liaquatabad. His father migrated to Pakistan as a child. His earliest memories include experiencing absolute terror during the night-time bombings of Karachi in the 1971 Indo-Pakistan war, frequent hunger, violence at home, and disturbing stories about Partition. Bollas argues that the individual who experiences annihilation terrors in early life, the 'murder' of his ability to feel safe, may later realise these fears through by reproducing traumatic shock in others through the use of violence (1995, 201). Howell suggests such individuals may 'turn the tables'; visiting their past experience of terrorisation on many victims, they recreate the 'timeless' (never-ending) loss of their safety and imagination (2005, 256).

Psychosis, whether quiet or florid, ubiquitously features the belief in one's exceptionality. Certainly Arshad was an unreliable historian who distorted events in many self-aggrandising tales. He drew comparisons with Indian film heroes to describe how he was 'chosen', 'destined' to be a martyr, saviour of the community, had sworn an oath of loyalty, and killed 'more than 400'. These stories buffered him against a fragmenting reality, and detached him from any 'normal' sense of reality. Wernicke theorised in the nineteenth century that surviving in psychosis entails creating a secret place to rationalise delusions of persecution. This allows the person to exist in yet also outside the world they inhabit (Leader 2012, 93). Being uniquely singled out by a party leader and entrusted with 'secret tasks' vitalised a fantasy space for Arshad within which real social power relations and a new self-image could be materialised. Killing became a way to distance from reality, to feel safe.

The Other in psychosis is vital for survival yet also highly destructive. The MQM's charismatic leader Altaf Hussain fulfilled this role, epitomising a supra-human, extraordinary, ethical icon to identify with, whose words Arshad described, were 'like magic, they pierced my heart, so powerful, he could make us cry, kill anyone for him.' Verkaaik (this volume) discusses how Mohajir religiosity in the MQM played in a very powerful way with Sufi, and to some extent Shia, languages of tyranny, betrayal and sacrifice, and ideals of the devotion of the *murid* (follower) to the *pir* (spiritual leader). The magical appeal of violence in the MQM, its martyrdom and treacherous power also bear aptly on Taussig's term 'fabulation' (1991). That is, on ways 'magic realism' 'created an uncertain reality out of fiction, giving shape and voice to the formless form of 'reality' in which an unstable interplay of truth and illusion becomes a phantasmic social force (101–2). For Taussig magic realism is also a powerful means by which 'liberators' discipline and control the desires of the people. Revered and feared, Altaf Hussain created terror and chaos at will, vitalising cults of death and redemptive violence as ways of acquiring and holding onto political power. Amidst the ferocity of the violence instrumentalised, many miraculous stories circulated. His image has appeared on trees and buildings across the city; during his hunger strike in 1990 throngs of birds alighted on his saintly body (in timely appearance for a press conference). Such practices transposed Altaf Hussain into a powerful charismatic icon able to provide the love, vision, guidance, and author-

Image 4: Graffiti in Liaquatabad district, Unit 161. The slogan in Urdu reads '*Masloomoon ka sathi ha Altaf, Altaf Hussain*' (Companion of victims Altaf, Altaf Hussain). Unit 161, Liaquatabad, March 2006 (Nichola Khan).

Image 5: Graffiti in Liaquatabad. The slogan in Urdu reads *Jeay Mohajir!* (Long Live Mohajirs!), Liaquatabad, 2006 (Nichola Khan).

ity necessary to renew hope for the future—and the imagined context for the restoration of Mohajir wholeness in Pakistan.

Despite their gruesome details, Arshad's stories about killing had an unreal quality, as if he were describing the imagery and events of himself playing centre role in a film—in which he felt afraid but also strangely detached, immune, or even protected. Arshad's and others' actions constitute a political culture which fosters modes of detachment and interpersonal disconnectedness. As a social, political, and psychic experience born of power relations, violence cannot simply be understood as punctuated by moments of either sanity or delusion. Political disorder has specific geographical, social, and historical forms; it reflects social discord and internal individual conflict. Freud argues that war externalises our psychic struggles and is enlivening. For Klein it 'cures' the intolerable depression and madness of the inner war experienced all the time by the individual. Importantly, individual disorder can become reality through being instrumentalised by political leaders and the state. Attention to biography can reveal its particular singularity.

Anthropologists have developed on these ideas through analysing the phantasmatic presence of colonial apparatuses in experiences of politics and madness. Certainly, individual paranoia may mirror local and national political events, the so-called 'madness of the state'. Alternatively, the 'insane violence' of radical nationalists such as Arshad may also rest in something more hidden, secretive, and problematic: in the presence of a traumatic history not altogether resolved—the phantom of Partition. This has to do with the tainted birth of the nation: the foundational violence which has not disappeared, but has been nurtured and used by Pakistan's political powers to legitimate the very form of democracy, or military rule. This produces a 'sense' of continuity with the violence of Independence and colonial rule. Whilst resistance is the 'story' of many like Arshad, it is highly paradoxical. It produces the passionate desire to banish violence, but to also hang on to it, and push it to its limits. Writing on Basque nationalism, Aretxaga suggests that the fantasy of radical nationalists 'hides something unspeakable and rather shameful' (2008, 60). This is the belief that achieving the goal of the nation-state will entail the loss of an idealised, unified, national collective with which they deeply identify.

The paradox for Arshad's generation, whose grandparents and parents constituted part of the divine migration from India, is that pursuing Mohajir rights in Pakistan (and on behalf of his parents) so ferociously ensures the desired form of the nation will never emerge. Instead, what happens is the present perpetuates itself *ad infinitum*; the future is always coming but never fully arrives. Perhaps what is really feared is the dissolution of a unity of identity, which is bound to occur with the disappearance of an enemy. I reiterate: the real madness in political violence is the sense of safety it ensures. This is the idealised unity of the nationalist project. In Homi Bhabha's terms, it characterises the profound ambivalence of the postcolonial situation that cannot be acknowledged, and is one reason it remains the same (1994).

In Arshad's case the dream ruptured. I have written elsewhere in detail about the killing that haunted him: when he decapitated the pregnant wife of a police superintendent in her home (Khan 2010c, 240). He described being ordered to 'make it horrible' so it might be published in the newspapers, and terrorise the populace. After this killing, Arshad continued; killing to forget about killing, to try and regain his sense of detachment. What happened was the collapse of the distance between reality and the film. Severe trauma may deprive a person of fantasy and illusion: 'when the terrible becomes true, not only are we unsafe, we lose the ability to imagine' (Howell 2005, 256). This killing took away Arshad's hiding place. It forced him to become the hero, and confronted him with the evidence of a permanent dissociation, from any possibility of returning to a 'normal' life. In making the film a reality, he lost control of the story. The life he extinguished remained immutably present. At the point he desperately wanted to reverse an irreversible act and erase the image, the story and reality became permanently joined. Although he never 'recovered' after this killing, there was some residual satisfaction. His fantasies were vindicated.

* * *

Arshad and Javaid since left Pakistan. I felt compelled to write Arshad's story. I thought writing would help me grasp an understanding which seemed so difficult and elusive. This was a relational enterprise; Arshad wanted the shared fantasy, for me to see him as the avenging hero. I was the soundboard on which to reinforce the story as reality. I assumed a minor part in his film. His story became a personal mythology to make sense of himself, and keep his terrors at bay. It described a man who failed to get a government job, joined the MQM, became a killer, and span dramatic stories about the violence he committed. This made him feel uniquely recognised, proud to be named on eighty-six murder charges. Turning those stories into reality became addictive. As did his victimhood: blaming those who recruited him, Altaf Hussain for deceiving him, the government for failing him, the broken promises of Partition, anyone except himself. My role was to uphold the story. And, given that I felt keenly attuned to experiences of 'madness', of dissolving selfhood and reality—in the context of the painful disintegration of my marriage that was occurring alongside—to an extent I did.

Arshad's unprompted confession of killing the pregnant woman shocked me deeply. It begs how far into violence a person can go before the mind unhooks from reality. It detached me too from reality—my head spinning afterwards sometimes, flying from my body, like that woman's. Was this his feeling when he cut into her body, half-living his story, half trying to absorb its finality? Was telling me an aggressive attempt to inflict on me the death-in-life experience he lived through? Relationships too are about telling stories. All that is needed is a series of facts to thread together. And so I followed Arshad into his extraordinary story, becoming deeply immersed, trying to make sense of it: a story in which he suffered, he was the pawn in a deadly game, free of guilt and shame. A story in which he was innocent.

Missing from Arshad's heroic account is any compassion for his victims whose stories are unspoken, or cannot be spoken because their authors are dead. More than any feelings of guilt, shame, or anathema, what Arshad describes is a deep narcissistic rupture to his self-image as a 'good terrorist'. His primary goal became to survive, and to maintain some coherence of selfhood. In Freud's ideas of psychosis, disturbing ideas are not forgotten, or their emotional charge displaced, but totally abolished. Erased from the psyche, the unacceptable, banished thought, 'I am a bad person', returns from the outside as a delusion, in the belief of being persecuted, victimised (45–61). Over twenty years since I first met Arshad, his story, likewise, has become increasingly intractable. It seems less about inflating his ego, as an essential way to survive. When I spoke to Arshad after the raids on Nine-Zero during the 2015 operations against MQM, he warned, or hoped for, a volcanic groundswell of retaliatory violence. If the trauma of killing and the experience of psychosis at one time held positive potential (Laing) for remorse or a new political position to emerge, it did not. Rather, Arshad re-attached himself to the dissociative thrall of the fantasy and the idea he would if 'necessary', kill again, this man sacrificed and victimised by Pakistani politicians. Killing, after all, was the one time he felt truly alive.

Byron Good's term 'postcolonial disorders' is germane in its emphasis on how relationships between powerful political economic and state entities are shaped by the violent experiences of colonialism; their insinuation into the institutional entanglements of the present as the historical legacy of violence and appropriation, traumatic memory, and the 'altered' mental states associated with living through the uncertain, threatening conditions of dislocation, disarray, and marginality (2012). Undeniably mental health problems—trauma, depression, anxiety, and 'nervousness' (Taussig 1992)—result from these conditions. When violence becomes endemic in a culture, any alternative becomes perceived as weakness, or surrender. Renouncing violence is very difficult because it threatens the established order on both sides. At the same time, many examples of non-violence around the world have been successful.

Becoming sensitised to the rhythm of violence as both life and death or decay does not imply a transcendence that redeems life from terrible moments of destruction. Rather it is to acknowledge the moments, days, and years of failure and unremitting sorrow in the task of going on, and surviving life as best one can. It means we might blur distinctions between madness and normality, play-acting and work, reality and unreality, the mundane and the spiritual—and accept the uncertainty that comes with allowing such components to remain in an 'unresolved, nondialectical tension' (Singh 2015, 123). While the inability to grasp experience is a difficult position to hold, it is not necessarily pessimistic. For Das it is in the fragility of relations revealed when madness cannot be absorbed in the everyday that change can be invited in. She writes:

> I saw too much suffering and violence to say that mental illness is all a matter of social construction or that symptoms are only forms of resistance. Instead, I offer the idea that the illness resides in the network of relations, in the movement over institutions, and that the pathology is trying to find an environment in which it could re-establish new norms (2015, 104).

Perhaps then it is in the inscrutability of these movements, despite Arshad's singular refusal to move, is where we might find momentum for change.

To conclude: the trouble with stories is they are seductive. They become the fabulations of very different realities. Killers do not live in a vacuum. We must question our addiction to phantasmagoria, the collective dissociation and collusion that allow us to accept and detach from atrocities; the cultural and cinematic enfolding of violence into subjectivity and experience, the ease with which Arshad followed a pathway into killing, and with which political leaders pursue mass murder. Can such stories become a way to write against political practices that resort automatically to violence? Telling stories involves being changed—and becoming open to being changed—by them. Telling Arshad's story created a dissonance; a space of transformation which polarised our parts in the film. His story did traumatise me. It is also sad. Now, I feel a different kind of incomprehension at his refusal to entertain the idea that his actions were wrong. This means, for Arshad, that I have betrayed him. Perhaps he fears if he allows the guilt to touch him, he might break. But as it engulfed him, and took on a life of its own, so did his film animate another truth: in the end we are accountable for our stories.

References

Aretxaga, Begoña, 'Madness and the Politically Real: Reflections on Violence in Postdictatorial Spain', in Mary-Jo DelVecchio Good (ed.), *Postcolonial Disorders*, Berkeley: University of California Press, 2008, pp. 43–61.

Bhabha, Homi, *The Location of Culture*, New York: Routledge, 1994.

Bollas, Christopher, *Cracking Up*, New York: Hill & Wang, 1995.

Das, Veena, *Affliction*, New York: Fordham University Press, 2015.

Freud, Sigmund, *The Neuropsychoses of Defence*, 'Project', Standard edition, Vol. 3, London: Hogarth Press, 1966 (1894).

Good, Byron, 'Theorizing the 'Subject' of Medical and Psychiatric Anthropology', *Journal of the Royal Anthropological Institute*, 18, August (2012), pp. 515–35.

Howell, Elizabeth, *The Dissociative Mind*, New York and Hove: Routledge, 2005.

Jaspers, Karl, *General Psychopathology, vols. 1 & 2*, Baltimore and London: Johns Hopkins University Press, 1997 (1913), trans. J. Hoenig and Marian W. Hamilton.

Kapferer, Bruce, 'How Anthropologists Think: Configurations of the Exotic', *Journal of the Royal Anthropological Institute*, 19, November (2013), pp. 813–37.

Khan, Nichola a, 'On the Limits of Empathy: a Note on Psychoanalysis and a Case of Extreme Violence in Pakistan. *Clio's Psyche, Special edition, Anthropology and Psychoanalysis: Intersections of the Intrapsychic and Social*, Aaron Denham (ed.), March (2014), pp. 408–12.

———— b, *Mohajir Militancy in Pakistan. Violence and Practices of Transformation in the Karachi Conflict*, London and New York: Routledge, 2010.

———— c, 'Violence, Anti-/convention and Desires for Transformation amongst Pakistan's Mohajirs in Karachi', *Cultural Dynamics*, 22, November (2010), pp. 225–46.

Laing, Ronald D., *The Divided Self*, London: Penguin, 1960 (2010).

Leader, Darian, *What is Madness?*, London: Penguin, 2012.

Singh, Brighupati, *Poverty and the Quest for Life. Spiritual and Material Striving in Rural India,* University of Chicago Press, 2015.

Taussig, Michael, *Shamanism, Colonialism and the Wild Man. A Study in Terror and Healing*, University of Chicago Press, 2001.

————, *The Nervous System*, New York: Routledge, 1992.

3

KARACHI

A PASHTUN CITY?

Zia Ur Rehman

On 20 December 2014 a seminar entitled 'I am Karachi' was organised in a Karachi hotel by the Pakistan Institute of Labour Education and Research, a Karachi-based civil society group. One of the speakers, Dr Kaiser Bengali, a prominent Pakistani economist and researcher, began by stating that Karachi, a Sindhi-majority city at the time of Partition (1947), was now an Urdu-speaking majority city. This came as no surprise to the audience. 'However,' he continued, 'by 2045, Karachi will be a Pashtun-majority city.' Reporting on the seminar, I observed several participants, mainly political workers, journalists, and development sector activists, react with astonishment. Yet undoubtedly Karachi hosts the world's largest urban Pashtun population, surpassing those in Peshawar, Quetta, Kandahar, and Kabul. Karachi is the largest Pashto-speaking city in the world; more Pashtuns live in Karachi than any other city in the world. Pashtuns have lived in Karachi since Partition. For many, Karachi is their first home.

Bengali cited the rapid demographic changes that had accompanied the arrival of migrants from the North West Frontier Province (NWFP, renamed Khyber Pakhtunkhwa in 2010) and the Federally Administered Tribal Areas (FATA) in the 2000s. He also cited high birth rates, increasing household sizes, and the lack of employment in Khyber Pakhtunkhwa and FATA as reasons for Pashtun migration to Karachi which is a major industrial centre, and Pakistan's only commercial port. Sindh's ethnic parties and civil society organisations have responded with persistent concerns about the influx of people displaced by military offensives in Khyber Pakhtunkhwa and FATA into Karachi, where local and foreign migrants are numerous. They fear the large-scale migration of internally displaced persons (IDPs) would even further alter Karachi's disturbed ethnic balance (Rehman, July 2014). This chapter develops on Bengali's extraordinary claim. It draws political economic, social, and demographic connections between historical and contemporary analyses, and on decades of professional fieldwork on issues concerning Pashtuns, Pashtun political mobilisation and grievances, nationalism, and religious politics, as a Karachi citizen and a Pashtun myself.

Prior to Partition, Pashtun neighbourhoods existed in Lyari, one of Karachi's oldest neighbourhoods near to the seaport. After the 1960s, rapid economic development and industrialisation led many Pashtuns from Pakistan's north-west to seek opportunities in Karachi's construction, textile, and transport sectors. These migrants, as journalists and scholars have noted, contributed significantly to Karachi's economy through low paid wage labour, petty jobs, and small trade. Many Karachiites at this time employed 'honourable' Pashtuns as guards, watchman, drivers and cooks, and enjoyed the delicious Afghan dishes, naan, and unique 'Pashtun' tea from Balochistan they prepared.

Census reports expand on a more worrying picture. For Sindhis the loss of Karachi has been severe. In 1947 Sindhis comprised 60 per cent of Karachi's population, but by 1951 they had been reduced to a mere 8.6 per cent, owing mainly to the large-scale influx of 'Mohajir' Muslim migrants from divided India into Pakistan. The secession of East Pakistan in 1971 resulted in another large-scale in-migration from what would become Bangladesh. Census reports in 1981 and 1998 put Karachi's Sindhi population at 6.29 and 7.22 per cent respectively. The

1998 census recorded over a million Pashtuns—11.42 per cent of Karachi's entire population—numbers which Pashtun politicians and civil society activists argue are even so underestimated. Hassan Buneri, a population science researcher at Karachi University, suggests first, 'a lack of awareness and organised civil society organisations among Pashtun communities as one reason for non-participation in the 1998 census'. He cites the 'myth of return' as a second reason. Here he refers to the widespread belief amongst Pashtuns that they will eventually return to their hometowns, which dissuades people from participating in census surveys.

Karachi additionally incorporated a large number of Afghan refugees who fled to Pakistan in the 1980s after the Soviet invasion, as well as during the Taliban regime (1996–2001). UNHCR figures estimate around 1.5 million registered Afghan refugees currently in Pakistan carrying Proof of Registration (PoR) cards. According to Afghanistan's Ambassador in Pakistan, Janan Mosazai, approximately 65,000 registered Afghan refugees currently reside in Karachi (as of March 2015).[1] However, Afghan tribal elders and researchers estimate actual numbers to be much higher at nearer 5 million. While many Pashto-speaking Afghans have received Pakistani citizenship cards, many are not registered, and many Dari-speaking Afghans still live in Afghan camps established near the northern by-pass, and in the slums of Sohrab Goth.

Karachi's Pashtuns mostly live in western and eastern Karachi, including settlements around the super highways such as Sohrab Goth, Sindh Industrial Trade Estate (SITE), Landhi Industrial Area, Korangi Industrial Area, Keamari, Baldia Town, Sultanabad, and Pipri. Almost all are unplanned settlements built on the hillside. The majority of these residents originate from Malakand, Hazara and Mardan Divisions of Khyber Pakhtunkhwa, South Waziristan, Bajaur, the Momand and Khyber tribal agencies of FATA, and Pashtun districts in Balochistan. Again, severe poverty, unemployment, and high population growth are key reasons Pashtuns from these areas migrated to Karachi.

Recognising the contested nature and unavailability of official statistics, Karachi's Pashtun population is nonetheless estimated between 4 and 7 million, totalling some 25 per cent of Karachi's population,

[1] Personal communication.

and around 15 per cent in Sindh. Karachi's Mohajir population is estimated at between 7 and 9 million, or 45 per cent of Karachi's population and 23 per cent of Sindh (Saleem, 2010). Thus, after the Mohajirs,
Pashtuns represent the city's second largest ethnic group.

During my work as a journalist and researcher from 2005 to the present, I analysed military operations against Taliban groups across Khyber
Pakhtunkhwa and FATA, Taliban militancy in these areas, and those
operations begun in 2009 which forcibly displaced millions of people
from their hometowns. Large numbers of internally displaced persons
(IDPs) in Swat, Bajaur, and South Waziristan joined relatives in Karachi,
and settled with their assistance. These demographic and political transformations and migrations further intensified after the 2005 earthquake.
The earthquake, of a 7.6 magnitude, occurred on 8 October 2005 in
Pakistan-administered Kashmir. It also severely affected six northern
districts of NWFP. Reports by the Pakistani government, aid organisations, and the International Organisation of Migration (IOM) estimate
that in excess of 73,000 people died overall in Pakistan, and around
69,000 were injured. In the affected areas, the earthquake devastated
entire infrastructures and communication systems, and left around 2.8
million people homeless. In NWFP, Mansehra was the worst affected;
parts of Battagram, Shangla, Kohistan, and Swat were also severely
affected. Reporting on the earthquake, I witnessed the large-scale
destruction of houses and businesses. Many Pashtuns also migrated to
Karachi, to join relatives living in different parts of the city.

In 2009 in Swat a peace agreement failed between Taliban militants
and the Khyber Pakhtunkhwa government of the liberal, ethno-nationalist Awami National Party (ANP). Taliban militants led by Maulana
Fazlullah took over large parts of Swat, and the neighbouring districts
of Buner and Upper Dir. I conducted interviews with Swat-based journalists, governmental officials, and aid organisations. They suggest that,
in the subsequent military operations, as many as 2.2 million IDPs fled
to other parts of Khyber Pakhtunkhwa, including Mardan, Swabi, and
Peshawar. Many other displacees moved to Karachi where a large Swati
community has existed for two to three decades. Although official statistics on Swat's IDPs in Karachi are not available through government
or aid organisations, independent social researchers working extensively on militancy-related issues in the region suggest around 20,000

Swati families migrated to Karachi at this time, and settled in different Pashtun neighbourhoods (Ali Arqam, personal communications, 30 December 2014).

Similarly, in late 2009, military operations across Bajaur district compelled many families to flee; a significant number headed to Karachi. Certainly seasonal migration from Bajaur to Karachi existed before 2009. Since the1970s, Bajaur's freezing winters have tempted many young men to Karachi where they worked mainly as cobblers, road diggers, and truck loaders. These men initially over-wintered on a temporary basis of three to five months, and shared rented accommodation. Over time, they purchased properties and settled their families.

Regarding migration from Waziristan, since 2004 four major military operations have been launched against Taliban militants in South Waziristan, especially in its Mehsud areas. The Operation *Rah-e-Nijat* (Path to Salvation) offensive began in October 2009 and continued through 2012 (Rehman April 2012). In 2010 around 364,000 inhabitants of the five districts (*tehsils*) Ladha, Makeen, Sararogha, Sarweki, and Khaisor belonging to the Mehsud tribe were displaced during the operation (January 2010). Whilst some displacees migrated to the adjacent settled districts of Tank and Dera Ismail Khan, and the Bannu and Peshawar districts of Khyber Pakhtunkhwa, the majority came to Karachi. Mehsud activists in Karachi suggest one reason was that law enforcement agencies were pressurising locals in Tank and Dera Ismail Khan not to offer shelter to Mehsud IDPs. They estimate that around 60 per cent Mehsud IDPs joined relatives in Karachi. They also cited tribal feuds as additional reasons for migrating (IRIN November 2009). The majority of IDP families in Karachi settled to form a very low-income class, rent the cheapest accommodation, and compete for the lowest paid employment.

After the government announced it had cleared their areas of Taliban militants, the majority of IDPs from Swat and Bajaur returned to their hometowns. Whilst their stay in Karachi lasted only three or four months, the Mehsud IDPs' situation is different. Although government officials claimed several times that the Mehsud area of South Waziristan was cleared of militants, and sent displacees back, many were unwilling to return to their villages for fear militants were hiding in mountains, or had escaped to adjacent areas. Most displaced Mehsud tribesmen I spoke to in Karachi were not ready to return owing to security concerns, their damaged homes, and the lack of livelihood opportunities, electricity, food, and basic amenities. Again in mid-2014, the Pakistani military started operations in North Waziristan and the Khyber Agency districts of FATA, forcing local populations to flee. These residents did not come to Karachi but travelled to the neighbouring towns of Bannu, Lakki Marwat, Kohat, and Peshawar. Unlike the Mehsuds or Swatis, the main two tribes of North Waziristan—the Utmanzai Wazir and Dawar tribes—do not have relatives or settled communities in Karachi. For similar reasons, the IDPs from Khyber Agency tended to go to Peshawar and Nowshera.

Paying attention to later transformations should not detract from older Pashtun settlements in Karachi. Certainly, the last two decades have produced a new Karachi-born Pashtun educated and professional class. Success in business and public transport industries, in trade in trucks and heavy machinery, and in acquiring government contracts to supply NATO forces for the war in Afghanistan, moreover led many Pashtuns to become exceedingly wealthy. Alongside their economic successes, Pashtun activists argue they are discriminated against in government sector employment, in admissions to Karachi's academic institutions, and in city and district government representation. Political experts cite historical and contemporary factors, in combination with unchecked and unmanaged mass migration, in their explanations of societal breakdown involving Pashtuns, the rise of criminality and serious conflicts, and the ways these acquired the cultural and ethnic patina of irrevocable difference—not only between Pashtuns and other communities, but amongst Pashtuns themselves. How have these issues shaped Pashtun politics in Karachi?

Political mobilisation

Despite being Karachi's second largest ethnic community, Karachi's Pashtuns are politically under-represented at all governmental levels. ANP leaders complain Pashtun communities have been held back by MQM-led district and provincial governments. Anti-Pashtun discrimination was particularly severe during General Pervez Musharraf's regime (2001–08). Pashtuns accused Musharraf of the wholesale handover of Karachi and Hyderabad to the MQM. In May 2011 I conducted an interview with the President of the ANP in Sindh, Shahi Syed. Syed clearly iterated this position: 'The fight in Karachi is not limited to Pashtuns or the ANP. It is against the control of Karachi by MQM who assumes Karachi and Hyderabad belong to them and none other. According to the 1973 constitution, every Pakistani can live and do business in every city of the country.'

Correspondingly, ANP leaders complain that Pashtuns are facing multiple forms of discrimination, especially severe in employment and hiring practices. They are not employed at governmental organisations such as the Karachi city district government, the Karachi Port Trust (KPT), or the Karachi Water and Sewerage Board (KWSB), and experience wholesale discrimination at the Karachi Electric Supply Corporation (KESC). In 2011 the Human Rights Commission reported that students with matriculation certificates from Khyber Pakhtunkhwa and FATA were not granted admission in Karachi's colleges. The situation thus became entrenched. At the same time, Pashtun-dominated areas across Karachi remained less developed.

Karachi's Pashtuns traditionally aligned themselves with various political and religious parties. In the main these are the ANP, the Pakistan People's Party (PPP), the Pakistan Muslim League-Nawaz (PML-N), Jamaat-e-Islami (JI), and since its founding in 1996, the Pakistan Tehreek-e-Insaf (PTI). During the 1980s, some Pashtun ethnic groups, particularly the Punjabi Pashtun Ittehad (PPI) led by Ghulam Sarwar Awan and Irfanullah Marwat, became active when ethnic violence erupted between Mohajir and Pashtun communities. On 15 April 1985 a bus accident in the Nazimabad area led to the death of a Mohajir girl, a college student named Bushra Zaidi. Zaidi's death precipitated ethnic riots and violence in the city. According to media reports, fifty people were killed and more than 300 injured in just one week (Imtiaz and Ahmed, 2012).

The reckless driver, who was caught and pursued in the courts, was a Pashtun. Pashtuns, moreover, dominated Karachi's transport industries. Karachi's Mohajirs, mobilising around an ascendant MQM, began distributing incendiary leaflets against Pashtuns in Mohajir-populated areas. For their part, the leaders of the PPI and Pashtun Federation (PF) themselves began organising rallies and delivering inflammatory speeches against Mohajir communities in Pashtun neighbourhoods. Zafar Abbas (1998) documents that in the following three years (April 1985–May 1988) 358 deaths ocurred and 1,355 people were injured in 2,606 riots across the city. Orangi Town, Liaquatabad, and North Nazimabad became virtual battlefields. The army imposed curfew conditions for 353 days during those three years in response to wholesale failures by the partisan police to curtail ethnic violence.

The MQM and ANP leadership realised that state forces were fuelling communal hatred, and sought to resolve the problem. Altaf Hussain, who was in jail at the time, invited the ANP head Wali Khan to Karachi, but Khan was prevented from travelling by government sanctions. He eventually came on the eve of the PPP leader Benazir Bhutto's wedding, where he met MQM leaders. Afterwards, Wali Khan and another senior leader, Ghulam Ahmed Bilour, got agreement from Pashtun communities for a ceasefire between Pashtuns and Mohajirs, during a rally at Banaras Chowk in Lyari (*Express Tribune* 2013). To mark the occasion the chowk was renamed Bacha Khan Chowk by the MQM city mayor, Dr Farooq Sattar. After the truce, peace prevailed for almost a decade, save when the notorious 1998 Riffat Afridi case brought Karachi to a standstill, after a Mohajir boy, Kanwar Ahsan, married a Pashtun girl against her family's wishes. The marriage sparked widespread riots. A council (*jirga*) of Pashtuns led by Tariq Khan, a Pashtun leader affiliated to the PML-N, and Amir Nawab who later joined the ANP in 2011, sought to exploit the situation to fuel ethnic violence and hatred. The ANP leaders were not, however, in universal agreement. Amin Khattak in particular opposed the *jirga*'s aggressive politics. Peaceful relations between MQM and the ANP subsequently prevailed largely up to 2007, when renewed ethnic violence occurred. This time, the ANP emerged as a more aggressive force under the leadership of Shahi Syed.

Syed was in his late fifties. A businessman who owned numerous petrol stations in Karachi, he migrated to Karachi in 1971 from the small town of Babuzai in District Mardan of Khyber Paktunkhwa province. In 2001 he joined the ANP and owing largely to his standing as a wealthy patron, was appointed Central Finance Secretary by the ANP head, Asfandyar Wali. Before Syed, ANP leaders mostly came from the lower or lower middle classes, and could not afford financial donations. In 2003, Syed was unanimously appointed President of the ANP in Sindh. This followed the 2002 general elections, in which the ANP fielded nine candidates in different Pashtun-majority constituencies of Karachi, but did not win a single seat. Following voters' trends in their home town districts in NWFP, FATA and Balochistan, Karachi's Pashtuns voted for the Mutahida Majlis-e-Amal (MMA), a nation-wide electoral alliance of six religious parties led by the Jamiat-e-Ulema Islam-Fazl (JUI-F) and JI.

In early 2006, Syed sought to unite Karachi's Pashtuns on a single platform. In April he formed the Pashtun Action Committee, which he also named the Loya Jirga (Grand Assembly). He mustered support from wealthy Pashtun transporters and influential political figures, especially those belonging to the Pakhtunkhwa Milli Awami Party (PkMAP), the PPP, and the PML-N. According to Syed, the alliance was formed in direct response to the Sindh government's decision to demolish many *katchi abadis* (unplanned settlements) and ban two-stroke rickshaws in Karachi, at the behest of the MQM which was then part of the ruling coalition at the federal level, and in Sindh. In the beginning, many Pashtun leaders from different political and religious parties, clan-based organisations, and transporters' associations joined the Loya Jirga. Seeking to pressurise the government, they organised a number of public rallies during June 2006 across the city, and called a strike on 30 June (*Dawn*, June 2006). After some negotiations, the government accepted the Jirga's key demands which, analysts believe, served to recognise its strength and help boost ANP support in Karachi.

A watershed moment for the ANP in Karachi came on 12 May 2007. The Chief Justice Iftikhar Chaudhry had been removed from the bench by General Pervez Musharraf. The deposed Chief Justice planned to fly to Karachi to address lawyers at the High Court. Gunfights and violent clashes ensued when the MQM, an ally of Musharraf, attempted to prevent Chaudhry's entry into the city. Forty-eight people were killed in subsequent clashes between the ANP and the PPP, who had supported Chaudhry and the MQM. The MQM was implicated in the widespread violence. The majority of victims were Pashtuns.

Journalists likened the 12 May incident to the Bushra Zaidi case of 1985 which marked the beginning of renewed violence between the two parties. Academics such as Gayer note that 12 May 'signalled the emergence of a new political and military force determined to challenge the domination of the MQM over Karachi' (2014, 118). The ensuing ANP-MQM violence led hundreds of innocent people, mainly apolitical and daily wage workers, to be targeted. The situation continued largely up until 2013 when the emergence of Taliban groups threatened both parties.

Syed tactically used the *jirga* to mobilise Pashtuns over the killings of 12 May, and called for strikes. In the general elections of February 2008, the PPP made an alliance with the ANP who won the provincial Labour Ministry and, for the first time, two seats in the Sindh Assembly in two Pashtun majority neighbourhoods—Landhi Industrial area, and SITE Town. The ANP had also positioned itself as a crucial ally at the federal level, inviting increased support in Karachi. This stronger PPP-ANP alliance boosted each party's political standing against the MQM and increasingly violent clashes between the MQM and the ANP ensued.

Whilst the Loya Jirga was a major factor behind the ANP's rise on Sindh's political scene its public presence declined gradually as member parties, including the JI, PMAP, and PML-N, failed to sustain momentum in their zones (Khattak June 2012). Notably, whilst the Loya Jirga was a non-political body originally formed to protect the rights of Pashtuns in Karachi, leaders of political parties within the Loya Jirga became progressively unhappy with the ANP's dominance. 'We participated in the Loya Jirga's first meeting, but it was a one-party show,' said Abdul Ali Ghourghushti, a Karachi leader of the PkMAP. In an interview I conducted with Ghourghushti in May 2010, he criticised how the ANP's assumption of control over decision-making had sidelined other parties: 'After the 12 May 2007 tragedy, Loya Jirga leaders decided to hold a three-day strike in the city, but later withdrew their decision without consulting us'.

Of the 168 seats in the Sindh Assembly, Karachi has forty-one seats. In the 2008 General Elections, the ANP and PPP won two and six seats respectively. The remaining seats went to the MQM. Based on population statistics, Karachi's Pashtuns comprise 25 per cent of the population, and might proportionately be expected to gain ten seats in the provincial legislature, not two. For analyst Farrukh Saleem (2010) this political power reality was way out of sync with demographic realties. Likewise, the PPP had ninety-three members in the provincial assembly, 95 per cent outside Karachi, and only six in Karachi.

The Pashtun vote

I turn next to consider how these events were influenced by wider forms of political mobilisation involving Pashtuns, and progressive divisions that formed between nationalist, religious, and more extreme affiliations. Pashtun votes in Karachi have traditionally been influenced by political trends at the national level, especially those in Khyber Pakhtukhwa. Pashtun localities are known for their diverse political support base. One sees flags, graffiti, and the offices of almost all the political and religious parties active in Pashtun communities (Arqam, April 2013).

Before the ANP's emergence as a popular nationalist party, the Pashtun vote bank largely inclined towards religio-political and national parties. Throughout the ethnic violence of the 1980s, many Karachi

Image 6: Candidates from the Awami National Party, Pakistan Tehreek-e-Insaf, Ahle Sunnat Wal Jammat, and Jamaat-e-Islami display party flags in Sohrab Goth in local government polls, 25 November 2015 (Zia Ur Rehman).

Pashtuns supported the PPI, led by Malik Sarwar Awan and Ifranullah Marwat. The PPI's influence declined in the early 1990s. This became clear when in the 2002 general election Karachi Pashtuns voted on religious lines. The Muttahida Majlis-e-Amal (MMA), an electoral alliance of religious parties, had four Pashtun members in the Sindh Assembly and one in the National Assembly from Karachi. Other political party leaders, especially JUI-F, JI and PkMAP, complained that the media had unintentionally (or intentionally) promoted the ANP by assuming it was the official mouthpiece of Karachi's Pashtuns. When I interviewed Qari Muhammed Usman, Karachi President of the JUI-F in August 2012, he claimed: 'I challenge, there are many more Pashtuns in JUI-F than the ANP because these are traditionally, and culturally religious-minded people.' Thus we see the articulation of a schism between nationalist, religious, and more extreme mobilisations, which would subsequently become severe.

By January 2014 the ANP's presence in Karachi's Pashtun-dominated areas had significantly declined, owing to continuous attacks by the Tehreek-e-Taliban Pakistan (TTP), including more than 120 ANP activists, between June 2012 and December 2014. The JI began working to form a *jirga* comprising representatives of various Pashtun clans, traders and civil society groups. For the task, they chose Abdul Razzaq, a popular figure among the city's Pashtuns. Razzaq had twice been elected mayor of the Metroville Union Council of SITE Town. When I interviewed him that month he explained that whilst JI enjoyed immense support among Pashtun communities, by contrast the *jirga* had no political ambitions. Its main objective was to pressurise the police authorities to stop the extra-judicial killings and harassment of Pashtuns, especially those from tribal areas.

The MQM rejected outright the ANP's claims that they usurped Pashtuns in Karachi. It insisted its support and representation extended beyond Mohajirs exclusively and cited as evidence its name change in 1997 from the Mohajir (refugee, or migrant) Qaumi Movement to the Muttahida (united) Qaumi Movement. The rationale for the name change was to extend MQM representation to all ethnicities, sects, religions, and classes. Earlier, the party had formed the Pashtun Punjabi Organising Committee (PPOC), which it transformed into the Muttahida Organising Committee. In its early years, there was no

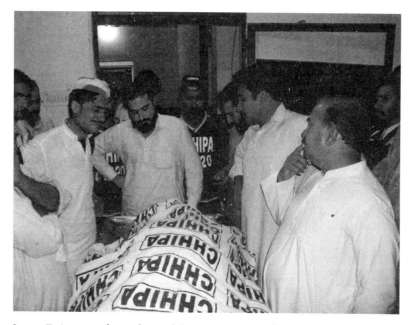

Image 7: Aggrieved members of the Awami National Party gather around the body of district president Saifullah Khan who was assassinated by the Tehreek-e-Taliban Pakistan, 5 January 2015 (Zia Ur Rehman).

Pashtun representation in the MQM's policy-making forums. Over time they introduced Pashtun representation. By early 2015, two Pashtun members sat on the MQM's Coordination Committee, the party's most powerful policy-making forum. One of them, Gul Faraz Khattak, granted me an interview. The ANP was spreading misperception and hatred against other ethnicities, especially Mohajirs, Khattak claimed: 'Pashtuns have no economic clashes with Mohajirs. This is a misperception. Nor do all Pashtuns support the ANP. Some elements fuel ethnic violence to protect illicit businesses.' Khattak added that the MQM was interested in discussing strategies to end ethnic violence with the ANP, and regretted the ANP leadership had expressed little interest (Rehman September 2011). Haider Abbass Rizvi, another central leader of the MQM, claimed 85 per cent of Karachi citizens, including Pashtuns, had voted for the MQM. Nonetheless, he continued, some forces wished to curtail the MQM in Karachi's Pashtun-dominated areas. Whilst ethnic riots and violence did occur between 1985 and 1988, both party leaders, Altaf Hussain and Wali Khan, had met and reached a conclusive peace accord. The late Wali Khan and Altaf Hussain had wished to end communal violence and indeed were successful. Rizvi also stated that the ANP Sindh leadership did not want peace, and therefore would not negotiate a new truce (Buneri 2012). Illustrating this line, in June 2012, the MQM arranged a huge gathering of Pashtuns wherein the MQM chief Altaf Hussain asked his workers to protect the businesses of Pashtun traders in their areas (*MQM News*, June 2012).

Enter the Taliban

After June 2012 most of Karachi's Pashtun-populated areas fell under the complete influence of the TTP. I have written extensively around controversies concerning the 'Talibanisation' of Karachi in my work as a journalist. I revisit some of these questions here. These are relevant to this chapter's emphasis on detailing historical and contemporary alliances, political and economic, and on bringing these to contextual-ise representations of Pashtun politics in an increasingly Pashtun-dominated city.

On the evening of 9 August 2012, ANP workers began closing their offices, removing party flags and graffiti in Sohrab Goth, Manghopir, Pipri, Ittehad Town, and other Pashtun-populated areas where Mehsud tribesmen comprise a majority. ANP leaders from the Mehsud tribe in Sorabh Goth revealed that TTP leaders had asked Mehsud tribes-people in Karachi to leave the party, or be killed. A week later, the TTP Swat chapter, led by Maulana Fazlullah, now central chief of the organisation, claimed responsibility for killing a Karachi ANP leader and the former Union Council Mayor Amir Sardar in Frontier Colony. ANP leaders cite August 2012 as the month the TTP openly targeted the ANP. Police offi-cials and Pashtun activists associate the TTP's rise in Karachi with insur-gencies and military operations in Khyber Pakhtunkhwa and FATA since 2009. Militants from Swat, South Waziristan, Mohmand, Bajaur, Dir and elsewhere began taking refuge after the government launched military operations. Karachi, with a population of about twenty million including approximately five million Pashtuns, provided manifold sanctuaries.

Many militants-in-hiding shaved their breads, cut their long hair, worked as petty labourers, and organised their activities after nightfall. One Mehsud tribal elder living in IttehadTown told me: 'In the beginning, the TTP were not involved in subversive activities. It was aTTP policy to use Karachi only for fund-raising, rest, and recuperation from theWaziristan insurgency. But since, they seemed to have changed their strategy.'

After June 2012 law and order deteriorated most in those areas where TTP factions had joined hands with local sectarian outfits and criminal syndicates in order to increase insurgency-related activities, and scale-up their fund-raising campaigns. These became total 'no-go areas' for law enforcement agencies, for liberal political activists— especially those belonging to the ANP—for polio vaccination programme administrators, and for non-governmental organisations (Walsh and Rehman 2013). It must be emphasised that theTTP is not a monolith. It is, in fact, composed of different groups. AsTTP militants moved into Karachi, they predictably organised into factions according to their regional origins. In Karachi, there were three TTP factions—the Mehsud, Swat, and Mohmand. These groups have been actively running networks in various neighbourhoods. Swati and Mehsud militants migrated to Karachi after military operations began in Swat and South Waziristan in 2008 and 2009 respectively; the TTP Mohmand chapter sent their militants to Karachi for fund-raising in 2011. The three groups have their own internal leadership structure but support each other in their broader shared objectives (Rehman, May 2013).

Analysts suggest TTP tribal militants did not possess the resources, skills and expertise to conduct specialised operations in Karachi and for this reason combined forces with local sectarian and jihadi outfits, Lashkar-e-Jhangvi in particular. In an interview in June 2014, the senior police official Chaudhry Aslam fearfully expressed to me how this deleterious nexus had increased the risk of terrorist attacks in Karachi.

Mehsud militants dominate the most powerful TTP faction in Karachi which is divided organisationally into two groups, one loyal to TTP's central chief Hakimullah Mehsud, and the second to the TTP chief in South Waziristan, Waliur Rehman Mehsud. In August 2013 Waliur Rehman's faction expelled the Hakimullah group from Karachi. Internecine fighting broke out when militants loyal toWaliur Rehman killed Sher Khan, a key commander of the Hakimullah group in the Manghopir area, that month. Between August and November 2013, rivals killed thirty key members of Hakimullah's Mehsud-led faction (Rehman October 2013). Khan Saeed, popularly known as Sajna, was appointed successor of Waliur Rehman after his killing in a drone attack in North Waziristan in May 2013, a change which strengthened the group in Karachi. That is, the Sajna faction depends on militants of its own Mehsud tribe, but also supports other factions. It additionally resolves business disputes between Mehsud tribesmen through *jirgas*. It is active in many suburban areas including Ittehad Town, Mingophir, Kunwari Colony, Pashtun Abad, Sohrab Goth, and settlements on Super Highway, Pipri, Shah Latif Town, and Gulshan-e-Buner (Landhi)—areas all dominated by the Mehsud tribe.

The TTP Swat faction is loyal to its leader in Swat, Maulana Fazlullah, who is also the organisation's chief. Whilst little information exists about the leadership of Swati militants in Karachi, Karachi CID officers claim Azizullah Shamzai is the head of the Swat TTP's Karachi faction. Most Swati militants operating in Karachi belong to the Kanju, Kabal, Matta, and Charbagh sub-divisions of the Swat valley. The Swati TTP militants operate in Ittehad Town, Pirabad, Qasba Colony, Frontier Colony, Banaras, Metrovel, Future Colony, Sherpao Colony, and Gulshan-e-Buner. In keeping with regional tribal methods of resolving family and business disputes, Swati and Mehsud militants do not intervene in the disputes of people from Malakand division.

The TTP Mohmand chapter also organised in Karachi in order to collect protection money from people from Mohmand Agency. Like Mehsud and Swati militants, they did not arrive in Karachi as displacees. The TTP Mohmand chief Abdul Wali, popularly known as Omar Khalid Khorasani, together with his deputy Qari Shakeel, dispatched a group to Karachi to raise funds. Several TTP Mohmand faction leaders in Karachi have been killed by law-enforcement agencies. Little information exists about their Karachi leadership. They are not concentrated in any specific areas; most likely their sanctuaries are in settlements on Northern by-pass and in Manghopir area. Interestingly demonstrating the autonomy of different factions, in September 2014 Mohmand militants defected from the TTP and formed a new faction named 'Jamaat-ul Ahrar'.

The TTP's key target in Karachi was the ANP. From June 2012 to December 2014, the TTP, especially its Swat faction, killed more than 120 ANP activists, including key leaders. Party offices across the city, including the provincial party headquarters Baacha Khan Markaz in Pirabad, have been closed since 2012. Through an organised campaign of killing influential Pashtun political leaders and elders in Karachi and forcing the ANP from most of its traditional strongholds, all Pashtun-majority areas of the city fell under the influence of the TTP. Several ANP party leaders left Karachi in the face of TTP threats, and returned to their native towns in Khyber Pakhtunkhwa.

The ANP did well in the 2008 general elections, and won two provincial assembly seats in Karachi's two largest Pashtun-populated areas. The situation was very different in 2013. In the general elections, rallies and offices of ANP candidates from the two areas, Bashir Jan and

Image 8: Paramilitary Rangers personnel in targeted operation against the Tehreek-e-Taliban Pakistan, Swat chapter, in Qasba Colony, 20 February 2015 (Zia Ur Rehman).

Amanullah Mehsud, were targeted by the TTP militants, who killed and injured several party activists. The TTP also claimed responsibility for killing Sadiq Zaman Khattak, an ANP candidate from NA-254 Korangi, in Bilal Colony on 2 May. A large number of party leaders and workers felt compelled to leave the party and join right-wing political parties such as the JI, the Pakistan Tehreek-e-Insaf (PTI), and the sectarian Ahle Sunnat Wal Jamaat (ASWJ).

Connections between Karachi and Swat have proved highly interesting. In June 2011 my work as a journalist took me to Swat. Here a TTP Swat faction had killed dozens of Swati pro-government elders, and those who supported security forces during the operations. Since 2009, a number of influential political figures and members of anti-Taliban committees from Swat who travelled to Karachi for personal or business reasons were murdered there (Rehman April 2011). Futhermore, dozens of Swati families resident in Karachi for three to four decades migrated to Swat because of the worsening security conditions in Karachi's Pashtun neighbourhoods. All three TTP factions have been involved in extorting from Karachi's Pashtun traders and transporters, school and hospital owners, and *madrassa* owners since June 2012. Several Pashtun traders I interviewed suggest many incidents go unreported because of the immense pressure the TTP effects; not least their practice of hurling hand grenades and killing those who do not pay. This is now common in Pashtun areas. A Mehsud transporter described to me in chilling terms: 'They are well aware of the exact wealth of everyone in their tribe'. The TTP Mehsud faction also systematically infiltrated the trade bodies of the heavy machinery and heavy-duty vehicle business, and local truck and minibus associations of Sohrab Goth. They imposed fixed taxes on the traders and transporters. TTP Mohmand militants were, moreover, collecting extortions from Mohmand tribesmen in Karachi, who are well-off and mainly involved in selling timber and construction material. These developments reflected the severe financial difficulties faced by the TTP following measures by Pakistani authorities to seize their main sources of foreign income, especially from the Gulf countries. Subsequently the leadership of all three factions instructed their Karachi members to collect funds through extortion and kidnapping for ransom, and to target Pashtun businessmen and transporters in order to re-stock diminishing resources for equipment, weapons, and national operational expenses. In response, law enforcement agencies, especially the Rangers, claimed they arrested several suspects from banned militant outfits in their continuous crackdowns. Yet this contradicts reports by the ANP, other political leaders, and Pashtun residents who reported that throughout the entire operation, the agencies failed to challenge the TTP. These are ominous developments for the city.

Karachi-Afghanistan connections?

Finally, let me draw distinctions and reflect further on divisions between the TTP and the Afghan Taliban. Karachi's religious leadership and Islamic seminaries historically played leading roles in the Afghan resistance against Russia (1979–89), in subsequent fighting against the Northern Alliance, and lending support to the Taliban regime in Afghanistan. Pakistani jihadi groups, having a strong influence in Karachi, dispatched significant numbers of fighters to the 2001–14 Afghan war. During the Taliban regime, its Karachi consulate remained fully functional. Following the US invasion in November 2001, the Taliban consul in Karachi, Maulvi Rahmatullah Kakazada, financially supported Karachi's seminaries and encouraged their students to join the Afghan Taliban.

The arrests of high-profile Afghan Taliban leaders in Karachi indicate the Afghan Taliban are using Karachi as an organisational hub. Police officials in Karachi believe that Karachi is not an operational command centre for the Afghan Taliban, and that its members are not involved in criminal networks and activities in the city. Mullah Abdul Ghani Baradar, second in command to Taliban leader Mullah Omar, was arrested in February 2010 in Karachi in a joint raid by Pakistani and US intelligence agencies. Other significant arrests that year by Pakistani authorities include Akhunzada Popalzai, also known as Mohammad Younis, a one-time Taliban shadow governor in Zabul province and former police chief in Kabul during Taliban rule; Ameer Muawiya, Afghan Taliban's liaison officer for al-Qaeda militants based in Pakistan's tribal areas; and Abu Hamza, who served as a former Afghan army commander in Helmand province.

Prior to 9/11, the Afghan Taliban relied heavily on funding from Islamic Gulf states and private donors. After 9/11, the Taliban greatly diversified its funding schemes to generate income. They allegedly established businesses in Pakistan, Karachi particularly, and in construction and transport firms in the United Arab Emirates. According to well-informed Afghan tribal elders in the city, all three key factions of Afghan Taliban—the Quetta Shura or Afghan Taliban, led by Mullah Omar until his death; the Haqqani Network led by Jalaluddin Haqqani; and the Hizb-i-Islami led by Gulbuddin Hekmatyar—operate in Karachi. The Quetta Shura-linked Afghan militants have the largest presence in the city. Afghan elders in Karachi say that the lower cadres of Afghan Taliban live in Karachi's Pashtun-populated areas, while its leaders reside in the city's wealthy areas and move freely in and around the city. Afghan militants have suggested that since the fall of the Afghan Taliban regime, 7–8,000 Taliban fighters are living in Karachi's suburban and Pashtun majority areas. Hussain reports that most Taliban fighters in Karachi were either born or raised in Pakistan during the 1980s (2011). They are now Pakistani citizens, and their role as fighters purely voluntary. Many travel to Afghanistan every year or so to join the Taliban insurgency for a few months. Whilst the Haqqani network depends largely on residents from Afghanistan's Khost province, in Pakistan they recruit fighters from Pakistani jihadi groups. Contrary to the support they enjoy in Peshawar, the Hizb-i-Islami has failed to establish significant support in the Pashtun-populated areas of Karachi. Their supporters are mainly from the Kharoti sub-branch of the Ghilzai Pashtuns from Kunduz province in Afghanistan. Karachi, clearly, represents a different political beast.

Conclusion

Pashtuns are undeniably becoming ascendant in Karachi. Correspondingly, they are the 'natural' key competitors of the city's Mohajirs. The evidence refutes analyses which suggest that in the coming two decades Karachi's ethnic diversity will increase to the extent that no ethnic group will dominate the city. Whichever scenario comes to pass, it seems clear that the city's rulers should abandon a narrow-minded communal vision in favour of uniting all of Karachi's ethnic groups, especially Pashtuns, and work toward a pluralistic mainstream politics and political culture. At the time of writing, there has been evidence of this occurring. In March 2015 the co-chairperson, former President of Sindh's ruling PPP and former President of Pakistan (2008–13) Asif Ali Zardari visited a Pashtun neighbourhood in Keamari area where he met a group of Pashtun elders at a local function in order to listen to their grievances. PPP leaders claimed their party was carefully monitoring the impact of demographic changes on Karachi, and using this information to prepare a new political direction around PPP policies in the city. One key reason behind such moves certainly points to the rapid rise of the PTI, which has succeeded in creating a mass base across many ethnic and class lines. Many Pashtun activists additionally believe that the PTI provides a fitting opportunity for Pashtuns to exit the 'sense of isolation', unrepresentativeness, and alienation they feel because of violence between the MQM and the ANP.

Karachi's Mohajirs and Pashtuns certainly share commonalities. Both groups originally migrated from their home towns for a better life, many without any intention of return. The late ANP leader Amin Khattak succinctly summarised the situation when I interviewed him in late 2009: 'Whether or not Karachi continues in its current position or becomes a separate state, neither can five million Pashtuns afford to go back to Khyber Pakhtunkhwa and FATA, nor can more than ten million Mohajirs return to India'. By drawing on and sharing in each other's potential, initiating joint businesses and most importantly, participating in non-ethnically based party politics, the two communities may yet forge a more peaceful urban environment. Notwithstanding, many Pashtun victims of Pakistan's military operations in Khyber Pakhtunkhwa and FATA who migrated to Karachi may yet return to their hometowns if the government provides them with security and economic opportunities. Certainly a widespread belief persitsts that large-scale migration into Karachi, especially from Pashtun regions, combined with the issue of voting rights, is the primary cause of political unrest. Speakers at the December 2014 seminar, the example with which I opened this chapter, proposed policymakers grant voting rights to individuals only after they have lived in Karachi for fifteen years, while at the same time they advocated imposing no restrictions on new migrants' right to work. It is unsettling that the outcome of such debates has significant implications for policies which may be implemented, regardless of whether they have widespread acceptance, are just, or are even feasible.

References

Abbas, Zafar, 'The road to anarchy', *Herald*, June 1988.

Arqam, Ali, 'The Pashtun vote in Karachi', *Pakistan Today*, 12 April 2013.

Buneri, Aziz, 'Urdu interview with MQM's deputy parliamentary leader Haider Abbass Rizvi', *Hum Shehri*, 6 July, 2012.

Dawn, 'Karachi: Loya jirga gives strike call', 19 June 2006.

Express Tribune. 'History lesson: ANP, MQM relations worsened in Mid 1980', 31 January 2013.

Gayer, Laurent, *Karachi: Ordered Disorder and the Struggle for the City*, London and New York: Hurst & Co., 2014.

Human Rights Commission of Pakistan, 'Karachi, Unholy Alliances for Mayhem', September 2011.

Hussain, Tom, 'Karachi, Besham choice home bases for Afghan Taliban', *The News*, 17 September 2011.

Imtiaz, Saba and Noman Ahmed, 'March 8: Bushra Zaidi, the woman who changed Karachi forever, by dying', *Express Tribune*, 8 March 2012, http://tribune.com.pk/story/346933/march-8-bushra-zaidi-the-woman-who-changed-karachi-forever-by-dying/, last accessed 11 May 2015.

Jan, Reza Nasim, 'Trickling Home to South Waziristan', *Foreign Policy*, 10 December 2010, http://foreignpolicy.com/2010/12/10/trickling-home-to-south-waziristan/, last accessed 11 May 2015.

Khattak, Sohail, 'Politicking: as LG polls approach, ANP eyes revival of loya jirga', *Express Tribune*, 3 June 2012.

MQM News. 'MQM will hold public meeting of the Pashtuns on 24 June in Karachi—Press Conference', 21 June 2012, http://www.mqm.org/englishnews/83/mqm-will-hold-public-meeting-of-the-pashtuns-on-the-24th-june-in-karachi-press-conference, last accessed 1 May 2015.

Rehman, Zia Ur, 'Karachi targeted killings of Pashtuns tied to militant groups', *Central Asia Online*, 1 April 2011.

————, 'No space for Pashtuns', *The Friday Times*, 2 September, 2011.

————, 'The Pakistani Taliban's Karachi Network', CTC Sentinel, 23 May 2013, https://www.ctc.usma.edu/posts/the-pakistani-talibans-karachi-network, last accessed 1 Nov. 2015.

————, 'Taliban factions fight over Karachi turf', *The Friday Times*, 25 October 2013.

————, 'Fear of small numbers', *The Friday Times*, 4 July 2014.

Saleem, Farrukh, 'Why Karachi is bleeding', *The News*, 21 October, 2010.

Walsh, Declan, and Zia Ur Rehman, 'Taliban spread terror in Karachi as the new gang in town', *New York Times*, 28 March 2013.

4

THE SUNDAY FIGHTER

DOUBTS, FEARS, AND LITTLE SECRETS
OF AN INTERMITTENT COMBATANT

Laurent Gayer

On 10 May 2013, as final preparations for Pakistan's general elections were underway, Iqbal and three other young men from his locality in eastern Karachi received a phone call from their political supervisor within the Muttahida Qaumi Movement (MQM). Karachi's dominant political force since the late 1980s, the MQM was in a belligerent mood. Its opponents claimed the party's support was waning in the city, and its leadership was determined to prove these prophets of doom wrong by registering yet another electoral triumph. Time was running short, however, and at this stage any mishap could prove disastrous. This is how Iqbal and his three companions were entrusted with a sensitive task: striking back at a group of party dissidents (the Haqiqis), who had recently infringed on their party's turf and 'captured some area' which the latter considered an integral part of its jurisdiction. The four young men were provided with weapons and, along with other party workers, were tasked to repel this intrusion, which besides the '*Haqiqi-wala*s' involved some Baloch fighters affiliated with the Peoples Aman Committee (PAC), a militia projecting itself as a social welfare organisation, at that time ruling the roost in Baloch-dominated inner city neighbourhoods and in urban villages scattered across the city (*goths*). Between two rounds of fighting, Iqbal found time to visit a local cyber-café, where he logged on to his Facebook account and started narrating to me the events of the day, before apologising for having to shorten our online chat: he now had to 'head back to the battlefield'.

The casual way in which Iqbal negotiated his involvement with these skirmishes and related them to me bears testimony to the routinisation of political violence in Karachi over decades of chronic civil strife. The timing of these events was particularly significant, as it showed that while political parties were completing their final preparations for the elections, they were also busy settling scores by deploying armed fighters, and in particular those intermittent combatants recruited from time to time by all major political forces to battle it out in the streets of the city. Far from being alien to the democratic process, these forms of political violence extend it and regulate it. In Karachi as in many other parts of South Asia, the path to electoral success often involves the control and public display of force. So much so that, for the rank and file of Karachi's political parties, the episodic exercise of violence has become an integral part of political work. To be a political activist, in this context, is tantamount to being recruited, at least part-time, into militant activities.

This casual nature of political violence in Karachi raises important questions on the lived experiences of militancy among the rank and file of the political parties competing for the control of the city and its resources. In Pakistan as elsewhere, violent forms of political, ethnic, and/or religious activism are generally perceived as the outcome of large-scale processes of disenfranchisement and, at the individual level of combatants, the result of a firm commitment to a specific set of beliefs, ethnicity, or ideology, which would encompass the entire personality and lifestyle of these young men. In this perspective, which remains dominant in conflict studies, violent mobilisations are primarily perceived as as symptom of societal ills, diagnosed through the identification of root causes and individual motivations. Against this fetishisation of background explanations, I have pleaded elsewhere for a study of conflict in motion, as it transforms its social environment and feeds on these societal changes (Gayer 2014, 12). Violence is no longer perceived as the symptom of collective dynamics or individual cognitions predating it, here. As suggested by Danny Hoffman in his anthropology of West Africa's Mano River War, it is first and foremost 'a form of labor', which can be exchanged for cash, land, or consumer goods. Another important contribution of Hoffman's study lies in his suggestion to avoid disaggregating individual psychology, economic motives, cultural logics, and political projects. All too often, scholars of conflict tend to consider these spheres of experience separately as they examine the lives of combatants, which inevitably leads them to give precedence to one of these spheres and to make it an explanatory variable for everything happening in other spheres. Against these dichotomies, Hoffman pleads in favour of a dynamic and 'holistic' anthropology of violence, which is brimming with promise for the study of other protracted crises such as that characterising Karachi since the mid-1980s. This is particularly true for its emphasis on the creative potential as well as the disruptive effects of these situations of prolonged conflict, where chronic uncertainty hinders the stabilisation of class positions, psychic states, and life projects. This 'deterritorialization of life itself', to use Gilles Deleuze and Félix Guattari's terminology (2009 [1972]), is most pronounced among combatants, whose entire life-sphere is at the mercy of forces beyond individual control (Hoffman 2011, 104–106).

The following pages also question the assumption that becoming an armed fighter would systematically induce a re-socialisation process setting the individual apart from his original milieu (Schafer 2001), a process which would amount to an 'initiatory rebirth as men of power', through the severing of kin ties in particular (Jackson 2005, 63). This might be true for some underground organisations and irregular armed groups waging guerrilla war against state forces, which often strive to produce a counter-society around their (wo)men in arms. This assumption is more debatable in the case of Karachi, however, at least for the rank and file of political parties who are only mobilised intermittently for militant activities (a situation which contrasts with that of full-time 'shooters' (Khan 2010)). Rather than a full-time occupation and state of mind, militancy can here be exercised part-time, in concert with other forms of political, professional or leisurely activities. This is not to downplay its significant challenges: part-time fighters always face the risk of being carried away by their high-risk activism, while their private lives are not immune to severe safety breaches. However intermittently they may be involved into violent activities, they are constantly under threat from their rivals. Preserving the sanctity of their personal realm, their own safety, and that of their family members is a daily struggle and a source of constant anxieties.

A self-restrained fighter

Iqbal is somewhat of an anomaly in Karachi's deeply ethnicised political landscape. In a city where every political party draws the bulk of its supporters and workers from a specific ethnic group (Mohajirs for the MQM, Pathans for the Awami National Party, Sindhis and Balochis for the Pakistan Peoples Party), it is relatively rare for young men to join a group which does not represent 'their' community. Of course, there are notable exceptions to this rule. Thus, the most (in)famous militant ever of the ANP, the late Liaquat Bangash, alias Liaquat 'Tension', was reputed to recruit his 'bodyguards' among Mohajirs, for fear of betrayal by his own party men. These remain isolated cases, however, which makes Iqbal's recruitment into the MQM an oddity. Indeed, Iqbal is not a Mohajir and while sympathising with the MQM's secular orientation and anti-establishment rhetoric, he was not drawn to the party on ideological grounds either. His enrolment into the party was guided by more mundane concerns (namely, a search for social status and upward social mobility), which only translated into actual engagement under the influence of micro- and macro-social events that radically altered his life's course, such as a series of individual 'career contingencies' (Goffman 1961, 133–4) and a sudden transformation of the political opportunity structure, following a reform of the legislation on local governments.

The turf wars waged by Karachi's political parties for the control of votes, territory, and economic rents (land, water, *bhatta* or extortion, *etcetera*) were part of Iqbal's life for as long as he can remember. He grew up and continues to live in one of the city's most notorious 'no-go areas', those neighbourhoods of disputed sovereignty where the authority of the state, without having entirely faded away, is exercised intermittently and shared with violent entrepreneurs. This impoverished locality has seen its share of political and criminal violence (I have purposely withheld topographic and social coordinates which could have compromised the anonymity that I guaranteed him when we first met in the mid 2000s). Throughout the 1990s, his *katchi abadi* and its surroundings, which include more affluent colonies, were a major terrain of confrontation between the MQM (Altaf) and the rival Haqiqi faction. In 2003 the MQM reasserted its authority over the neighbourhood, but in recent years the party has been facing multiple challenges, from the 'muscular Sufis' of the Sunni Tehreek (ST)—founded in 1990, the group has evolved into a more mainstream religious party in recent years, but it remains a well armed sectarian organisation with considerable muscle power—to Sindhi nationalists, to the Baloch gangsters of the PAC, to the Pakistani Taliban. From time to time, fighting erupts along the 'borders' of the locality, those contact zones between ethnically differentiated neighbourhoods then turning into front lines between political parties with distinctive ethnic vote-banks. Occasionally, violence strikes even closer to home. Over the years, Iqbal has lost several friends to incidents of inter-party violence or to confrontations between militant groups and law enforcers. Among them were fellow party workers but also more distant acquaintances who had joined rival groups, whether the Haqiqis or the Jihadis. Here as elsewhere in Karachi, while political parties tend to recruit workers within a specific ethnic group, this does not preclude social relations—as well as economic transactions across political, religious, and ethnic divides.

His father was relatively well-off (he had earned some money as a migrant worker in the Gulf) and Iqbal managed to pursue his education until university level. If he had to interrupt his studies before their term it was for less economic than political reasons. After intervening in a brawl between two student factions, he feared possible retaliation by an influential Islamist student union and dropped out of College. Iqbal then tried his luck in the army and spent some time in Balochistan as a *jawan* (infantry man). However, he soon realised that prospects of rapid upward social mobility in the military were more limited than he had anticipated, and when his first contract reached its term, he decided not to renew. He returned to Karachi and was resigned to 'timepass' while waiting for a new opportunity to present itself.

One day, as he was taking part in a demonstration for religious freedom, in the late 1990s, he was arrested and sent to jail together with several participants. The motives behind his arrest and his lack of political protections made him a prime target for the more religiously inclined detainees. However, before the latter could carry out their threats, a group of prisoners affiliated with the MQM stepped in and threatened the jihadis with dire consequences if they picked on their protégés. 'Remember, they won't be here for long, while we're here to stay,' the leader of the MQM-*walas* told the Islamists (who, at that time, remained in limited numbers in Karachi's Central Jail and, thus, were in no position to challenge the dominance of MQM-affiliated inmates). Even if Iqbal was indeed released after a few days, the episode left a deep imprint. Following the incident, he developed—as they say in Pakistan—a 'soft corner' for the MQM: 'They did what they said. They were protecting us. That was the motivation factor'. This motivation did not immediately translate into actual engagement, however. At that time, Iqbal was learning Japanese and toyed with the idea of moving to Japan to start a new life. What prompted him to enter into politics was the 2001 reform of local bodies, following the implementation of the Sindh Local Government Ordinance (SLGO). This reform transferred new competencies and financial resources from the provincial government to local bodies (the Karachi Municipal Corporation, as well as the Towns, and Union Councils representatives) and opened up new opportunities of upward social mobility to lower-income educated youths such as Iqbal.

By then the MQM leadership had determined to break away from the radical nationalism of yore (as the renaming of the party from *Mohajir* Qaumi Movement to *Muttahida* Qaumi Movement in 1997 demonstrated). Thus, it was eager to recruit and showcase non-Mohajirs to counter those who claimed these changes were purely cosmetic. Iqbal himself never felt completely at ease within the party, but in the initial years of his political career he convinced himself the party was indeed determined to reject its ethno-nationalist past. Or maybe he just chose to look the other way, and focus on the more ethnically neutral component of its ideology. In the aftermath of the 9/11 attacks, this made sense, as the MQM was the only party in Pakistan to take a strong secular, pro-Western stance. Thereby it appeared a beacon of cultural liberalism and modernity for young urbanites like Iqbal, who were searching for a political roof and could not find one in their own ethnic group. Finally, after allying itself with Pervez Musharraf, the MQM was now more powerful than it had ever been. No other political group in the city offered such a promising career option. Facing a few racial slurs occasionally from his party men was a small price to pay, after all, and maybe it would not last, thought Iqbal, as the party was bound to evolve into the pan-ethnic force it was publicly aspiring to become.

The decisive push, which translated Iqbal's 'motivation' into actual engagement, came from his family entourage. Taking notice of these emerging opportunities, his father encouraged him to join the party—a pragmatic rather than ideological choice, considering the dominance of the party in their locality—and to strive to earn a party ticket in local elections. While his father passed away a few years later, Iqbal put his advice to good use and, after formally joining the party (a process involving a six-month probation period during which every aspiring worker is placed under observation), he was elected a councillor in the following municipal elections (2005). He made the best of this new position of influence and 'took money from builders, contractors, everyone', justifying his practices of wealth accumulation by invoking the 'ethics of illegality' (Roitman 2005) allegedly prevailing in his milieu, which enabled him to deem his act illicit and yet legitimate: 'taking bribes is common and not considered a crime'. His lack of experience in this tricky trade provoked suspicions and earned him serious enmities. Soon enough, he was denounced to the party—probably by one of his relatives following a dispute—and forced to resign. After making amends, he resumed his political activities and a party cadre took him under his protection. In 2005, this cadre became a Union Council Nazim (local representative) of the MQM, and Iqbal seemed well positioned to accompany his rise towards the upper echelons of the party. However, some years later, Iqbal's patron was murdered by the Haqiqis. Iqbal considered leaving the party, where he felt discriminated against for his ethnicity. But his exit plan did not materialise and, instead, he became increasingly involved in militant activities in his locality.

Iqbal's fairly conventional entry into local politics did not divert him from its murkier side. While fulfilling his first electoral mandate in the local Union Council, he found himself increasingly involved in his party's dirty work—those displeasing or discrediting chores inherent in any profession that encompass its most exhausting, dull, degrading, or dangerous tasks (Hughes 2009, Strauss et al. 1997). Within Karachi's political parties, this dirty work involves a wide range of practices, such as extortion (*bhatta khori*), land grabbing (*qabza*), public disturbances aiming to create panic (*hara huri*), electoral rigging (*dhandli*), targeted assassinations, and street battles with rivals. Within the MQM, these activities are highly compartmentalised, and party workers (*karkuns*) generally shy away from the most sensitive operations such as *bhatta* collection and targeted assassinations. It is however common for the party's rank and file to be involved in rigging elections and armed clashes with electoral rivals. Thus, during the summer of 2011, which saw the ruling parties fight each other around a new reform of the legislation on local governments, Iqbal was repeatedly sent to battle with local activists of the ANP, who maintained close links with a local criminal group involved in the drug trade. This remained a part-time job, however and, in all, he participated in around a dozen 'encounters' (*tasaddum*).

As with many combatants, Iqbal's military assignments primarily consisted in killing time. He sometimes spent entire nights without firing a shot, watching the slightest movement on the other side of the frontline, a few streets away. Beyond the risks inherent in these militia activities, their tedious nature devalues them among the rank and file of his party. Because of his ethnicity and humble origins, Iqbal sometimes took charge of an additional burden of dirty work, at the behest of Mohajir activists from higher social status. Thus, during the clashes of July and August 2011, these 'senior activists' often deserted their posts and left Iqbal with their weapons as soon as they reached the 'bunker' from where they would monitor the enemy position. While the elite troops of the MQM, the 'shooters', have access to high-grade weaponry such as sniper rifles, night vision goggles, and rocket launchers, intermittent fighters such as Iqbal only have old Kalashnikovs. Because Iqbal is not a Mohajir, having access to such 'merchandise' (*saman*, in the MQM's lingo) cannot even be taken for granted. More often than not, he only managed to get hold of old *klashnis* (Kalashnikovs) after the so-called 'senior *karkun*s' deserted their post and left their weapons in his care.

The relegation of the least qualified to unglamorous tasks, like orderlies in hospitals, does not mean employees are entirely deprived of autonomy in completing their tasks. In every profession, workers have developed strategies for preventing, minimising, or avoiding dirty work. In the medical sector, for instance, nurses and orderlies have developed a wide array of responses to 'scut work' or 'shit work', from delegation to dark humour, to sabotage, to upward transvaluation (turning it into gratifying work) (Strauss et al. 1997, 250). Among the intermittent fighters of the MQM, it is mostly for their dull and exhausting nature that military assignments are perceived as distasteful. As Iqbal's account suggests, the most common way for part-time fighters to cope with these chores is to delegate them to lower level activists. While such subcontracting practices may not be an option for lower rank workers, the latter still find ways to negotiate their share of dirty work. On some occasions, Iqbal simply exited from the scene, to avoid being compromised in activities he found reprehensible. This was the case, for instance, on 12 May 2007, when he found himself involved in street battles with rival political parties (the PPP and the ANP), following an attempt by Chief Justice (CJ) Iftikhar Muhammad Chaudhry to lead a protest in Karachi, a project that was opposed by the MQM (which at the time was allied with the regime of Pervez Musharraf, who had recently suspended the CJ and strove to prevent the movement for the latter's restoration from expanding to Karachi). Iqbal was present on one of the 'fly-overs' overseeing Sharah-e-Faisal, the road leading to the airport, when fighting erupted between MQM workers on one side and their PPP/ANP rivals on the other. After firing a few shots, he decided to slip away, as the rules of engagement did not fit with his ethics of war: 'I was shooting and I was not happy. This is not the way to treat your enemy. This is just duck hunting [I thought]. My moral, my rules don't allow me to engage into fights like this.'

Iqbal's negotiation with his burden of dirty work also took *ex-post facto* forms, through sarcasm in particular. He is particularly prone to taunt the actions of 'so-called senior *karkun*s', as indicated in the following extract from one of my conversations with him, during which he related an episode of fighting in his locality during the month of Ramadan in 2011:

They [the MQM unit-in-charge for his locality] called me and I went there [to the place where the fighting was about to start]. It was 12am and I started my duty, eight hours. At 2am, they told me I should accompany two senior *karkuns*. They were supposedly senior because they were Urdu-speaking, and I was non-Urdu speaking. I accompanied them. Both were carrying guns. Only I was empty-handed. Then we reached the [firing] post. It was a sensitive post. The distance between our post and the enemy post was around 200 metres. When we reached there, it was completely dark. You could not even light a matchstick, or it would have revealed our position to the enemy. There, one of the so-called senior *karkun*s handed me his rifle, and retreated twenty or thirty metres from the frontline, where he picked up his cell-phone and telephoned his girlfriend.

Another way Iqbal coped with his burden of dirty work was to conceal biographical resources and technological skills which, if made public, would make him vulnerable to additional military assignments. The fact that he served in the Pakistan Army for a few years provided him with much greater military expertise than standard party activists. However, he feared that if he revealed these skills, his superiors might involve him further in illicit or paramilitary activities, and eventually make him a full-time militant, 'shooter', or 'target killer' in the jargon of Karachi. If this meant relegation to menial tasks, he was adamant he would avoid assignments which were valued higher, but contrary to his ethics. Thus he fought occasionally, but refused to 'become a killer'. This is also why Iqbal considered leaving the party. Besides continuing to endure racial discrimination which, he now understood, seemed little likely to abate, his growing involvement in the party's dirty work exposed him to greater risks, moral and physical, while his prospects of 'making it' appeared downright bleak.

Everyday struggles of a part-time fighter

To date, Iqbal's attempt at upward social mobility through party politics remains frustrated. His financial situation remains fragile and while local politics momentarily seemed to have opened a window of opportunity for him, in terms of wealth accumulation, he had to revise his ambitions promptly. Not only did the prospects of financial gain through party politics proved more limited than he initially anticipated, but his political activities prevented him from taking a regular job.

While taking some odd jobs in his locality, Iqbal feared that a more regular professional activity would put his life at risk, especially since his commuting routines would make him vulnerable to an attack by the many groups he has antagonised in the past, from electoral rivals of the MQM to the 'drug mafia' to religious extremists. 'I've learnt the trick to survive: always be on the move,' he told me in November 2013, a few months after his house was attacked by a rival group, which suspected him of being involved in poll rigging and held him partly responsible for its defeat in the local constituency.

While showing me the bullet holes piercing through the corrugated iron door to his house, Iqbal wore a devil-may-care smile: 'Now, this is living on the edge!' he bragged. For all his boldness, Iqbal never struck me as reckless. For several years he had trod a dangerous path, but he was not one of those 'violent few' who, in every militant group, deal with danger by seeking it out rather than avoiding it (Collins 2008). Iqbal's days in the army had endowed him with a capacity of 'interactional dominance', which proved useful during armed clashes—a capacity which distinguishes the actively violent from the competently violent and which amounts to 'being cool in the midst of other people's hot emotions' (Ibid.). His bravado, while pointing at the bullet-riddled door, did not fit well with his usual reactions to danger and, before anything, it felt like an attempt to conceal his anxieties and reclaim control over a life going adrift. Following the attack on his house, he left his family and, for a couple of months, stayed with friends and relatives. This was not the first time he had gone into hiding. Every now and then, when he started feeling the heat, he left his home and disappeared for weeks. When things went really bad, such as in the aftermath of the attack on his house, he headed back to his natal province. He was a city-dweller to the bone and village life held very few attractions for him. But these periods of self-imposed retreat from the hurlyburly of city life also had their charms.

During his latest stay in his natal province, he made the acquaintance of a 'cute chubby girl'. I was asked to validate his claim on the basis of some photographic evidence. For the first time in his life, Iqbal discovered the pleasures of the flesh. Ever since I knew him, Iqbal had recounted his travails with largely virtual romances. Like many unmarried Pakistani men, Iqbal turned to digital courtship to approach women, sending unwanted text messages to many he had never met or even seen. Surprisingly, some occasionally responded and even sent photographs of themselves. However Iqbal was aware he was not the most suitable boy in town. While I could sense some genuine affection for this girl, and he even considered marriage, at the same time he was not ready to return to his natal province, and did not envisage how he could provide a wife with a decent living in Karachi.

Iqbal was even unsure about remaining in Pakistan. After contemplating moving to America, where one of his brothers had settled, he now considered applying for asylum in Thailand or Sri Lanka, where he had heard refugee status was granted less parsimoniously than in the West. He was still hesitant: he knew that if he pursued his political career, he might be re-elected a councillor—a potentially lucrative position, although one fraught with risks for himself and his family in the next municipal elections.

His family encouraged him to quit politics altogether. Both his parents had passed away. His siblings remained unaware of the exact nature of his political activities, but nonetheless feared for his life. His sister, a local school teacher, confided to me she wished he would renounce his political activities and take a 'proper job', lest he be killed. Iqbal, aware of his family's concerns for his safety, revealed the minimum about his activities. As we saw earlier, these attempts at self-occultation were not limited to the private realm. They extended to his public activities: by hiding parts of his past from his party, he denied himself a militant career, which his past in the military could have accelerated. Living in fear (of his 'enemies', and also his own party) and denial, Iqbal lived in chronic uncertainty. He remained uncertain about his future, but had nowhere else to go.

Far from providing a vehicle of upward social mobility, politics exerted a severe constraint over Iqbal's life options, and maintained him in a prolonged state of limbo. The deleterious effect of party politics on his college studies prompted him to drop out, and to search out less conventional routes towards social and economic success. Following his departure from the army, Iqbal turned to the dangerous and impure realm of party politics, mainly out of desperation. His enrolment was not truly cynical, however: he felt ideologically closer to the MQM than any other Karachi party, and his 'soft corner' was reinforced by its 'virtue in efficiency' (Piliavsky & Sbriccoli, 2014). This was a party that practiced what it preached, whose violent proclivities were neither a liability nor a mere protection against the shortcomings of the Pakistani state, but an integral part of its 'performative politics'. That is, he admired its capacity to 'deal with everyday problems rapidly, visibly, and though rarely aimed at transforming institutions or practices, with some immediate effect' (Blom Hansen 2005, 116). Following his formal enlistment into the MQM, Iqbal discovered he had overestimated the prospects of empowerment and self-aggrandisement that direct political action held. Becoming increasingly aware of the blind alleys and ever higher risks of activism, he allowed himself to be recruited into increasingly illicit activities. As a result, could not insulate his private life from politics; at the same time he remained constrained by his opposition to illegality which prevented him from jumping headlong into a life of crime. Besides his reluctance to conduct more militant activities for his party, he became uneasy with some practices of wealth accumulation in which he was involved.

In 2012 Iqbal participated in some land grabbing operations along the National Highway. Like most *qabza* work in those days, this operation aimed to capture agricultural land surrounding a local *goth*, or urban village with a majority of Sindhi and Baloch residents. This particular operation was not overseen by the MQM but by a prominent Sindhi nationalist leader. The fact that Iqbal was recruited attests to the porosity of party affiliations amongst participants in Karachi's unofficial economy. In the southern outskirts of the city, local leaders of the MQM and Sindhi nationalists cooperated in *qabza* operations (interview with Perween Rehman, Director of the Orangi Pilot Project (OPP), February 2013). This time, however, the MQM was not involved and Iqbal acted on his own. The middlemen who recruited him were undoubtedly aware of his party affiliation but they ignored it, and prioritised his ethnicity. Indeed, the *modus operandi* of this particular *qabza* group rested upon the co-optation of impoverished members of Iqbal's *biraderi*, who were provided accommodation at a subsidised rate on the illegally encroached land. The occupation of the land would make it harder for public authorities to oppose its development, and could pave the way for the construction of higher-grade accommodation. Despite the risks involved, especially if news of his involvement reached his party bosses, Iqbal considered this was a 'good money-making opportunity'. He was aware such *qabza* operations served the electoral and larger strategic interests of the MQM's rivals, assisting their vote banks along the National Highway, and providing them an important source of leverage. Indeed, the control of Karachi's entry and exit points is vital for the city's political parties. It allows them to monitor goods, legal and otherwise, entering the city, and endows them with the capacity to shut down the city at will, especially during outbursts of collective violence such as those witnessed in summer 2011.

More than his contribution to an operation working against the interests of his own party, what truly upset Iqbal was the exploitation of weaker sections of his community. He felt they were used because of their vulnerability and, as the operation went on, his guilt increased. Within a few days, he backed out of the operation. Doing otherwise would have compromised his self-image, which he had cultivated with consistency over the years. This was one of the selfless defender of his own folk, one aware of the shortcomings of the Pakistani state as far as the provision of justice to society's weaker sections was concerned, but who worked without despair for their recognition as proper citizens entitled to basic legal rights. For example, he had campaigned on several occasions for their right to register FIRs against wrongdoers.

As Janet Roitman writes in the context of the Chad Basin, 'the practice of illegality is an ethic insofar as it is a practice of truth'—that is, insofar as it acknowledges and authenticates representations of economic normality and efficiency (Roitman 2005, 21). Inscribing the illegal domain into a legitimate world of acceptable practices, through ideas of 'this is the way it's done', always involves an active engagement not devoid of tensions. The ethics of illegality does not entail transcendental truths and prescriptions on how to act. Rather, it entails a self-reflexive process through which moral subjects test and constitute themselves in practice, through a tensile engagement with a series of codes and rules related to economic behaviour (Ibid., 190–91). The 'truths' acknowledged, here, are contingent. Thus, while Iqbal found comfort in widely held assumptions about graft, to legitimate his experiments with 'corruption', his involvement in shady real estate operations was a source of greater anxiety. As I expressed surprise at his indiscretion, or concern for the risks involved, he made no attempt to conceal his economic motives. On the contrary, he inscribed them into a mode of reasoning which proclaimed the supremacy of economic considerations over party and ethnic affiliations. He endowed the pursuit of the quick buck with an aesthetic and moral aura, as if it were the embodiment of a cunning economic reason. This was not a sufficient defence against Iqbal's sense of guilt, which had less to do with disloyalty to his party than with his impression he had betrayed his kith and kin, and ultimately himself, in doing so. All these years, he had preserved an image of himself as an uncompromising servant of his community, eager to sacrifice his personal interests and even his life. This commitment was reinforced by his intuition that his community was his last refuge and possibly his last chance of 'making it', socially and economically. All things considered, his best option to succeed economically without endangering his ethical convictions was to act as a representative of his people at the local level, a role the MQM seemed most prone to bestow upon him. By serving his community Iqbal also served himself, in the most practical sense of the word.

More than cynical calculation, the collapsing of opportunism and political activism for Iqbal was a reminder that, in Pakistan as in other contemporary terrains of conflict, combatants are simultaneously political subjects who carry an agenda of social, political, and economic reforms and social actors and economic agents with material interests inscribed into various communities of belonging (Hoffman 2011, 111–12). In contrast to the 'greed versus grievance' thesis, these combatants are 'no more greedy than other laborers in the postmodern global economy, and their work [is] inextricably tied to their understandings of the rights and political responsibilities of citizens and men' (Hoffman 2011, 111). Thus, Iqbal continuously strove to reconcile his affiliation to a party which closely surveyed its workers, with his search for a livelihood and commitment to uplift his *biraderi*. These three spheres did not coexist smoothly. Iqbal's attempts to reconcile them was a source of great anxiety, which he only partially overcame by fashioning his own ethics of illegality. As an 'experiment with truth', to use a Gandhian phrase, this ethics was validated by his proclivity to risk his life in the line of duty, rather than by the intrinsic moral value of the 'codes' he invoked. Thus, in August 2014, he was struggling to register an FIR against members of a rival ethnic group who had assaulted a labourer from his neighbourhood, following a minor scuffle between local youths. He revealed he would 'start the fight for right soon', even if he were 'targeted and eliminated', as 'this happens all the time here in Pakistan'. *Biraderi* politics offered the prospect of reconciling his self-image as a sincere servant of the people with his aspirations for upward social mobility. What allowed this reconciliation was also what made it unsustainable—the prospect of an early death. However rhetorical his self-sacrificial commitment initially was, he took his role increasingly seriously. At this juncture, I wished my friend Iqbal would draw a line under his projects of self-aggrandisement. But would he prove capable of renouncing this life on the edge which, in the absence of tangible material benefits, had imbued his precarious existence with a sense of purpose and urgency?

References

Blom Hansen, Thomas, *Violence in Urban India. Identity Politics, 'Mumbai' and the Postcolonial City*, Delhi: Permanent Black, 2005 (2001).

Collins, Randall, *Violence. A Micro-sociological Theory*, Princeton University Press, 2008.

Deleuze, Gilles and Félix Guattari, *Capitalism and Schizophrenia, vol. 2. Anti-Oedipus*, New York: Penguin, 2009 (1972), trans. Robert Hurley.

Goffman, Erving, *Asylum. Essays on the Social Situation of Patients and Other Inmates*, New York: Anchor Books/Doubleday, 1961.

Hoffman, Danny, *The War Machines. Young Men and Violence in Sierra Leone and Liberia*, Durham/London: Duke University Press, 2011.

Hughes, Everett, Cherrington, *The Sociological Eye. Selected Papers*, New Brunswick/London: Transaction Books, 2009 (1951).

Jackson, Michael, 'Custom and conflict in Sierra Leone: an essay on anarchy', in *Existential Anthropology. Events, Exigencies and Effects*, New York, Berghahn Books, 2005, pp. 53–74.

Khan, Nichola, *Mohajir Militancy in Pakistan. Violence and Practices of Transformation in the Karachi Conflict*, London and New York: Routledge, 2010.

Piliavsky, Anastasia and Tommaso Sbriccoli, 'The Virtue in Efficacy: Goonda Raj (Rule of Strongmen) and Political Authorisation in Northern India', *Democratic Cultures* conference, King's College, Cambridge, 5 September 2014.

Roitman, Janet, *Fiscal Disobedience. An Anthropology of Economic Regulation in Central Africa*, Princeton University Press, 2005.

Schafer, Jessica, 'Guerrillas and Violence in the War in Mozambique:

De-socializationof Re-socialization', *AfricanAffairs*, 100, April(2001), pp. 215–37.

Strauss, Anselm Leonard, *Social Organization of MedicalWork*, New Brunswick: Transaction Publishers, 1997.

5

LIFE IN A 'NO-GO AREA'

EXPERIENCES OF MARGINALISATION AND FEAR IN LYARI

Nida Kirmani

Introduction: wading into a 'no-go area'

I first visited Lyari in August 2012 when Laurent Gayer and I con-ducted a focus group discussion with members of a community-based organisation in the neighbourhood of Baghdadi. Until this visit I had only heard snippets about this part of the city in terms of its reputation for violence and criminality, but having not grown up in Karachi and having only done limited fieldwork in the city, I knew very little of substance about this 'no-go' area. The members of the community organisation, who were largely Baloch, talked about how Lyari had been maligned by the media, how people in Lyari were discriminated against in employment, and how the Muttahida Qaumi Movement (MQM) in particular had waged a campaign against the people of Lyari. The people in the focus group also kept mentioning 'Sardar Uzair Jaan', a way of affectionately and respectfully referring to Uzair Baloch, who was the head of the People's Aman Committee (PAC) and the *de facto* leader of Lyari at the time. The themes they discussed—marginalisation, stigmatisation, political manipulation, and state neglect—were issues I had explored before in my previous work on Muslim women in Delhi (Kirmani 2013). However, the context in Lyari was extremely different.

After the focus group discussion, one of the most vocal and articulate young women in the group, Saniya Naz, pulled me aside and asked whether Laurent and I wanted to meet 'bhai' in person, referring to Uzair Baloch. Despite the fact I knew little about him, I was admittedly excited by the prospect of meeting Karachi's most powerful 'gangster'. I agreed without hesitation and found myself nervously sitting in his reception room a few days later along with Saniya Naz, Laurent, and a journalist friend, Aziz Sanghur. While his home, situated in a typically narrow, dusty street littered with rubbish in the neighbourhood of Singhu Lane, was ostentatious to say the least, particularly when juxtaposed with its humble surroundings, I was struck by Uzair's own slight frame and soft-spoken manner. This man certainly did not have the air of a gangster. After a brief meeting, the men left for an *iftari* party (meal to break the fast during Ramadan), and I was ushered across the street by Saniya Naz to Uzair's mother's house to take *iftari* with his mother, wife, and children. At this point I had little understanding about what was actually going on in Lyari, but I knew I wanted to know more.

Although my interest in Lyari was immediate, my relationship with the area developed gradually. In spite of the warmth and hospitality of the people I met and the desire of many of them, particularly people such as Saniya Naz who would later be elected as Lyari's first woman Member of the Provincial Assembly (MPA), to show me the 'true picture' of Lyari, in my first year of fieldwork my visits were sporadic. One reasons for this was simply because I worked in Lahore and only came to Karachi every couple of months to visit my family. Even when I was in Karachi, travelling to Lyari seemed daunting. Despite the fact that Lyari was only around ten kilometres away from the Defence Housing Authority (DHA) where most of the city's elite reside, and where my family also lives, it seemed to inhabit an entirely different country altogether.

The name 'Lyari' itself has become synonymous in Karachi with violence, crime, and gangs. Consequently, every fieldwork visit I made involved a complex set of negotiations with my family members who could not understand why I would risk my life in this feared locale in the city. No amount of assurance I offered would ease their fears. Even my friends expressed concerns over my interest in the area. Some questioned whether my research was worth it. Others were in awe of my bravery, as if I were travelling to administer aid in some far-flung, war-torn region. This is not to argue, as many Lyari residents often did, that Lyari was safe. Rather, the reactions I received were disproportionate to a much more complex reality, one in which violent events did periodically occur, but most of the time targeted particular individuals, groups, or areas. Ironically, and to the chagrin of my friends and family, these reactions served to feed my interest in Lyari, not because I am stubborn or a thrill seeker, but because of the deep ethnic and class divisions within Karachi itself that they reflected. These divisions exist in the minds of all people living in Karachi, including my own. They have continuously grown in the last decades alongside the escalation of violence. Oskar Verkaaik argues that one impact of the increasing violence in the city is that the space one calls 'home' in Karachi has become progressively restricted and increasingly tied to one's own ethnically-defined neighbourhood (2009). Lyari's marginalisation and stigmatisation must be viewed within this context.

From 2012–2014 I conducted several formal interviews in Lyari alongside just 'hanging out', or engaging in what social scientists call participant observation. I also became involved personally with a community-based youth organisation there. Most of my time was spent with members of the Baloch community, which is extremely diverse. I spoke to members of other ethnic groups including Pashtuns, Kutchis, Punjabis, and Sindhis. My research was mostly conducted in Baloch-majority areas in which the gangs had seized control. However, I also interviewed people living in the contested Kutchi-majority areas of Lyari, such as Agra Taj and Hingorabad that had not been seized by the gangs. As is the case with ethnographic research, I became increasingly emotionally involved in Lyari. I grew closer to some people I met and actively distanced myself from others, particularly those with formal links to the PAC and afiliated gangs. I have taken pains to protect the identities of the individuals involved in this research. Hence, unless I am referring to a public figure, all names have been changed, and details altered to preserve my respondents' anonymity.

This chapter reflects on material I gathered in Lyari, focusing particularly on ways residents narrated their own experiences of violence and fear within and outside their locality. In Karachi as a whole, fear has certainly become a 'way of life' for residents of the city (Green, 1994). Ali highlights multiple fears in Karachi around poverty, unemployment, and physical violence, that 'reverberate like a spectre' (2009, 57). Gayer describes fear as being experienced as a 'chronic condition' in Karachi and explores the ways in which 'geographies of fear' impact on the socio-spatial formation of the city itself (2014). Kaker highlights the impact of fear on the spatial layout of the city in terms of increasing residential fragmentation (2013). While fear is pervasive in Karachi, it must be understood as socially and spatially situated in particular contexts. This chapter, therefore, aims to tell the story of Lyari focusing particularly on how residents of this 'no-go area' express multiple fears in relation to political parties, the state's security forces, and the gangs.

A history of marginalisation and resistance

Referred to by outsiders as 'the Colombia of Karachi' because of its perceived control by drug mafias, Lyari has increasingly become known as one of the most violent and crime-ridden parts of the city. However, many residents would argue otherwise. They refer to Lyari as '*Karachi ki maan*' (the mother of Karachi), emphasising that it is one of the city's original settlements. The area that is now Lyari was named after the *lyar* trees that grew along the banks of the river where people first settled. This area developed gradually during the eighteenth century as a fishing settlement, and was one of the few majority-Muslim areas of Karachi before Partition. The area's population grew significantly during the period of British colonial rule when the British began modernising Karachi's port and people began migrating in larger numbers from Balochistan and Sindh in search of better livelihoods. Much labour for the port was drawn from Lyari at this time, and many residents continue to work there.

Covering approximately 1,800 acres of land in Karachi's South district and with a population estimated between 1 and 1.7 million, Lyari is highly densely populated. As in most parts of Karachi, many of Lyari's conflicts are rooted in the struggle for control of land by various powerful groups. Because Lyari is adjacent to the port and many of the city's major wholesale markets, its land is valuable, economically and politically. Although Lyari is often framed as a Baloch area, with the Balochis comprising approximately half its population, Lyari is actually multi-ethnic and includes Punjabis, Mianwalis, Kutchis (from the Kutch region of Gujarat in what is now India), Memons, Sindhis, Pashtuns, and a small number of Urdu speakers at its outskirts. It is also religiously diverse, including a large number of Hindus, Christians, and members of the Zikri community, a heterodox Sunni sect originating in Balochistan. This diversity is often cited as a great source of pride for Lyari's residents.

Despite its geographical and historical significance in Karachi's landscape, Lyari has been consistently neglected in terms of infra-structure and development since Karachi was founded during British rule. Forming the largest part of 'the native city', Lyari was home to the Muslim working classes before Partition, and has retained its working class character. Lyari developed in a haphazard fashion around unplanned settlements, and it faced degradation during the late nineteenth century when the city's most polluting industries were located within its vicinity. This pattern of neglect continued after Pakistan was created, and worsened with the influx of migrants from India who were given priority in terms of housing by city plan-ners because of their symbolic importance to the nation-building project, to the detriment of older working class areas such as Lyari (Slimbach, 1996).

A sense of abandonment by the state continues to colour the narra-tives of Lyari's residents, many of whom feel the dominance of the MQM over Karachi's political landscape since the 1990s. During that first focus group discussion I conducted with community activists in August 2012, one young Baloch man articulated this sense of marginalisation:

> Look Lyari is blacklisted by the banks.... They won't give people from here credit cards or include them in loan schemes.... The people of Lyari are poor. If they received a loan, they could make something of them-selves. This is an injustice that has been committed against the people from Lyari. Wherever you go, Lyari is viewed as is if it is bombarded, as if a storm has descended, or as a battlefield. If you go to the airport, out of all of the cabs, perhaps only one will go to Lyari.

Others mentioned difficulties in finding a job because they were from Lyari. Nasreen, from the Kutchi community who I interviewed a year later in August 2013, described this:

> Even now if you look, wherever we apply for a job, regardless of whether we have completed an MA, we are blackmarked as being from Lyari and our applications are rejected. This pains me so much. Just because we are from Lyari, we are rejected…is this a crime or a sin that we have committed?

This sense of being marginalised on multiple levels, in terms of access to social services and jobs particularly, along with a sense of spatial isolation due to the area's violent reputation, cut across social boundaries of gender, age, and ethnicity and emerged repeatedly in discussions with Lyari residents. Many argued that it was employment discrimination that had led to growth of gangs in the area, as many young men were unable to find formal employment. Perhaps because of its strong working class roots, Lyari has been an important site of struggle and social activism since the colonial period, when it provided a space for anti-colonial resistance movements such as the Reshmi Rumal Tehreek, and the Khilafat Movement. During the 1960s, several leftist student organisations, political parties and Baloch nationalist organisations made Lyari their base (Gayer 2014, 130). Although his own leftist leanings were themselves questionable, Lyari's association with progressive politics might have made the area more attractive to the founder of the Pakistan People's Party (PPP), Zulfiqar Ali Bhutto, who campaigned from there in the 1970s and is still venerated by the area's residents as the person who brought development to Lyari, ensured people acquired jobs in the public sector, and opened up opportunities in the Gulf. More importantly, Bhutto is remembered as the first politician to give the people of Lyari respect, something residents feel few politicians have done since. Benazir Bhutto is similarly venerated, having held her *valima* (wedding reception) in Lyari's Kakri Ground. Since this time, Lyari has remained Karachi's main PPP stronghold.

Residents of Lyari also speak proudly of having resisted the military regimes of Zia-ul-Haq in the 1980s and Pervez Musharraf in the 2000s. Habib Hasan, the Vice President of the PPP's Karachi division and a long-time social activist in Lyari, spoke proudly of this history of resistance while also citing this as a source of Lyari's troubles: 'Whenever there has been an anti-government movement in the entire country, it has started in Lyari. Lyari has never supported any dictator until this day. Look at our history: whether it was Ayub Khan or Yahya [Khan] or Zia-ul-Haq or Musharraf. They [the state] know that if they don't keep these people [the people of Lyari] down, then they will come out, and if they come out then a whole movement will emerge from every place' (September 2012). The idea that the people of Lyari are both secular, democracy-loving (*jamooriat-pasand*), and tolerant was mentioned again and again in interviews with residents as a kind of counter-narrative used to subvert the negative image of Lyari that is so often depicted in the media.

The criminalisation of politics

Lyari's *badnaami* (bad image) stems partially from the fact it has been home to various criminal groups which have become powerful over past decades. Gangsters have existed in Lyari since the 1960s, with the names of the earlier gangsters, Kala Nag (Black Serpent), Dadal and Sheru, still periodically mentioned in conversations about local history. However, residents paint a picture of that generation of gangsters as relatively harmless, at least for local residents, minding their own criminal activities and only engaging in periodic knife battles with each other. The 1980s is cited as the period when local gangs started impacting the wider population, as the Afghan War increased flows of heroin and weapons across Karachi (Gayer 2007, 2014). Drug use spread rapidly in Lyari during this period as knife battles turned into gun battles between rival gangs.

Although the early generation of gangsters served as strongmen for local and national politicians, it was not until the appearance of Rehman Dakait (Rehman 'the Bandit'), Dadal's son, in the late 1990s that the gangs' presence in Lyari increased, and criminality and politics became more directly intertwined. Rehman cultivated a violent image from an early age, reportedly stabbing someone at the age of thirteen and killing his own mother in 1995 (Imtiaz 2010; Gayer 2014, 138–9). He quickly rose to power in the area, dominating the drugs and arms trades along with another local kingpin, Haji Lalu. The two eventually split over a rift about sharing profits, and Haji Lalu's son, Arshad Pappu, took over his activities after his arrest. The two groups engaged in a gang war, instigated after a local transporter, Faiz Mohammad (or 'Mama Faizu'), the father of Uzair Baloch, was kidnapped and killed by Pappu in 2003. This conflict continued for five years and ravaged the area, creating widespread insecurity amongst its residents. It is widely believed that the gang war was a proxy turf war between the PPP and the MQM, with the PPP supporting Rehman's group and the MQM supporting Pappu's.

The gang war officially ended in 2008 when, with the support of the PPP, Rehman Dakait called a truce between the two rival groups and created the People's Aman Committee (PAC). The end of the gang war did not signal the end of gangs. Rather, the size and control of the gangs expanded after the creation of the PAC, with neighbourhoods divided between various 'commanders' and PAC offices established in most neighbourhoods, mirroring the MQM's sector and unit offices. According to residents, the collection of *bhatta* (or extortion money) was also introduced in Lyari at this time—a practice popularised by the MQM in Karachi during the 1990s, but now involving a variety of groups. Rehman became more involved with the PPP, and he and his men were allegedly central to the security apparatus of Benazir Bhutto and later Asif Ali Zardari (Imtiaz, 2010). During the last years of his life Rehman also shifted from simply supporting the PPP to fashioning himself as a leader in his own right, transforming from 'Rehman Dakait' to the more respectable 'Sardar Rehman Baloch'. During these years, he built a reputation as the 'Robin Hood' of Lyari, engaging in large-scale charitable works in his community, distributing rations to families, setting up medical clinics, and supporting educational and sports-related activities. After his death in 2009 in a police encounter, many speculated it was his increasing designs on political leadership that led to his demise. Uzair Baloch, the son of Mama Faizu, took Rehman's seat as the head of the PAC.

Until 2008 Uzair Baloch remained a relatively minor figure in Lyari's political and criminal scene. Uzair demonstrated political ambitions early on in 2001 when he contested the municipal elections on an independent ticket, and lost to the PPP's Habib Hasan. He became involved with Rehman Dakait's gang after his father's murder, but was prominent in the orchestration of violence. Perhaps this perceived distance from violence combined with his earlier political ambitions made him an attractive candidate to assume the reigns of the PAC after

Rehman, as the PAC sought to frame itself as a political rather than a criminal organisation. Many in Lyari argued that Uzair resembles a politician more than a gangster, one forced to join the gangsters in order to avenge his father's death—a socially acceptable reason for engaging in violence—and whose intention was to persuade the gangsters away from crime and onto the 'straight path' of community development and social work. It is this perceived 'softness' that many find attractive, including myself when I first met him. This is also seen as a source of his weakness as a leader, and his inability to keep the lower-level commanders in check.

Creating a siege mentality

Two sets of events occurred in the year prior to my fieldwork which considerably increased support for Uzair and the PAC in Lyari. The first was the wave of violence between the MQM and the PPP, with the PAC acting as its armed wing, which peaked during summer 2011. After the bloody events that summer in which hundreds were killed, in September Zulfiqar Mirza, the former Home Minister of Sindh, declared at a public rally in Lyari that he had issued 300,000 weapons licenses in order for people to defend themselves. Stories of men being targeted on the basis of their ethnicity were reported across the city, including Lyari, where the MQM was blamed for abducting, torturing, and killing innocent Baloch men. Many in Lyari, who had witnessed *bori band lashein* (bodies in gunny sacks) being returned to the area, viewed the PAC as their only defence. The state's security forces were viewed more of a threat than a source of protection. Similar stories circulated throughout the city about the PAC indiscriminately targeting young Mohajir men, thus increasing ethnicised fears between communities.

The naming of the MQM as the people of Lyari's primary enemy, and the notion that it had had systematically targeted the area and Baloch men there, emerged repeatedly in my research. In one interview I conducted with a Baloch family living in the Shah Baig Lane area, this sense of fear emerged clearly in Qudsia's narrative about her son, Bilal:

> Before this was not an issue. It began three or four years ago. Bilal used to work in a bank. This harassment began with him as well, but thank God he

was saved and managed to escape in another direction. That is why everyone is afraid that if they travel too far outside the area, there will be an issue. So people stay in Lyari. Everyone says, 'Mohajirs are killing Baloch, and Baloch are killing Mohajirs'. Now only God knows the truth.... We are ladies, even when we go shopping for our children with our husbands, we are scared that, God forbid, something will happen. A person is scared even to go shopping (May 2013).

Bilal told me some months later that he made employment choices based on whether the job was in an MQM-dominated area or not. He eventually took a job as a welder in SITE, a Pashtun-majority area, because he felt Pashtuns and Baloch were allies in relation to the MQM. Another man I spoke to who later moved to Dubai resigned his job when he was assigned the night shift because it was located in an MQM-dominated area and he was afraid to travel after dark. Similarly, Arif, a university student, thought twice before leaving Lyari. In an interview in May 2013 he revealed, 'I haven't left for three months. I only go out to buy things, and come straight back. There's a lot of fear. When I go into the city on my bike, I hope I don't cross any signals where I need to stop. I go to university, then straight home.' I asked, 'But why are people scared? Is it because they are Baloch or because they are from Lyari?' 'Both,' Arif replied, 'but the fear of being Baloch is greater.'

Several men recounted similar stories of restricting their movements within Lyari for fear of being targeted the MQM. Although everyone in Lyari felt insecure at this time, this particular fear was experienced more by young Baloch men and by their family members, rather than women or members of other ethnic groups, and it greatly restricted their mobility within the city. Many later acknowledged that one never really knew who was responsible for the violence during this period. Some quietly suspected the gangs might have orchestrated it in order to increase their support. This opacity, and not knowing, reinforced people's insecurity within and outside of Lyari, and made them less likely to vocally protest against the gangs.

The second key event that allowed Uzair to consolidate his support in Lyari was a seven-day police operation conducted in April–May 2012. The Lyari operation was led by the late Superintendent of Police and Karachi's own 'Dirty Harry', Chaudhry Aslam. It was initiated after a PPP worker was killed, allegedly by members of the PAC.

Residents of those areas near Cheel Chowk in Lyari faced severe difficulties. Water and electricity supplies to their homes were cut off and
their mobility severely curtailed. Several people were killed in the
crossfire between the police and PAC workers, including innocent
bystanders. Arif, who lived in the neighbourhood of Nawa Lane adjacent to Cheel Chowk, spoke about residents' fears: 'During this operation, we mostly feared the police. People would say the gangs were the
most feared people. Now when we see the police, we run away for fear
we might get shot. Children see them and run away. Instead of seeing
them as our protectors, we fear them' (August 2012).

Later Arif admitted he had to keep his fingers in his eight-year-old
sister's ears all night so she could sleep. This operation was a turning
point in many of residents' narratives, in terms of heightening the
sense of marginalisation and the fear and distrust of the state's security
forces, which were no longer merely abandoning Lyari's residents but
actively targeting them. The anger that resulted from the operation
increased support for Uzair Baloch and the PAC, who capitalised on
residents' fears of the state's security forces and the MQM, framing
themselves as the only true protectors of the Lyari people. The PAC
reinforced the narrative that Lyari's residents, the Baloch in particular,
were a besieged minority targeted by the MQM and the state: thus
both sides, the PAC and the MQM, mirrored each other's discursive
tactics in an escalation of violence (Khan, 2010).

The enemy within: living with the gangs

These events combined with the support of some branches of the state
meant the gangs could expand significantly. By the time I conducted my
research, only a few neighbourhoods within Lyari were not officially
controlled by a gang 'commander'. Neighbourhoods dominated by the
Kutchi community were under constant threat, and were the sites of
violence between the supporters of the PAC and the Kutchi Rabta
Committee, which claimed to represent Lyari's Kutchi community and
were rumoured to be supported by the MQM. Though exact numbers
are unknown, residents estimated that thousands of people were
employed in some capacity by the gangs. Tasks not only included engaging in direct acts of violence, but collecting *bhatta*, 'picketing' or

patrolling certain neighbourhoods, and acting as informers, with women and children often performing this task. This fed an atmosphere of fear and mistrust amongst residents and weakened communal bonds, as one never knew who might be an informer. It also made conducting research particularly challenging.

Uzair cultivated his popularity by expanding the social work activities begun by Rehman. Like his predecessor, he provided financial assistance to needy families and supported educational and health-related activities in Lyari, and several community-based organisations through the donation of funds and equipment. The PAC either approached community-based organisations itself to offer support or was approached by them. According to local community activists, this support did not come without strings attached, and the organisations that took funding were expected to support the PAC in regard to public relations, and sometimes also provide practical support such as space for the storage of weapons. Uzair also established his own organisations including the Sadia-Ishba Foundation Trust, named after his daughters, which provided educational support in Lyari. Much of this social work undertaken by the PAC was cosmetic. For example, thousands of school copies were distributed to children in Lyari with pictures of Uzair on the cover, while the schools themselves were hardly improved and sometimes used for gang-related activities. One government school reportedly even served as a torture cell at night.

The PAC was also viewed as keeping 'order' in Lyari after the long period of chaos of the gang war after 2000. Residents approached the PAC offices in their neighbourhoods in order to solve their problems quickly and efficiently. This ranged from family-related disputes to the provision of civic amenities. These issues were previously dealt with by local *anjumans*, representing different communities in Lyari. While *anjumans* still exist in Lyari, their activities were severely curtailed by the gangs' growing influence. Furthermore, several people talked about how the PAC also controlled crime, often brutally punishing thieves, and other transgressors. The fear this provoked was also seen to impose order, and to reduce crime, as punishments by the PAC were severe. Although most people I spoke to were aware that this parajudicial power was dependent on individual gangsters and often abused, they also believed some order was better than none.

The image of Rehman Dakait and Uzair Baloch as champions of the common people in Lyari can be linked to Hobsbawm's idea of the 'social bandit' in his study of the veneration of outlaws by peasants in Southern Europe as a form of social protest (1959). Several people I encountered, particularly in my early fieldwork in summer 2012, spoke of Rehman and Uzair as local heroes, explicitly referring to them as 'Robin Hoods'. Most were also realistic about the gangsters' motivations. Iftikhar, a community activist working in Lyari for over thirty years, explained to me why the PAC engaged in 'social work': 'They undertake community service to soften their image, but they also openly carry weapons that even the army does not have. They are attached to the PPP to soften their image, and the PPP needs them' (interview, March 2013).

Many others felt the gangs served the PPP and were supported by state agencies in order to curtail Baloch nationalist activities in Lyari. As Blok points out, bandits often serve the interests of the ruling classes, which allows them to remain protected (1972). This was the case in Lyari, where most residents I spoke to fully believed the gangs were protected and supported by powerful state actors. Blok also points out that myths and legends surrounding the bandit figure deserve our attention in terms of what they represent. The veneration of Uzair and Rehman, while ambivalent and difficult to gauge, expressed the deep sense of disillusionment and betrayal that many Lyari residents felt towards the state, the PPP particularly, and their feelings of marginalisation from the wider city at large.

The extent of genuine support for the gangs amidst the violence and fear that pervaded the area was not straightforward. This became more evident the longer I spent in Lyari. One might argue that the people of Lyari had no choice but to support the gangs, who controlled their neighbourhoods economically, socially, and politically. While it was easy to speak openly about the violence committed by the MQM and the state, at least within Lyari, the gangs were closer to home; they represented the enemy within. It was only after I had been going to Lyari for over a year that stories started to emerge about the violence committed by gang members of the gangs, or 'gang war'. I heard story upon story of people who had directly faced harassment and intimidation by the gangs or knew others who had. Most people did voice their fears openly. Respondents might begin talking about the gangs and then stop in mid-sentence or backtrack, or steer the conversation back towards 'safer' subjects such as the MQM, or the failed state. In this way, there was a 'code of silence' operating within Lyari with regard to the gangs. As Green's research on Guatemala reveals, silence operates as a survival strategy, but also 'silencing is a powerful mechanism of control enforced through fear' (1994, 239).

Thus, cracks in the PAC edifice started to appear. Two violent events took place during the summer of 2013. The first was a bomb blast on 8 August at a football match in which eight people were killed, including six young fans. This was followed the next month by the murder of Zafar Baloch, the PAC's spokesperson and political mastermind. Whilst the perpetrators were never identified, many blamed it on infighting between the gangs. A rift eventually developed between Baba Ladla, a powerful and feared gangster, and Uzair Baloch. This led to a bloody conflict reminiscent of the 2003–08 period between gangs that supported Uzair and those that supported Baba Ladla. Lyari's neighbourhoods became divided once again, leading to hundreds of casualties in cross-fire and from rocket propelled grenades (RPGs), known locally as *awans*, which were launched randomly on enemy turf. Residents could not cross from one street to the next for fear that they might unknowingly step into the rival gang's turf. Those who had feared stepping outside Lyari the previous year were now afraid to leave their immediate locality, planning their routes out of Lyari carefully to be direct as possible. Many were afraid even within their own homes, as *awans* could land on their roofs at any time.

A paramilitary operation led by the Rangers was launched under the direction of the PML-N government in September 2013 across Karachi. The Lyari gangs were a prime target. The main leaders, including Uzair Baloch, successfully fled the country as the operation began, arguably confirming their close links with the state. While many in Lyari were relieved by the operation and felt the Rangers were acting sincerely, they were also sceptical of their motives. The insecurity of young Baloch men increased, and I heard several stories of innocent men being picked up by the Rangers, arrested, and killed in 'encounters'. Similar to the violence committed by the gangs and political parties, state violence existed in an opaque realm where the identities of the perpetrators remained known, and the innocence or guilt of victims was never proven. This combination of looking towards the Rangers for protection mixed with fear and mistrust, also echoed many ambivalent feelings expressed about the PAC during my first year of fieldwork.

Conclusion: breaking the code of silence

The story of Lyari sits within the wider polarisation of Karachi's localities. The sense of marginalisation and insecurity expressed by Lyari's residents is similarly experienced by millions of others across the city, particularly those who live on the territorial faultlines between political turfs. Amidst such violence, Karachi's residents depend on various non-state actors for protection, whether these actors be gangs, mafias, party workers for the poor and working classes, or private security agencies. The result is a 'fortress city' (Davis, 1990) ruled by competing mini-sovereigns (see Hansen and Stepputat, 2005). The collusion of state agencies, political parties and non-state actors is also common throughout the city, and this blurring of boundaries increases the climate of fear and insecurity. That said, Lyari is an area that, despite its geographical centrality, has been gradually marginalised by multiple waves of migration, economic transformations, and political manipulation. The growing isolation of Lyari and the expansion of gangs are the direct result of these structural shifts taking place across Karachi as a whole.

While the situation seems grim, occasionally one can see small rays of hope struggling to break through the wider fog of fear and violence. On 2 March 2014 around midday, fighting between warring gangs broke out in Jhat Phat Market, one of the busiest markets in the centre of Lyari. At least sixteen people were killed, including several women and children. For Lyari's residents, this was a tipping point. Although they had endured months of violence at the hands of the gangs, no major protest had taken place. However, this incident, involving the killing of women and children in particular, crossed a line. Calls immediately began circulating about organising a protest at the Press Club the following day. I arrived at the protest not knowing what to expect. I was surprised that several hundred Lyari residents had turned up, mostly members of the Baloch community. I was even more astonished when they began shouting slogans openly condemning Uzair Baloch,

Baba Ladla, along with the PPP and the law enforcement agencies. This was the first time I heard people speaking out publicly against the gangs. As the protest continued, the tone gradually changed, and the gang leaders' names were taken less and less. I subsequently discovered that Uzair's representatives had been alerted and several had turned up in order to intimidate the residents. A peace deal was hastily struck, mediated by political parties, and for a few weeks the violence abated. However, most Lyari residents knew the peace deal was a temporary measure taken to appease the public. For a brief period after these events, residents began to mobilise against the gangs, but after several people were threatened and a few were killed, the code of silence was reimposed and violence resumed.

While this may seem like a story of defeat, it is also an indication of the growing discontentment and anger building amongst Lyari's residents with all the competing powers-that-be. Importantly, it demonstrated that the spirit of resistance that residents spoke so proudly of as characterising Lyari was not completely extinguished, even after enduring years of violence. This spirit is growing in Lyari as in other parts of the city. It represents the last hope to bridge the divides created between the people of Karachi, one that may someday topple the violent political order that has come to characterise it.

References

Ali, Kamran, Asdar, 'Men and their 'problems': notes on contemporary Karachi', in Asdar Ali, Kamran and Martina Rieker, *Comparing Cities: The Middle East and South Asia*. Oxford University Press, 2009, pp. 49–64.

Blok, Anton, 'The Peasant and the Brigand: Social Banditry Reconsidered', *Comparative Studies in Society and History*, 14, September (1972), pp. 494–503.

Blom Hansen, Thomas, and Fenn Stepputat, 'Introduction', in *Sovereign Bodies: Citizens, Migrants and States in the Postcolonial World*, Princeton: Princeton University Press, 2005, pp. 1–36.

Davis, Mike, *City of Quartz*, London: Verso, 1990.

Gayer, Laurent, 'Guns, Slums, and "Yellow Devils": A Genealogy of Urban Conflicts in Karachi, Pakistan', *Modern Asian Studies*, 41, May (2007), pp. 515–44.

————, *Karachi. Ordered Disorder and the Struggle for the City*, London and New York: Hurst & Co., 2014.

Green, Linda, 'Fear as a Way of Life', *Cultural Anthropology*, 9, 2, May (1994), pp. 227–56.

Hobsbawm, Eric, *Primitive Rebels: Studies in Archaic Forms of Social Movement in the 19th and 20th Centuries*, New York and London: W.W. Norton and Co. 1959.

Imtiaz, Huma, 'Kingdom of fear', *Express Tribune*, 18 July 2010, http://tribune.com.pk/story/27844/kingdom-of-fear/, last accessed 15 Feb. 2014.

Kaker, Sobia, 'Enclaves, Insecurity and Violence in Karachi', *South Asian History and Culture*, 5, December (2013), pp. 93–107.

Khan, Nichola, *Mohajir Militancy in Pakistan. Violence and Practices of Transformation in the Karachi Conflict*, London and New York: Routledge, 2010.

Kirmani, Nida, *Questioning 'The Muslim Woman'. Identity and Insecurity in an Urban Indian Locality*, New Delhi: Routledge, 2013.

Slimbach, Richard, 'Ethnic binds and pedagogies of resistance. Baloch nationalism and educational innovation in Karachi', in Paul Titus (ed.), *Marginality and Modernity.*

Ethnicity and Change in Post-Colonial Balochistan, Karachi: Oxford University Press, 1996, pp. 137–67.

Verkaaik, Oskar, 2009, 'At Home in Karachi: Quasi-Domesticity as a Way to Know the City', *Critique of Anthropology*, 29, March (2009), pp. 65–80.

6

'OUR RULE'

THE MQM, THE DAWAT-I-ISLAMI, AND MOHAJIR RELIGIOSITY

Oskar Verkaaik

At the end of the 1990s, when I was rounding up my research on the Mohajir Qaumi Movement (MQM) in urban Sindh, I became more and more interested in the Dawat-i-Islami, a religious movement, in the tradition of proselytising movements like the Tablighi Jamaat, that in many ways contradicted the MQM. The MQM was a political party and an ethnic movement, whereas the Dawat-i-Islami condemned politics as a dirty, meaningless business and promoted Islam as an antidote to ethnic strife. Since 1992, when the army had begun to prosecute MQM leaders and harass MQM sympathisers, members of the party had got used to a life in hiding, avoiding as much as possible public expressions of support for the party. Members of the Dawat-i-Islami, in contrast, were easily recognisable by their white tunics and green turbans, a uniformed style of dress that spoke of social equality and religious piety. Whereas the MQM then appeared to be losing its firm grip on the

Mohajir communities in Karachi and Hyderabad, the Dawat-i-Islami seemed to become more and more popular and visible.

And yet, there was also at least one thing that both movements had in common. In Karachi they were largely dominated by the Mohajir population of Karachiites with a family background of migration from India to Pakistan in the early years of independence. To some extent, they were opponents, competing between themselves for the support and membership of young, male Mohajirs. Although in principle a young Mohajir could be involved in both movements—one political, the other religious—in practice such dual membership turned out to problematic, for one thing because the Dawat-i-Islami denounced political engagement as corrupting the pious lifestyle it sought to promote. For young Mohajirs, the choice between ethnic politics and religious piety became an either/or question that ran through several of the groups of friends I had got to know in Karachi and Hyderabad. Within such groups, some youngsters continued to support the MQM, while others wore the green Dawat-i-Islami turban. Still others refrained from both. Such choices did not harm friendships, but they were a matter of mild, mutual teasing—a kind of joking relations in the tradition of Radcliffe-Brown (1940), meant to regularly unleash structural tension.

The origins of the Dawat-i-Islami go back to the 1980s when it benefited from state policies designed by the Zia-ul-Haq regime to financially support *madrassas*. Although it operated all over Pakistan, in Karachi it only became a powerful public presence in the second half of the 1990s. As a missionary movement, it copied some of the methods of the Tablighi Jamaat, an originally South Asian proselytising movement established in the 1920s to spread amongst fellow Muslims a reformist kind of Islamic conduct influenced by the nineteenth-century Deobandi tradition. Like the Tablighi Jamaat, the Dawat-i-Islami trained its members to 'invite' fellow Muslims to lead a more pious life closely modelled upon the lifestyle and everyday conduct of the Prophet Muhammad, including such mundane practices like eating, drinking, greeting, sleeping, etc. These self-disciplining practices in imitation of the Prophet were known as the spiritual path to Medina. More than the Tablighi Jamaat, however, the kind of Islam preached by the Dawat-i-Islami included several mystical and magical practices and beliefs, including the belief in the magical powers of Quranic texts or the wearing of amulets (*tawiz*). Popular stories about miraculous events played an important role in missionary activities, both orally told and printed in cheap booklets. Besides, a central element of the weekly routine were the *zikr* sessions, held at night, when large groups of followers would gather in a mosque. After some introductory speeches, mostly addressing everyday moral dilemmas and how to solve them, the lights would be switched off and the congregation would work itself into a state of trance by rhythmically repeating the name of God (*Allahu*). These sessions were a source of considerable attraction for the young Mohajir Dawat-i-Islami enthusiasts I knew.

I participated in two such sessions—one held in the movement's centre near the former wholesale market (*sabzi mandi*) in downtown Karachi, the other in Hyderabad—and in both cases the crowd was dominated by young men, although some older men were also present, some of them in the company of their young sons. What struck me most about these events, apart from the extremely physical quality of the *zikr* sessions that included crying, caressing, embracing, and other forms of close bodily proximity, were the speeches that directly related to the everyday anxieties and aspirations of young Karachiites. One speech I remember addressed the wish to leave the country and seek prosperity abroad. Although the speaker made it clear that he could understand the fellow Muslims who desired to go to America or Canada—to make that point he even graphically depicted the luxuries of these places—the point of his talk was that the better journey was the spiritual path to Medina, that is, the personal search for devoutness. Together with the mystical *zikr* practice that followed such speeches, these talks seemed personally and emotionally to move many of the practitioners.

In the last month of my research I came to interpret the Dawat-i-Islami as a third available option for young Mohajirs who were aspiring to give a sense of purpose to their lives that went beyond the daily concerns of work and education, recreation and care. The other two options I had learnt about earlier. One was the prospect of travel, if not to North America or Europe—parts of the world that were increasingly closing their borders to the average Pakistani—then to the Gulf or East Asia. The other was to join the MQM, which meant more than a political party to Mohajirs growing up in the 1980s and 1990s. It was also a generational movement that gave a sense of direction, urgency, and comradeship to groups of young men living in the lower-middle class areas of Karachi. But outmigration and politics were either difficult to achieve or dangerous. With travel becoming more difficult and costly, and the MQM under siege by state forces and plagued by internal violence, an alternative presented itself in such movements like the Dawat-i-Islami.

In this chapter I want to explore the differences and similarities between the MQM and the Dawat-i-Islami as they presented themselves to young male Mohajirs in Karachi, focusing particularly on how they evoked and redefined religious traditions that have been part of a particular kind of popular Mohajir religiosity during the 1980s and 1990s. Saying this, I am acutely aware of the sensitivity and danger of such a statement. Elsewhere I have written extensively about the ways in which religion has been subject to a process of ethnicisation in Pakistan, giving way to ethnic stereotypes and essentialist notions of, for instance, Sindhi, Pashtun, or Mohajir religiosity (Verkaaik 2004 and 2007). To talk of a 'popular Mohajir religiosity' seems to endorse this stereotyping, which is of course not my intention. Rather than painting an essentialist view of Mohajir religiosity, my aim is to look at how religious and political movements competing for Mohajir support have tapped into popular religious traditions that bind together, as much as they separate, Mohajirs and other segments of the Pakistani population. That is to say that there is, on the one hand, nothing essentially Mohajir about the religious traditions I will explore, as they are shared by non-Mohajirs as well. On the other hand, however, some of these practices have become associated with Mohajir ethnicity precisely because of the ways they have been mobilised by political and religious movements targeting the Mohajir population.

I will argue that the kind of Islam put forward by the Dawat-i-Islami highlights at least two elements of this popular Mohajir religiosity. On the one hand, there are the ecstatic practices like *zikr* that enabled young Mohajirs to temporarily lose one's sense of self, which share a family likeness with some of the ecstatic political practices of the MQM, rooted in certain Sufi traditions that informed Sindhi contentious politics since the 1960s onwards. On the other hand, there is the centrality of Medina, place of arrival of the original *Mohajireen*, who took part in the Islamic exodus (*hijra*), which has been a central trope in reformist movements like the Deobandis as a model of both personal and social transformation, and gave the Mohajirs of Karachi their name after their migration from India to Pakistan.

Transgressing ethnic stereotypes

Although the MQM made a name for itself by way of its involvement in a series of ethnic conflicts with Pashtuns and Sindhis, it is somewhat forgotten that one of the first of the MQM's adversaries was the Jamaat-i-Islami, a political party founded by Maulana Maududi and known in the 1970s as a party popular with large segments of the Mohajir population in Karachi. Although the Jamaat-i-Islami never managed to win the support of Mohajirs as massively as the MQM would a decade later, it was popular among many underprivileged Mohajirs. Emphasising the sovereignty of the Islamic law (Nasr 1994, 77), it propagated a kind of political Islam that was opposed to two other powerful forms of political Islam. First, it opposed Islamic modernism, with its roots in the writings of Muhammad Iqbal, particularly his interpretations of *ijtihad* (independent reasoning), which had been the dominant state ideology of the political elite during the 1950s and 1960s. Second, it denounced the political Sufism of the Sindhi separatist movement that came up in the 1960s and was later stripped of its separatist connotations by the Pakistan People's Party (PPP) and turned into a new form of popular Islamic nationalism that opposed elitist modernism. If during the regime of Ayub Khan Islamic modernism had gradually become inflected with Punjabi domination, the political Sufism of the PPP had become associated with Zulfiqar Ali Bhutto's ethnic policies that were perceived as a threat by Mohajirs. Opposing both Islamic modernism and political Sufism, the Jamaat-i-Islami won many of the Mohajir votes.

In the 1980s, however, the Jamaat-i-Islami allied with the Zia-ul-Haq regime, particularly in its support for the Afghan muhajedeen, which increased its numbers of Pashtun supporters, in the Northwest Frontier Province and among Pashtun settlers in Karachi. This put the party in an awkward position during the 1985 riots between Pashtun settlers and Urdu-speaking Biharis and other Mohajirs. Its reluctance to choose sides was fiercely criticised by the MQM, which took the opportunity to make a name for itself by attacking the Jamaat-i-Islami for its 'betrayal' of Mohajirs. Young MQM leaders accused the Jamaat-i-Islami of being 'fundamentalist' and 'hypocritical'. It also argued that Mohajirs were devout Muslims who had made the sacrifice of migration for Pakistan, while at the same time being educated, modern, liberal-minded Muslims, wary of religious extremism. The MQM would continue to cultivate this notion of Mohajirs as moderate Muslims opposed to fundamentalism in the years to come.

This emphasis on educated, modern Muslimness seemed to reinforce the public image of Mohajirs as 'cool', 'reasonable' Muslims as described earlier by Richard Kurin (1988). Analysing popular forms of ethnic othering, Kurin showed how oppositional pairs like hot and cool (*jalal* and *jamal*), and passion and reason (*nafs* and *aql*), informed the ways ethnic groups were categorised in these terms. As city-dwellers, Mohajirs were on the 'cool' and 'reasonable' side, in contrast to the more 'passionate' and 'hot' Sindhis. This also related to popular images of ethnicised religiosity. To give one example, the Sindhi intellectual Ibrahim Joyo once described to me what he considered the Mohajir inclination to a 'bookish' form of Islam. In contrast, he said, the Sindhi Islam was primarily characterised by mystical and bodily practices.

Such notions, however, were already the result of ethnic stereotyping in a political context in which ethnicity mattered. The actual practices of individual Mohajirs generally did not endorse these imaginations. From my long-term fieldwork in a Mohajir-dominated neighbourhood in the city-centre of Hyderabad I learned that Mohajirs actively took part in the mystical practices deemed typical for Sindhis, such as the revering of Sufi saints, those buried in Sindh as those in India. It is also true that others frowned upon such activities, saying that visiting shrines was the preserve of women and the uneducated, thereby drawing the boundary between 'hot' and 'cool' differently: not between ethnic categories, but in terms of gender and caste. But these boundaries, too, were often permeable and those who condemned shrine-visiting as idol-worship (*shirk*) could still engage in long discussions about, for instance, how Islam was disseminated in the intimate relation between saint (*pir*) and follower (*murid*) as much as by reading the Quran.

The novelty and ingenuity of the MQM was that it tapped into these neglected aspects of the popular religious experience of average Mohajirs. Like the Sindhi parties before it, the MQM introduced a sense of loyalty and sacrifice into its style of politics, rooted not in reformist traditions of personal transformation, but in Sufi, and to some extent Shia, practices of leader-disciple loyalty. The charisma of the MQM leader, Altaf Hussain, was cast in these terms, for instance when he was addressed as *Pir Sahib* or when new recruits pledged oaths of loyalty to him. Some of the best-known MQM political manifestations were popular spectacles of loyalty and sacrifice, such as the hunger strike of Altaf Hussain in protest against state persecution, which played in a very powerful way with the Shia language of tyranny, betrayal, and sacrifice, merged with the model of self-effacing loyalty to the spiritual leader. Such political practices returned to Mohajirs the public recognition of popular religious practices that ethnic categorisation had denounced as unfitting for an educated Mohajir, attributing them to ethnic others. In the heyday of the MQM, the saying went that 'the MQM had given Mohajirs a platform', meaning that it had united Mohajirs politically. But it could also be taken to mean that the MQM recognised the average Mohajirs on their own terms without telling them to live up to some elitist ideal of Islamic modernism or ethnic stereotype of dispassionate Islam.

This is of course not to say that the MQM's main objective was one of religious identity. In fact, the MQM mostly presented itself as a secular party, particularly in its early years when it pitted itself against the strong mixture of politics and religion during the Zia-ul-Haq regime and its links with Islamic parties like the Jamaat-i-Islami. The MQM's turn to ethnic identity politics and its claim that Mohajirs form an ethnic group (*qaum*) could in fact be seen as a move away from religious politics. According to a strong current in Pakistani nationalist discourse, Islam and ethnicity are separate and, in some views, even mutually exclusive forms of identification. Before the MQM, Mohajir politicians had generally denounced ethnic identity politics on the basis of the perception that with their migration Mohajirs had made the sacrifice of ethnic ties in favour of an all-Muslim solidarity. The MQM subscribed to this view but also argued that Mohajirs formed a separate group because their sacrifice had not been accepted by other ethnic groups in Pakistan. Contrary to nationalist discourse that separated Islam and ethnicity, then, the MQM's notion of Mohajir ethnic identity contained many religious elements. The association of the migration experience with the *hijra* was one such element, but the MQM also included other powerful elements of popular religiosity, such as religious traditions of sacrifice and loyalty. In this sense, the ethnic political rhetoric of MQM was pervaded with elements of popular religious experience.

It is doubtful to what extent this ethnicisation of popular religion was the result of a strategic or deliberate choice on the part of MQM leaders. It rather followed the model set by Sindhi separatists who had mobilised up-and-coming Sindhi students and professionals against the Ayub Khan regime by construing a Sindhi ethnic identity on the basis on mystical Sufi practices and theology. Rather than acknowledging Islam as monolithic, Sindhi separatists argued that Islam allowed for various regional traditions. Their portrayal of Sindhi Islam as essentially rooted in the mystical notion of the oneness of being (*wahdat ul wujud*) and a range of ecstatic bodily techniques to bring about such mystical experiences did much to construe the ethnic division between 'passionate' Sindhis and 'bookish' Mohajirs. In opposing the Zia-ul-Haq regime and especially the Jamaat-i-Islami, however, the MQM acted together with Sindhi nationalists and adopted some of the ways of their strategic allies. In particular, the charisma of Altaf Hussain was modelled upon the charisma of Zulfiqar Ali Bhutto which, in turn, was modelled upon the mystical loyalty to a Sufi saint or *pir*. To describe their devotion to the party, one MQM member told me: 'If Altaf commands me to stand up, I will stand up. If he commands me to sit down, I will sit down.' Another MQM member said: 'If Altaf commands me to tear off my skin, I will obey.' Not only did Sindhi activists describe their relation to the late Bhutto to me in a similar way, this was also how some Mohajir inhabitants of Hyderabad talked about their *pir*.

Writing about the Hindu nationalist movement in India—the rise of which coincided with the rise of the MQM in Pakistan—Thomas Blom Hansen used a Lacanian perspective to interpret 'the recuperation of masculinity' by young male Hindu nationalists. Their hatred for Muslims, Hansen argued, concealed a secret wish to become like Muslims and incorporate their stereotyped reputation of manliness, a wish that could only be realised in hate speech and violence (Hansen 1996). On first sight, the MQM's 'recuperation' of passion seems to resemble Hansen's interpretation. Still, my analysis of how the MQM transgressed ethnic-religious stereotypes differs from Hansen's view on at least two points. First, I would maintain a much more historical analysis of the MQM's adaptation of Sindhi passion, locating it rather specifically in the political moment when Mohajir and Sindhi activists strategically and temporarily united in their opposition to the military regime. Second, there was, strictly speaking, no need for the MQM to 'recuperate' religious passion from the Sindhis, for in their popular religious practices Mohajirs could already engage in the activities, which in practice were quite common and accepted across ethnic fault lines, even though they were labelled as essentially Sindhi in political discourse. What the MQM did, and what was new in Mohajir politics, was that it incorporated these practices in its political language and mobilisation methods. In doing so, it made such practices acceptable and public for Mohajirs. It was a matter of 'coming out' rather than of 'recuperation'.

Another way of putting this is that the appropriation of passionate politics was in an implicit way as much a class-based phenomenon as an ethnic-religious one. That is to say that the language of religious passion originally was not directed against the ethnic other from which the model was borrowed. It is true that, after the initial agreement with Sindhi activists, ethnic relations between Mohajirs and Sindhis rapidly deteriorated, resulting in some of the worst cases of ethnic violence between both groups in 1988 and 1990. But the MQM's adoption of passionate politics originated from before these clashes, when relations were still friendly. The revanchist power of the MQM was rather provocative of a modernist denunciation of ecstatic religious practices that was largely elitist in nature. The public references to such ecstatic practices within the context of a new and increasingly powerful political party liberated a Mohajir generation coming of age in the 1980s and early 1990s from this elitist and condescending view of popular religiosity. In other words, like most other revanchist movements the MQM did not only depict itself as a defence force against intruding others by claiming Karachi (and Hyderabad) as Mohajir territory besieged by other ethnic groups, but also redefined Karachi (and Hyderabad) as popular Mohajir territory. That is to say that it contributed to the rift between the privileged segments of the

Mohajir population and 'the lower middle class' (in MQM's parlance) as much as it added to ethnic polarisation. Besides being an ethnic party claiming to represent Mohajirs vis-à-vis other ethnic groups, the MQM has always portrayed itself as a party of the 'common people' (*aam log*) and the oppressed (*mazlum*), stressed the humble background of its leaders and followers, and condemned the political elite of landlords, bureaucrats, and the military.

In fact, the sense of liberation that was palpable in large parts of Karachi when the MQM won its first election in 1987 primarily resulted from a shared feeling that power had been returned to the common people. MQM members of the first hour called this feeling '*raj hamara*' or 'our rule' to indicate they had finally seized power as the representatives of the common Mohajir population. The sense of strength particularly empowered the peer groups of young male party members which formed the militant backbone of the party in the Mohajir-dominated neighbourhoods of Karachi. For them, *raj hamara* meant that they could forcefully control the neighbourhood on the basis of their own rules. Later, when the army entered the city to bring the party to its knees, this was perceived as a violation of the sovereign power of the MQM, a perception that intensified the will to resist. What was violated according to the MQM militants was precisely their sense of legitimate power over the Mohajir-dominated neighbourhoods of Karachi as the representatives of the common man.

Multiple religiosities

In contrast to what I have elsewhere called the ethnicisation of Islam, which ascribes certain religious mentalities and passions to ethnic groups (Verkaaik 2007), anthropologists have consistently showed that Pakistani Muslims have often combined various forms of Islam, including mystical and magical practices commonly labelled as Sufism, as well as reformist and modernist mentalities that in theory, but not in practice, are opposed to more traditional Islam. In her book on Islam and modernity, Katherine Ewing documents how both Sufism and reformism influence the religious desires of Pakistani Sunni Muslims, desires that are contextual and fluid rather than ethnicised and fixed (1997). Similary, Pnina Werbner shows that Sufism and reformism are not mutually exclusive and that both traditions are vital, as is for instance evidenced in the continuing influence of both Sufi leaders (*pirs*) and learned spiritual leaders (*ulama*) (2002). In fact, both traditions are often difficult to distinguish in everyday religious practice. Attempts to do so may serve analytical or political purposes but rarely do justice to the religious lifeworlds of Pakistanis.

Barbara Metcalf has argued that the interweaving of various forms of Islam is particularly discernable in the Tablighi Jamaat (1998; 2002). Established in 1926 in India, the Tablighi Jamaat has become an international missionary movement that operates in many countries to invite Muslims to adopt a more spiritual way of life. It gained international publicity because of its plans to build a large mosque in London, known as the Abbey Mills Masjid. After 9/11, it was suspected of recruiting terrorists because it regularly uses the term jihad in its missionary activities. An offshoot of the reformist Deobandi School, it is one of the many revitalist movements—both Hindu and Muslim—that came up during the colonial period in India. As Metcalf argues, all of these movements struck some balance between individual religious regeneration and political intervention, and the Tablighis must be placed on the extreme end of the spectrum because they 'put their weight wholly at the end of reshaping individual lives' (Metcalf 2002, 8). They considered the correct following of the *hadith* the appropriate way to cultivate piety and devoutness towards the Prophet Muhammad and saw it as their task to invite fellow Muslims to follow this path. Although they did not recognise Sufi leaders as intermediaries of spiritual growth, new members to the Tablighi Jamaat were often recruited through existing Sufi bonds. Like the Deobandis themselves, the Tablighis cherished many stories about the Sufis. The notion of spiritual charisma (*baraka*) that is so central in the Sufi relationship of leader and disciple was not so much abandoned as impersonalised in the central metaphor of Medina as well as in the missionary activities themselves. As Metcalf argued, 'the heart of Tablighi Jama'at strategy was the belief that the best way to learn is to teach and encourage others' and to do so in travelling proselytising groups or *jamaats*. Metcalf continues saying that 'among Tablighis, the holiness associated with the Sufi pir was in many ways defused into the charismatic body of the *jamaat* so that the missionary group itself became a channel for divine intervention' (Metcalf 2002, 10–11).

Insofar as Islam mattered in the personal life of the people I got to know during my research on Mohajir identity politics, it was my impression that this composite picture of religious traditions quite accurately captured the religious mentality of many of my interlocutors during the 1990s. For instance, religious extremes were generally condemned as improper and immoral. Such extremes included, among others, the asocial practices of mystical world renouncers, but also the radical reformism of the Ahl-i-Hadith movement that most of my Mohajir informants denounced as 'Wahhabi', 'Arab', or 'foreign'. In particular, the Ahl-i-Hadith's opposition to grave worship was generally deplored as disrespectful and wrong. Ulama-led political parties like the Jamaat-i-Islami and the Jamaat-i-Ulama-i-Pakistan still continued to exert considerable moral and political authority among my interlocutors—despite the MQM's fierce language against the Jamaat-i-Islami—but the same could be said about a range of Sufi leaders or *pirs*.

Given these multiple religiosities, it is not surprising that the Dawat-i-Islami attracted considerable support in the 1990s as an alternative to the beleaguered MQM. The Dawat-i-Islami presented itself as a popular movement of the common Muslim as much as the MQM depicted itself as the representative of the ordinary Mohajir, but it did so in a significantly different way. Established in 1981 by Maulana Muhammad Ilyas and modelled upon the Tablighi Jamaat, it considered evil as resulting from personal corruption (rather than from political injustice), defined jihad or the quest for personal purification (rather than political power) as the panacea, and used *dawat* or religious mission (rather than political mobilisation) as its method. Like the Tablighi Jamaat, it considered the personal or heart-to-heart (*sina ba sina*) form of religious dissemination as the most effective and pure form of *dawat*, although it did use the internet and other forms of mass-media on a larger scale than the Tablighis. In the second half of the 1990s, it gained the momentum of a mass movement that the MQM had lost, speaking the language of ordinary Mohajir youth and giving them a sense of purpose, just like the MQM had done a decade before.

To give an example of how from the point of the view of young Mohajirs the MQM and the Dawat-i-Islami could be connected, let me end by quoting from a conversation I had with one Mohajir member of the Dawat-i-Islami whom I will call Bilal. He was in his early twenties and worked in a dairy shop. His colleagues and friend addressed him by the nickname Maulana because of his beard, his green turban, and his white tunic. He good-humouredly responded to the mild teasing that his outfit provoked. After he had taken me to the Dawat-i-Islami centre in Karachi, he talked to me about his decision to join the movement, which he had taken a few months earlier. Being from a Mohajir family background, he related how he had become disappointed with politics in general and with the MQM in particular. He described politics (*siyasat*) as inherently hypocritical and corrupting. Although he and his brother had supported the MQM as teenagers, he now thought that the party had not succeeded in its effort to liberate Mohajirs. Instead it had contributed to a political culture of violence, intimidation, self-interest, and ethnic polarisation. The problem with politics, he claimed, was that it drove people apart, whereas Islam was meant to bring people together. Echoing the revitalist point that true liberation starts with the purification of the heart, Bilal quite explicitly perceived the Dawat-i-Islami as an alternative to, if not an antidote for, the politics of the MQM.

Taking a step further, he also criticised the ethnicisation of the term Mohajir by saying that the MQM wrongfully connoted the term to a group of people, whereas for him it conveyed a religious aspiration. He conceived of the exodus to Medina as symbolical of the personal journey to spiritual purification. He criticised Mohajirs of his own generation for wrongfully flaunting a Mohajir identity. First, it had been their parents or grandparents who had migrated to Pakistan, not they themselves, and second, even migration to Pakistan did not make one a Mohajir if it had been done for other than spiritual reasons, as, he thought, had in fact most often been the case. For him using the term Mohajir in a political and ethnic sense was religiously improper and insincere.

For Bilal, then, the Dawat-i-Islami redefined the meaning of being a Mohajir by linking the term to religious mission and the cultivation of piety as it had been propagated in the tradition of the Tablighi Jamaat for several decades before it had been given a new impetus by the Dawat-i-Islami. The Dawat-i-Islami was a new and popularised form of the Tablighi Jamaat that to some extent filled the vacuum left by the MQM at the end of the 1990s. But it also built upon a multiplicity of Islamic passion and conduct that defied ethnic categorisation and that the MQM had revealed publicly and politically since its spectacular rise in the late 1980s. In other words, one of the lasting effects of the MQM may have been the erosion of an ethnicised view on Mohajir religiosity as essentially 'bookish'. Although the Dawat-i-Islami was partially an adversary of the MQM, if only because of its denial of the relevance of politics, both the MQM and the Dawat-i-Islami had at least one thing in common: their departure from a one-sided notion of Mohajir religiosity, which was rooted in the modernist condemnation of popular religious practice and exacerbated by ethnic stereotyping.

References

Blom Hansen, Thomas, 'Recuperating Masculinity: Hindu Nationalism, Violence and the Exorcism of the Muslim Other', *Critique of Anthropology*, 16, June (1996), pp. 137–72.

Ewing, Katherine Pratt, *Arguing Sainthood. Modernity, Psychoanalysis and Islam*, Durham: Duke University Press, 1997.

Metcalf, Barbara, 'Women and Men in a Contemporary Pietist Movement: The Case of the Tablighi Jama'at', in Amrita Basu and Patricia Jeffery (eds), *Appropriating Gender: Women's Activism and Politicized Religion in South Asia*, New York: Routledge, 1998, pp. 107–21.

———, 2002. *'Traditionalist' Islamic Activism: Deoband, Tablighis, and Talibs*. https://openaccess.leidenuniv.nl/bitstream/handle/1887/10068/paper_metcalf.pdf, last accessed 4 December 2016.

Radcliffe-Brown, Alfred, 'On Joking Relationships', *Africa: Journal of the International African Institute*, 13, July (1940): pp. 195–210.

Verkaaik, Oskar, *Migrants and Militants. 'Fun' and Urban Violence in Pakistan*, Princeton University Press, 2004.

———, 'Ethnicizing Islam: 'Sindhi Sufis', 'Mohajir Modernists' and 'Tribal Islamists' in Pakistan', in Shafqat Saeed (ed.), *New Perspectives on Pakistan. Visions for the Future*, Karachi: Oxford University Press, 2007.

Werbner, Pnina, *Pilgrims of Love. The Anthropology of a Global Sufi Cult*, Bloomington: Indiana University Press, 2002.

7

PROHIBITION AND 'SHARAB'
AS POLITICAL PROTEST IN KARACHI

Nadeem F. Paracha

This chapter discusses a much neglected and maligned political history surrounding alcohol, getting drunk (*sharab*), and prohibition in Karachi. The intersections of personal, national, and social histories this entails demonstrate how the sale and consumption of alcohol became lethally entangled with protest politics, and with popular forms of anti-authoritarian rebellion on Karachi's student campuses from the 1960s. The attendant issues of religion, morality, and personal revolution it entails also speak more widely to the leftist politics of Zulfiqar Ali Bhutto who founded the Pakistan's People's Party (PPP) in 1967, and the subsequent challenge the PPP, its student wing and other groups posed to Pakistan's religious right, particularly the military regime of Muhammed Zia-ul-Haq (1977–88). Far from frivolous or marginal, *sharab* was a core feature of mainstream party politics and the articulation of social unrest during the period around 1970–90. Coincidentally, this period also characterised my personal passage through the naivety of boyhood to a more weathered condition altogether.

135

The ban on the sale of alcoholic beverages in April 1977 in Pakistan was more a political than a morally driven decision. Under pressure from an animated protest movement by an alliance of right-wing political parties named the Pakistan National Alliance (PNA), Prime Minister Zulfiqar Ali Bhutto pragmatically acceded to demands by PNA leaders. Bhutto's largely secular government had won power through the popular vote and many socialist promises. However, by its fifth year in power Bhutto was facing harsh criticism, especially in the major urban centres. When he ran for re-election in 1977, his government was battling several thorny economic problems—triggered by the international oil crises stemming from the 1973 Egypt-Israel War. These were inflation and the failure of its nationalisation policies that had seen industries, banks, and educational institutions suffering from incompetent management and rising corruption.

The PPP won the 1970 election on its socialist manifesto. During his tenure Bhutto tried to fuse populist socialist and secular notions of social democracy with certain aspects of political Islam, termed Islamic Socialism. When he formed the PPP (in 1967), the idea was to blunt the opposition from the right-wing religious groups. For instance, just before the 1977 election, the PNA, led by fundamentalist parties such as the Jamaat-i-Islami (JI), Jamiat Ulema Islam (JUI), and Jamiat Ulema Pakistan (JUP), demanded that Pakistan be governed by *Nizam-e-Mustafa* (Prophet Muhammad's system of governance). This was justified via the writings of scholars such as JI chief Abul Ala Maududi. It gave credence to certain myths of state-nationalism advocated as historical facts, for example the 'fact' that Pakistan was divinely decreed to emerge as a bastion of Islam.

In 1973 during the second year of his rule, Bhutto purged the Pakistan People's Party and expelled a number of left-wing ideologues from it. However, he overestimated the threat posed to his government by the pro-Soviet far-left groups. He sought to deflect the opposition from Islamists by giving them free rein on university campuses that until then had been hotbeds of left-wing activism. Paradoxically, after 1973 some of the policies that Bhutto had devised from mixing socialism and political Islam began to strengthen the narratives of right-wing religious parties that had been roundly defeated in the 1970 election. By 1973 college and university campuses in Karachi had witnessed a surge in the popularity of the JI's student wing, the Islami Jamiat Taleba (IJT). Bhutto's opponents, particularly Karachi's Urdu-speaking Mohajirs, and the right-wing anti-Bhutto bourgeoisie in general failed to gain much ground in parliament and attempted to fight his populist 'socialist' regime through the vanguard of the IJT in educational institutions. During the 1977 election campaign, the PNA accused Bhutto of being a drunk and resolved to 'rid society of the evils of alcohol' (Hoodbhoy 2011, xxix). During a rally in Lahore the same year, Bhutto lashed out at PNA leaders that he believed were supported by the industrialists whose businesses he had nationalised, and responded: '*Haan mein sharab peeta houn, lekin awam ka khoun nahi peeta!*' (Yes I drink alcohol, but I do not drink the people's blood) (Ibid.).

This was not the first time the right-wing religious parties had blamed alcohol for Pakistan's economic, political and social suffering. Previously, the youth wing of the fundamentalist Majlis-e-Ahrar had attacked coffee houses serving alcohol in Lahore during the 1953 anti-Ahmadi riots. In 1967 the IJT began a movement against 'wine shops' and bars in Karachi after the progressive Islamic scholar, Dr Fazalur Rahman Malik, who had been appointed by the Ayub Khan regime to head the Central Institute of Islamic Research, claimed on television that according to the Hanafi *mathab* (jurisprudence)—which the majority of Pakistan's Sunni Muslims followed—only some alcoholic beverages were *haram* (unlawful) in Islam (Michalak and Trocik 2006, 523). He then suggested there was nothing wrong in consuming beer. In response, JI asked for Rahman's resignation. IJT activists in Karachi attacked wine shops, hoardings, and billboards advertising the Pakistani-made Murree Beer. Nonetheless, the IJT campaign did not resonate with a public already embroiled in the student and worker movement against the pro-US Ayub dictatorship and, with the weakening of the Ayub regime, Rahman resigned.

After the loss of East Pakistan in 1971 JI blamed the Pakistani generals' liking for 'wine and women' as a main cause of Pakistan's defeat in the war. In 1974 Prime Minister Bhutto banned alcohol in army mess halls, although he took no action against bars, nightclubs, coffee houses, and wine shops. Throughout Bhutto's regime, the JI and IJT initiated various campaigns against wine shops and nightclubs but failed to garner significant public support until 1977. After the PPP swept the

National Assembly polls in the 1977 elections, the PNA claimed widespread cases of election fraud by the government. It boycotted the Provincial Assembly elections, began a tense protest movement, and demanded Bhutto's resignation. Its strongest support was in Karachi where thousands of students, shopkeepers, businessmen, and professionals clashed head-on with the police in the streets.

Many wine shops and nightclubs were attacked and looted. In response Bhutto began a dialogue with the PNA and agreed to close down all bars, wine shops, and nightclubs. He also banned gambling at horse races and announced the Muslim holy day of Friday would replace Sunday as the weekly holiday. Just when a breakthrough seemed imminent between the PPP regime and the PNA, in July 1977 General Zia-ul-Haq instigated a successful military coup. He arrested PNA members, PPP ministers and Bhutto himself. Zia then adopted the PNA's Islamic overtones and invited JI leaders to help turn Pakistan into a 'true Islamic state'. To the existing prohibition on alcohol Zia added a punishment of eighty lashes. Although the sale and consumption of alcohol is still banned for Muslims, the last Pakistani to be lashed was in 1981. In 2008, the Islamic Ideology Council and the Federal Shariat Court declared the consumption of alcohol a 'minor offence'. The Court also revised down the number of lashes from eighty to forty 'light' lashes.

Murree Brewery Co. is one of the biggest tax-paying companies in Pakistan and Pakistan's oldest brewery, established in 1860 near the resort town Murree in Punjab (Foreman 2012). In the 1920s the brewery moved to Rawalpindi where it stands today. In the 1960s, Murree introduced malt whisky, and in the early 1970s produced vodka and gin. Before prohibition, foreign brands were widely available in Pakistan's big cities, but Murree remained the leading most affordable brand. Its popularity among young urban middle-class Pakistanis was reflected in widespread advertising on hoardings and billboards—the largest a neon image of Murree beer atop a six-storey building in Karachi's Lucky Star area in Saddar. In the 1970s Murree competed with various imported brands, but it thrived because it catered mostly to a growing middle-class market for whom imported brands were an expensive luxury. Unlike other brands which went under after 1977, Murree survived prohibition and various subsequent waves of imposed piety and expressions of state-sanctioned 'Islam'. It is also a valued export, not least personally. For example, in 2005, when cravings for *desi* food struck me on a visit to Paris, I was delighted to find a restaurant serving Murree Beer, for me a cherished Pakistani brand. Murree has licensed breweries in Belgium to produce and distribute Murree Beer in Europe.

Karachi and other urban centres in Interior Sindh have the largest number of Pakistan's legal 'wine shops'. They are permitted to sell local beer and brands of spirits to foreigners and to Christian, Hindu, Zoroastrian, and other non-Muslim consumers who have a government-issued permit. Buying alcohol from these shops has always been easier than elsewhere in Pakistan. According to Isphanyar Bhandara, the owner of Murree Breweries, almost 90 per cent of Murree's consumers are Muslim (Foreman 2012). Karachi still has some restaurants that serve alcohol, a rarity in a country declared dry four decades ago. Punjab province has very strict laws compared to Sindh. That is why the JI and IJT have persisted with campaigns against 'wine shops' in Sindh and Karachi. Whereas some anti-alcohol crusaders suggest such campaigns failed owing to the bigger urban problem of heroin addiction, JI

Image 9: A neon sign advertising Pakistan's beer brand, Murree, on top of a building Lahore in 1963 (Courtesy: *Dawn* newspaper, Pakistan).

Image 10: A 1966 newspaper ad of a famous Karachi nightclub, The Oasis (Courtesy: *Dawn* newspaper, Pakistan).

and IJT blame Karachi's leading political parties—the PPP, the Muttahida Qaumi Movement (MQM) and the Awami National Party (ANP)—of having economic interests attached to the alcohol business. Elsewhere in Sindh, JI accuses PPP ministers and members of nationalist Sindhi parties of being the 'real owners' of the wine shops and business. Although quality Murree brands are available, prices are high and smugglers profit from contraband alcohol. Trucks import vodka from China across the mountainous northern border, while ships unload cargos of European beer and whisky on Karachi's dockside. Yet Pakistanis largely remain silent about prohibition. Despite the deaths that routinely occur due to toxic brews, alcohol consumption remains widespread across the country, in all classes, and in urban and rural areas. While the conservative elements remain rigidly opposed, others suggest that lifting the ban will gradually rid the country of bootlegging, and help address rising rates of alcoholism. Yet: if the risk of being lashed, arrested, or harassed by the police failed to stop so many Pakistanis from drinking during the oppressive Zia years, why would they stop now?

Indeed, according to many surveys, cases of alcoholism doubled in the 1980s, and continue to grow (Haider and Chaudhry 2008). Illegal breweries producing cheap whisky for the poor and peasant classes are nothing new. But when alcohol was legal, bars, cafes, and stores sold drinks from established breweries. After prohibition, establishments were only permitted to sell to non-Muslims (even though their main clients were Muslims), and prices sky-rocketed. Poorer drinkers could not keep pace. They began to depend squarely on shady moonshine makers and many lost their lives owing to toxic whiskey (*katchi sharab*) produced by illegal brewers.

Murree continues to do a roaring business, as does Indus Brewery (established in 2008) which caters to clients who cannot afford Murree's rising prices. In short, prohibition failed to stop many Pakistanis consuming alcohol and whilst JI has initiated several campaigns in Karachi, these have failed to generate substantive momentum or public support. In addition, the use of deadly drugs such as heroin increased almost tenfold in Pakistan after prohibition in 1977. Although bootlegging mafias have grown up in response to prohibition, since the 1980s the number of chronic alcoholics in Pakistan has also increased tremendously (Walsh 2010). On the one hand, today there are more alcoholics in Pakistan than ever, and many privately-run detox and rehabilitation centres operate in Karachi. On the other hand, although Pakistan's first registered case of heroin addiction was reported at Jinnah Hospital in Karachi in 1979, by 1985 Pakistan had the second largest population of heroin addicts (Ibid.). The 1980s and 1990s also saw a dramatic rise in cases of heroin and tranquilliser addiction. Equally startling is the absolute lack of action by the country's mainstream religious parties on the issue of heroin usage and sale. Of course these transformations cannot be exclusively attributed to prohibition. The 1980s saw a dramatic influx of heroin accompanying the Afghan refugees from the Soviet-Afghan war (1979–88). With so many political and economic crises facing Pakistan since prohibition, alcohol has receded as a moral and political issue. Yet the desire amongst Pakistanis to forget their problems through intoxication has not. This must be attributed to the changing environment but also to the long-term effects of chronic, multi-layered experiences of violence facing people every day, in a city blighted by almost three decades of continuous ethnic and political conflict.

Although I have not been a big drinker now for over a decade, sharing drinks with close friends is still one of my favourite pastimes. Next I outline my personal experiences of vehement student protest and the rampant drinking that characterised one channel of rebellion available to Karachi's youth during the repressive Zia years. Student politics transformed my passion for *sharab* into participation in collective protest, and sometimes collective chaos. In their escalation to a situation that eventually became far from fun, these activities were also a catalyst for personal and political change.

In 1977 when I was eleven years old, alcohol was a pressing national, political, and religious issue. I had seen nightclubs, bars, and roadside cafes serving alcohol in Karachi, all operating just like any other business. My father and uncles drank and those who did not adopted a *laissez-faire* attitude. 1977 was the height of the religious parties' movement against Bhutto. One evening that year I was returning from a wedding when our family car got caught up in a riot in Karachi's Lucky Star area. I witnessed dozens of youths smashing traffic signals, and breaking into wine shops. Some raised slogans while smashing bottles of spirits and beer; others stole as much as they could carry and disappeared into the narrow lanes. Others swigged the stuff down right there outside, before torching the stores. The contradictions in these scenes, so glaringly obvious, were lost on me as an eleven-year-old.

Yet when I entered my teens, one of the most popular acts for rebellious youth was drinking alcohol. Memories of a time before prohibition were fresh, and for those young people who detested Zia's despotism, drinking was an act of defiance. Ironically, those problems that would eventually push the country towards the madness of sectarian and religious violence, bigotry, corruption and moral hypocrisy were sown by

Zia's dictatorship. But most of these seeds would start to sprout after his controversial demise in 1988. For example, whereas many women's organisations would regularly protest against Zia's anti-women laws by publicly burning their *dupatta*s, it is unimaginable women could do the same today without being threatened by religious groups. I grew up during a time when a military regime publicly flogged activists and journalists. It was common for Zia's opponents to be arrested in the night, tortured and 'disappeared'. I personally know about many young activists who lost their minds after such experiences. Some emerged from jails after Zia's death in 1988, looking gaunt and aged, but others never reappeared. Drinking was both a self-destructive and a self-preservative relief, and a form of self-medication.

Whenever I patronise a licensed wine shop in Karachi these days, I remember the ordeal it was in the 1980s. There were always police on bikes posted outside stores. Though they were paid bribes and received free booze from the store-owners, they nonetheless harassed the customers from whom they demanded the same. Those who refused could be arrested under the notorious 'Hudood Laws' introduced by Zia. These include fixed punishments for crimes deemed to be against 'edicts of God' including theft, fornication and adultery (*zina*), consumption of alcohol or other intoxicants, and apostasy. Consequently, buying alcohol from stores became highly risky and Muslims began depending on the rising numbers of bootleggers. Others struck up working relationships with police officers who would sell alcohol they had confiscated.

I had my first drink in 1983, aged seventeen. I had previously only tasted a few tablespoons of brandy as a child, administered by an Afghan doctor in the freezing winter of Kabul where our family lived in 1972. Many people will tell you that when Pakistanis drink, they drink like there is no tomorrow. Broadly this is true. Why? I would locate the emergence of this habit in the early 1980s, when laws and actions against the sale and consumption of alcohol became stricter. New Year's parties became a collective free for all. Since the nightclubs and hotel bars where New Year's celebrations traditionally took place were ordered to close down in April 1977, many Pakistanis held New Year's parties at homes. Ironically, many parties in spacious bungalows belonged to those industrialists and businessmen who had hailed the fall of the 'socialist' Bhutto regime, and had financed the PNA movement against him in 1977.

Image 11: A shop selling alcohol near a petrol station set on fire by a right-wing mob in Karachi, April 1977 (Courtesy: *Dawn* newspaper, Pakistan).

The zenith of public drunkenness may well have been on the last day of 1983, New Year's Eve. As my friends and I hopped from one New Year's party to another, we saw roads littered with smashed up cars, bikes, and empty bottles. Revellers came out on bikes and cars. They were chased down by hordes of policemen who were not only extorting money from those they booked under Zia's Hudood Ordinances, but were themselves also drunk! I vividly remember driving over Clifton Bridge and seeing cars and bikes upturned. Karachi's famous 'food street' in the congested Burn's Road area witnessed similar scenes. As Zia's so-called religious laws and repression increased, many Pakistanis went overboard with their drinking and partying. New Year's Eve 1983 was a stark example of how required public displays of piety nurtured ever more decadent desires for profligacy.

These desires also included an appetite for quick-profit schemes, criminal rackets, and general fiscal 'immorality'. After 1983, huge bungalows began appearing around Karachi, and indeed all Pakistan's major cities. These were owned by military officers or traders from the emerging nouveau-riche, including entrepreneurs in the lucrative new heroin smuggling business. At the same time an overt show of religiosity was supported amongst those businessmen who supported Zia. Amongst those in the 'import-export' business who profited from heroin and weapons trades in the early 1980s, a new fashion emerged large gaudy houses decorated with Qu'ranic quotations. These homeowners were blind to the hypocrisy, if indeed in each case there was any.

My proposition that drinking alcohol by young people during Zia's era became a political act of defiance typically produces surprise. Those Pakistanis who entered their teens and twenties after the late 1990s cannot relate to living under a military dictatorship that was far more oppressive than the 'softer' regime of General Musharraf (1999–2008). The terror that is committed by outlawed extremist and sectarian organisations today was directly perpetrated by the state during Zia's regime. To silence political and ideological opposition, Zia used increasingly more rigid, moralistic interpretations of Islam that until the early 1980s were marginal. Zia himself was an ideologue of the state-nationalist Islam of scholars like Maududi. By the mid 1980s, he had brought clerics with ever sterner and more myopic dispositions on faith and morality into the mainstream. These men, once only found on the fringes, helped recruit young Pakistanis and Afghans to fight the 'jihad' in Afghanistan; a jihad that guaranteed American support and an unprecedented flow of dollars and Saudi riyals.

Imposing morality was also lucrative in local communities. Backed by the controversial Hudood Laws, the police could easily extort money from anyone they accused of being immoral. They commonly stopped couples and ask them to produce marriage certificates. Failure to do so could result in jail on charges of committing *zina* (sex outside marriage). By 1986 the situation was so absurd the police were extorting money from married couples, even brothers collecting their sisters from college. Nevertheless, some enterprising restaurant owners began designating special corners in their establishments where couples could sit, have coffee, and talk. Others served alcohol. Dozens of such places sprang up in Karachi's Tariq Road and Nazimabad areas, and served a counter culture of anti-authoritarian, anti-establishment minded, or simply licentious youth.

Nemesis

In this final section, I examine how drinking alcohol and *shugal* (fun) became directly linked with protest in politics during my years as a college student in Karachi, 1983–90. The 1970s were the 'golden era' of student politics in Pakistan. The National Students Federation (NSF) had celebrated the PPP's sweeping victory in the 1970 general elections. In 1972 the Pakistan Peoples Party's student wing, the Peoples Students Federation (PSF) entered campus politics. Although the 1974 Student Union Ordinance officially encouraged politics on campuses, after 1973 student factions began opposing Bhutto. Several new leftist student groups formed. Bhutto began to view student politics as a mutable, volatile creature that could unpredictably change allegiances. At the same time his growing authoritarianism gave momentum to conservatives and Islamists such as JI and the IJT.

Fierce anti-Bhutto protests surrounding the 1977 general elections gave a pretext for Bhutto's handpicked Chief of Army Staff, General Zia-ul-Haq, to impose Pakistan's third Martial Law (5 July). When Zia

Image 12: Zulfiqar Ali Bhutto speaking at a rally of left-wing youth in Karachi in 1972 (Courtesy: *Dawn* newspaper, Pakistan).

appointed Jamat-e-Islami members to his first cabinet (to help 'Islamicise Pakistan'), IJT's notorious 'Thunder Squad'—formed in the 1960s to challenge leftist student activists—began freely harassing JI's opponents. Zia increased punishments against progressive groups, especially the PSF. Sophisticated firearms began appearing on university campuses, led by the IJT. At the University of Karachi (KU)'s 1979 student union elections Thunder Squad members were seen carrying AK-47s. The PSF had risen appreciably at Peshawar University. Their student leaders bought AK-47 assault rifles from Afghan traders who arrived in Pakistan during the Soviet occupation. At KU, the Progressive Alliance capitulated under government repression and the well-armed IJT. In 1978 Altaf Hussain, who was a student at KU, formed the All Pakistan Mohajir Students Organisation (APMSO). The APMSO held progressive views and supported the rights of Sindh's Urdu-speaking students (Mohajirs), who it claimed were disenfranchised by Bhutto's quota system.

With their cache of AK-47s, leading this group of activists at KU was the PSF's most notorious leader, Salamullah Tipu. Tipu formed a militant PSF wing that propagated armed rebellion against Zia's dictatorship. The PSF immediately clashed with the IJT at KU. After Tipu killed a senior IJT leader, Hafiz Shahid, at KU, he and several PSF militants escaped to Peshawar and then to Soviet-controlled Afghanistan. There they received training from the Afghan intelligence agency, KHAD. In 1979 in Kabul Bhutto's exiled sons, Murtaza and Shahnawaz, formed an anti-Zia guerrilla outfit called Al-Zulfikar Organisation (AZO). When Tipu returned to Pakistan he hijacked a domestic PIA flight with the help of three other PSF/AZO men. They diverted it to Kabul and demanded Zia release political prisoners. Despite such high profile activities, by 1984 Tipu had become a liability and was hanged by the Kabul authorities. His PSF counterparts in the hijacking escaped and settled in Libya.

By 1983 anti-government student alliances had gained strong momentum and were in a position to initiate a students' movement of the sort that helped topple Ayub Khan's dictatorship in the late 1960s. The government announced a ban on student union elections in early 1984, citing violence as a reason. 1983 was the last year countrywide student union elections took place in Pakistan. Consequently the IJT suffered heavy defeats in the 1983 union elections. The irony was that

IJT defied JI's approval of the ban and joined the student groups who protested against it. The IJT demanded JI withdraw its support for the Zia regime. Subsequently Karachi saw protest rallies, where for over two months members of the IJT, PSF and NSF burned dozens of government cars and buses, and fought battles with riot police.

I joined Saint Patrick's Government College in Saddar in 1983. St Pat's boasted an ethnic, religious, and economic diversity. Amongst my class fellows were rich and poor students, Mohajirs, Punjabis, Sindhis, Pushtuns, Baloch, Palestinians, Iranians, Bengalis, Sunnis, Shias, and Christians. The college union was dominated by an alliance of three progressive student parties, the NSF, PSF, and the Baloch Students Organisation (BSO). St Pat's enjoyed a reputation as one of Karachi's most *shugal* (fun) colleges. Its 'notorious' canteen was well-stocked with Murree beer. It also held regular games of Royal Flush. Several students were arrested in police raids for gambling and drinking alcohol.

I did not join any student groups until Zia banned student unions in 1984. Karachi's state-owned colleges and universities soon formed a united front against the ban. Across Karachi police and government vehicles were attacked. I joined in a large crowd at St Pat's throwing rocks at the police, who returned fire with teargas shells. The riots lasted three days. On the second day we began using empty bottles to make petrol bombs or Molotov cocktails and to burn government cars. The police fired rubber bullets. I was caught and thrashed with sticks. With several others, all bleeding, all shouting slogans against Zia, we were driven to the notorious policestation, '555 Thana', infamous for its torture cells. Dozens of students were locked in tiny cells. I spent ten terrifying hours there, slapped, kicked, punched, spat at, and insulted by the police.

This incident propelled me to join the PSF. Initially this largely involved sitting, and smoking, with friends in the canteen, sharing with bravado our experiences of 555. One day soon after, a student rushed up, shouting that the IJT were taking over all Karachi's campuses. '*Bhenchodh agey! Jamaati Tha! Jamaati Tha!*' ('The fuckers are here. Bang the Jamaatis!'). The IJT posse had arrived. In the violence that followed several students were severely injured. Our friend Akif's stomach was eviscerated, cut open with a knife. Soon afterwards the anti-Zia student movement collapsed after the IJT pulled out. Zia had asked JI to discipline its student wing. IJT protests were damaging Pakistan's role in the anti-Soviet 'Afghan jihad', and his Islamisation process. By 1984 the leaders of almost all anti-Zia student organisations were in jail or in hiding. At St Pat's, we had prevented the takeover of the college's union by the IJT, but the progressive alliance was lost. We entered 1985 in quite a different mood. *Shugal* and decadence had been replaced with ideology and politics. I became involved in forming a new political alliance—albeit one that still involved a personal commitment to the cause of *sharab*.

In May 1985, St Pat's reinstated the cancelled union elections of 1984. I was now heading the PSF. I asked some local PPP leaders for cash for the election campaign. 'Why?' they responded. 'You St Pat's boys will spend it on booze, women, and drugs.' Nonetheless they donated Rs.4000. I bought two pistols and printed some posters. We called our alliance the St Pat's Socialist Students Federation. We sprayed our leftie slogans and insignia on the walls (a hand holding a pen shaped like a sickle). Yes, pretentious, but fun! Elections were held on 3 June 1985. The SPSSF won. I became General Secretary of the union until we graduated in 1987. I think we did a decent job.

We mostly kept the IJT out—until December 1986 when we demonstrated against Zia. Over a hundred students gathered outside the common room (our 'recreational hall') chanting anti-Zia, anti-US, and pro-democracy slogans. We made fiery speeches denouncing Reagan's government for financing Zia and the Afghan jihad. Provoking the police outside, one hot-headed student whipped out an American flag (to burn it). Others filled empty bottles with petrol, to make Molotov cocktails. The situation degenerated when the IJT gatecrashed the rally. Despite bloody injuries, the police remained unmoved.

When I graduated from St Pat's in 1987, the PSF and APMSO took over the union. When Zia died in August 1988 (allegedly because of a bomb planted in the plane he was travelling in), I was a Master's student of political science at Karachi University. Then Benazir Bhutto won the 1988 elections. In December I joined the PSF at KU. By early 1990 clashes between the PSF and the APMSO were turning increasingly violent. The bloodiest episode occurred at KU. Intense firing between the two groups at NED University of Engineering and Technology saw PSF activists pushing their APMSO counterparts back into KU. Meanwhile, the APMSO gunmen re-entered NED, firing at the PSF militants. Before PSF assistance could arrive, the APMSO men had captured some PSF students. When the PSF forces reached NED with a trunk full of guns and bullets, the police had shut all entry and exit points. Driving into KU would have been suicidal because the APMSO militants had taken over. They took their PSF captives to the gymnasium. They opened fire, killing them all, splattering their brains across the walls. The incident shocked the city. Deadly PSF-APMSO violence ensued across Karachi's major colleges, and eventually the MQM quit the shaky PPP-MQM alliance.

Strung out amidst this escalation of violence, and afraid, I became incredibly paranoid. The killings had shaken me. I felt personally hunted by the PSF, APMSO, and the police. I told my father I was driving around, crazy, with a gun and knife. 'You are at a crossroads,' he said. 'Throw the gun way. Put your struggle in the past.' We agreed I should leave Karachi until tensions cooled down. And so I took a bus to Islamabad to stay with a friend at Quaid-e-Azam University there. From there I travelled to Peshawar and stayed at a cheap hotel. Here I borrowed money from my sister's in-laws and travelled to Lahore. After spending time in Lahore I took another bus south to Shewan Sharif, the colourful city in Sindh famous for hosting festivals around the shrine of the Sufi saint, Lal Shabaz Qalandar. There, in possession of just my small backpack, some Gold Leaf cigarettes and Rs.17, I survived for several weeks sleeping in various *jhugi*s (straw houses) visited by roaming *malang*s (spiritual vagabonds). I ate what they ate (dates and *rotis* given to them as charity), drank what they drank (muddy water and large quantities of the intoxicant *bhang* (a beverage prepared from cannabis plants), and smoked what they smoked (large quantities of hashish).

Finally, losing weight and running a fever, I made my way home and faced the consequences. One *malang* advised me to hitch a ride on one of the many trucks that transported fruit, sugar and wheat to Karachi. I did just that. I was dropped off at Karachi's congested area of Sorabh Goth from where I took a taxi home. I slept two whole days. Seeing my father again, he smiled: '*Jaag gaye?*' (You have woken?) 'Indeed, Papa. I have truly woken. The past is finished.' And so I quit university and student politics. Later that year, 1990, I became a reporter for Karachi's largest-selling English weekly, *MAG*. Protest politics and campus 'fun' had become too deadly. It is ironic that the rebellion which I pursued wholeheartedly, through means that were absolutely characteristic of the time and city I grew up in, finally straightened me out. Perhaps this is universal to the passage of youth, but whilst I survived my excesses and eventually even flourished, the cost, which reaches far beyond any cost to myself, has been prohibitively high.

References

Foreman, Jonathon, 'Ale under the veil', *The Telegraph*, London, 24 March 2012.

Haider, Waseem and M. Aslam Chaudhry, 'Prevalence of Alcoholism in the Punjab, Pakistan', *Biomedica*, 24, July (2008) pp. 80–84.

Hoodbhoy, Nafisa, *Abroad the Democracy Train*, Delhi and New York: Anthem Press, 2011.

Michalak, Laurence and Karen Trocki, *Alcohol and Islam*, New York: William S. Hein & Co., 2006.

Walsh, Declan, 'Alcoholism booms in Pakistan', *The Guardian*, London, 27 December 2010.

8

THE COST OF FREE SPEECH

THE MEDIA IN THE BATTLEFIELDS OF KARACHI

Razeshta Sethna

For years, Pakistan has been ranked by media watchdog organisations as one of the most dangerous countries for journalists facing violence from militant groups, political parties, feudal lords, separatists, the military, and intelligence services. Over 55,000 Pakistanis have been killed in terror attacks in the past decade, including over seventy journalists. This is the highest number in any single country for this period, ranking Pakistan among the most dangerous countries to practice journalism. In 2014 the Committee to Protect Journalists (CPJ) ranked Pakistan as the fourth most dangerous country in the world for journalists, while Reporters Without Borders placed the country 158th out of 167 documented countries in its World Press Freedom Index the same year. Additionally, in 2016 the International Federation of Journalists ranked Pakistan as the fourth most dangerous country for journalists, with 115 journalists killed since 1990.

Extremist groups threaten the media if they refuse to air their points of view, and the state relegates certain subjects as no-go areas, making journalism a dangerous profession. In Balochistan and FATA, journalists cannot travel and report independently. The spillover of the fight against militancy in the north-west tribal regions into Karachi has resulted in the assassinations, threats, and intimidation of journalists, influencing media coverage of a conflict that has resulted in over 50,000 civilians, soldiers and militants dead since 2004 (Buneri, 2015). In the tribal areas, media organisations offer negligible support to journalists. They are abandoned when threatened by militants or security forces, and the state is complicit in attacking and harassing journalists.

Where newspapers and broadcasters have sought to make politicians accountable, they risked being closed down, or denied advertisement revenue. Journalists are banned, dismissed, physically, and verbally attacked, and editors pressured. Lest they gravely offend the military, politicians, or the Pakistani Taliban, journalists select their words carefully. They use 'alleged', and remove terms such as 'outlawed', 'militant' or 'terrorist' for reports on the Pakistani Taliban. Some newspapers resort to self-censorship. The state's repression of press freedoms requires journalists either to dilute or hedge their own narrative, or to present the state's version, putatively for 'security reasons'. These measures curb public debate and dissent.

In January 2015 the Human Rights Commission of Pakistan reported that around 3,000 people including women and children were killed in Karachi in sectarian killings since 2011. Leaders of banned groups such as Ahle Sunnat Wal Jamaat and the Sipah-i-Sahaba Pakistan operated with virtual immunity, and used social media and text messaging for disseminating militant ideas and influencing mainstream political parties (Sethna and Rehman, 2014). Thirty years ago, my driver taught himself how to read the newspapers. Now, he watches television and discusses the extortionate price of petrol, how sewage water irrigates his growing vegetables, and, American dollars bolster the Taliban. This traditional man, who has been a keen political commentator for thirty years from behind the wheel, no longer attends his local mosque every Friday for fear of being killed by a sectarian party.

A war on words

This is a recollection, not a historical record. It is a collection of conversations and memories that bear witness to stories that might easily disappear. Events unfold at such a feverish pace in Karachi that they might easily be lost on a supply-line of aggregated news. This is the journalist's experience. Yet collecting stories also involves a fight for our country, for rights, women, dignity, and religion. It invokes a war of words, a story of dreams and nightmares involving numbers dead, neighbourhoods bombed, peaceful communities massacred, women with terrorised faces, radical preachers issuing death sentences, bloody images on television screens, a procession of ambulances carrying dead bodies to a mass funeral, a young woman in a white shroud buried by women, a black banner with white script proclaiming support for terror, presenters thrashed on live news programmes, civilians convulsed by tear gas. The callousness and impunity with which groups kill for profit, religious ideology and 'security', combined with a situation of proliferating weapons, has fuelled an exhausting civil war in Karachi. How long until we reach peace? Perhaps this writing may help explain the forces driving violence in our city, and direct attention to the indifference shown by our civilian leaders to violence. This examination of the media industry raises more questions and dilemmas than it answers. These relate to curbed editorial freedoms, the business-military nexus, and pressures from the state and security apparatus to 'ideologise' public minds.

I have never written about my personal experiences of working in newsrooms as a broadcast and print journalist. Indeed, I long preferred not to mention the patriarchal politics within the profession, the lack of editorial judgement, too much editorial control, insufficient television broadcast equipment, inadequate safety measures, lack of respect, and the blatant discrimination facing journalists. However, since I have experienced attacks and the killings of my colleagues and friends, I no longer wish to keep quiet. This chapter reflects on my work as a journalist in Karachi, as a presenter for Geo TV and later Dawn TV, and draws on interviews I conducted in 2015 with some of Karachi's key media figures in order to elaborate on various connections between violent politics, state violence, and the media.

The fortified media offices of *Dawn*, Pakistan's first English-language newspaper, have a long history, one that is entwined with pre-Partition India. The founder of Pakistan, Mohammad Ali Jinnah, began publishing *Dawn* as a weekly from New Delhi in 1942 in order to represent the view of Hindustan's Muslims. These days, on most Fridays the thoroughfare on which the Dawn Group's offices are now located is blocked to protect the chief minister's colonial style residence which is close by. Armed security guards, crouched under the barrel of a machine gun behind sandbags, are a familiar sight in Dawn's carpark. Fridays are dangerous because terror attacks typically occur during afternoon prayers. In 2008 and 2009 I was a presenter for Dawn TV. Every Friday for several months I reported with my colleagues on Taliban and sectarian attacks on places of worship, Shia *imambargah*s, Sufi shrines, the police, markets, military installations, and government infrastructure. There was no respite from the horror of body counts, innards strewn on the roads, body parts stuck on electricity poles after bombs exploded, and attacks on hospitals following suicide blasts. While I thought I had seen violence, knew what it meant, I was proved wrong by many subsequent killings in the city.

The media and the MQM

The Taliban's entry into Karachi as a topic for reportage is newer compared with the violence associated with sectarianism and ethnic politics. An older unforgiving political geography means that hospitals, colleges and even roads denote earmarked political and ethnic jurisdictions. For example, the Abbasi Shaheed Hospital provides medical assistance to Urdu-speaking Mohajirs, militants and supporters of the Karachi-based political party Muttahida Qaumi Movement (MQM). The MQM has effectively exerted control over the city, including over the print and broadcast media, through intimidation, violence or its media sympathisers. In 2011 the MQM was accused in the murder of Geo News reporter, Wali Khan Babar. Five witnesses in the case were killed between April 2011 and November 2012. The April 2015 operation to 'clean-up' Karachi's militant elements by the army and Rangers curtailed the party's influence. Consequently news channels and newspapers began publishing on the MQM with a free hand, and they increased their profits at the same time. Competition for TV ratings made breaking news a significant portion of news programming. Often broadcasters failed to corroborate their facts. During the operation one senior Karachi newspaper editor I interviewed (anonymous) felt certain the MQM's setback was temporary and the army would ease them into a deal. He chose personal safety in exchange for not writing all he knew. For this reason, he has 'friends' and informants within the party. In May 2015 another senior editor (also anonymous) described exchanges of information between military representatives and the media as quite the norm. Inferring the political role that the state, and the media, are forced to play, he described how months before Operation Zarb-e-Azb began the military decided that Karachi's political stakeholders should change. The city could not be held hostage to a single political party; nor could there be a political vacuum.

2015 and 2016 presented difficult times for the MQM. The party's exiled leader Altaf Hussain visited London's Scotland Yard for questioning in relation to money laundering charges. His party's Karachi headquarters were raided by paramilitary forces in March 2015 and weapons were recovered and suspects arrested. The arrestees included Faisal Mota, who had been sentenced to death *in absentia* in an anti-terrorism court for the murder of reporter Wali Khan Babar in 2011. Editors and reporters forced to provide airtime to Altaf Hussain knew well the party's methods. In control of Pakistan's economic powerhouse, the MQM has long been able to bring Karachi to a standstill, despite military operations against it, even from London.

In the eighties and nineties, the MQM burned the city's newspaper offices. Journalists were openly threatened for 'non-compliance'. Hussain demanded editors travel to Nine Zero, the party's headquarters in Karachi, to ask forgiveness for their 'misdemeanours'. Karachi's streets became dumping grounds for mutilated bodies. With a solid votebank, the MQM brutalised rival militants and anyone who criticised the party, journalists included. The 1990–92 MQM coalition with the Islami Jamhoori Ittehad government was the highpoint in its power. The press was targeted; party workers burned thousands of copies of *Dawn* and stopped its distribution, looted the offices of the Jang Group, and attacked journalists' homes. The MQM demanded prominent coverage of its activities to be placed in newspapers, condemned criticism of the party, and punished those who would not oblige. During Benazir Bhutto's government, when the Interior Minister (1993–6) Naseerullah Babar was widely reported to have ordered thousands of extrajudicial killings against the MQM, MQM leaders were highly effective in gaining support from international human rights organisations such as Amnesty International and Human Rights Watch. These organisations condemned the human rights abuses being carried out against the MQM, while downplaying the party's involvement in targeted killings. The media criticised the human rights abuses against MQM sympathisers.

The MQM has long had a fraught relationship with reporters and editors at the political monthly, *The Herald*. In March 1991, *The Herald* reporter Zafar Abbas, who later joined the BBC and subsequently became editor at *Dawn* newspaper, was viciously attacked at his Karachi home and hospitalised. On 28 March 1991, an editorial in the Lahore-based *The Friday Times* by Najam Sethi discussed a meeting between members of news agencies and the Prime Minister Nawaz Sharif. Sethi observed that in private, members of news agencies thundered against the party's excesses, whilst publicly yielding before Altaf Hussain 'who hectored them into a refresher course on the dos and don'ts of responsible journalism'. Sethi lambasted Sharif for his inability to defend and protect the press. Over two decades later, little had apparently changed during Sharif's third term.

In 1994 the *Herald* published many stories of police and army raids, massive round-ups and seize-and-search operations for MQM leaders, human rights abuses, extrajudicial killings, and MQM torture cells. The *Herald* predicted the MQM had gone underground during Operation Clean-up, but would reassert itself at a later date (July 1995, 34–5). On 29 June 1995, the Sindh government invoked the Maintenance of Public Order (MPO) Ordinance of 1960 and banned six Karachi-based Urdu language newspapers for sixty days because of their sensationalist reporting and incitement against the government. This muzzling of the press represented the harshest crackdown since the Zia years. In August that year, police raided the home of Razia Bhatti, editor of the independent political monthly *Newsline*, and searched the paper's editorial offices. Charges were brought then dropped against Bhatti, *Newsline*'s publisher who was known to be critical of the government's role in Karachi's violence, and also the journalist Mohammed Hanif who had been highly critical of Kamaluddin Azfar, Sindh's newly appointed governor.

Many reporters, editors and publishers had sordid experiences with the MQM in the nineties. Insecurity is so deeply ingrained that journalists, convinced the MQM will avenge all criticism, reluctantly curtail their reports. Certainly media narratives change when the establishment does not protect the MQM. For example the Pakistan Tehreek-e-Insaf has young supporters who do not support violence in the way the MQM does, and there is a definite establishment patronage of the PTI. Nonetheless PTI workers have attacked and verbally abused female presenters reporting on rallies after August 2014. Despite advances in press 'freedoms', the 2015 media honeymoon of abusive MQM bashing also begs the question of how far journalists should go in serving political agendas?

On 13 January 2011 twenty-eight-year-old Wali Khan Babar, a Geo News reporter gunned down in Karachi while driving home, reminded Pashtun journalists that investigating political stories is a dangerous proposition. In 2008 I worked with Wali, when he was a bright-eyed new reporter from Quetta just beginning to navigate the Karachi's complex politics. Wali dived into the turf wars between the Awami National Party (ANP) and the MQM, reporting on clashes, extortion, drug dealing, and land grabbing. His bosses at Geo News were informed he was an MQM target, but failed to grasp (or ignored) the gravity of his situation.

Around 2012 after the Taliban secured a hold in Karachi, targeting the media and murdering reporters escalated. The MQM was allegedly the most lethal in its retaliation against newspapers who would not publish its version of events, followed by the state and intelligence agencies, the Pakistani Taliban (TTP), and sectarian groups. In the 2014–15 crackdown on Taliban groups, the group issued threats on social media platforms and through text messages. Ethnicity makes targets of journalists. One Pashtun journalist told me he did not write exclusively on Pashtun politics for fear of being labelled an ANP sympathiser. Nor would he visit Nine Zero for fear of his safety. He described that when the new English language daily *Express Tribune* began recruiting reporters to work on their city pages, the editor specifically selected Pashtun reporters because they could access areas out of bounds for other reporters.

On many occasions when Altaf Hussain has addressed his followers by telephone from London, TV channels have been compelled to air hours of incoherent rambling. If any channel did not air the speech, the MQM's media committee pressured the news editor and forced cable operators to 'demote' the channel. In May 2013, I was privy to the making of a BBC Newsnight report about the MQM by the veteran journalist Owen Bennet-Jones. The BBC team exercised caution regarding the potential consequences of the report on their offices in Karachi. The report, broadcast in July 2013, focused on money laundering complaints that the London police were investigating, and suspicion that Hussain was using the UK as a base to incite violence in Karachi. The MQM leader, Dr Farooq Sattar, was interviewed in the documentary which began with Hussain's warning to journalists: 'We will prepare your body bags.'

Whilst few dared write about the MQM after Wali Khan Babar's murder, the 2015 operations against the MQM ushered in a sea-change. Speaking to me in April 2015, the Editor of *The News* Talat Aslam argued there had been an overreaction. He singled out the news channel ARY for offensive reporting, although he praised the media's safer working conditions. The Director General of the military's Inter Services Public Relations, Major General Asim Bajwa posted a series of tweets dated 1 May 2015 condemning Altaf Hussain's statements regarding the army's actions during the operation as 'uncalled for and disgusting.' Hussain's statements about the anti-MQM operation in Karachi were broadcast on most private channels, irking the establishment. When the Pakistan Electronic Media Broadcasting Authority (PEMRA) threatened to issue TV channels with notices, media experts noted the 'selective interest' in applying the law that prohibits hate speech. PEMRA, the media regulator, has done little to control hate speech between sectarian rivals and political enemies on television, and in other sections of the media (BBC News, 2015). Instead the regulator has instituted an informal ban instructing editors and broadcasters to permanently embargo news coverage, inciting 'sectarianism, hatred, or violence through [television] shows, reports, tickers'. Intending a blanket blackout, the twitter handle @reportpemra (in February 2016) 'warned' all television channels against reporting on the funeral of the convicted murderer Mumtaz Qadri, the police bodyguard, who shot the Punjab Governor Salman Taseer twenty-nine times in 2011, over the latter's call to reform the country's blasphemy law.

Unwelcome handlers: the military and the media

Certainly the press must muzzle itself when writing about the military and the ISI. Ayesha Azfar at *Dawn* has edited its opinion and editorial pages for a decade. She rarely submits to pressure, not even by anonymous callers purporting to be army colonels who disapprove of her columnists or editorials. Over the past decade, Pakistani journalists inquiring into certain subjects have risked getting killed: the religious-militant nexus, militant infiltration of the military, enforced disappearances of young men in Balochistan, drone strikes, religion, Pakistan's geo-political relationship with America, Afghanistan, and the rest of the world all represent contentious issues. The press has little choice but to tread carefully, or give in to state control. When I interviewed Ayesha in April 2015 she emphasised the strong commitment amongst media professionals to hard-won press freedom in the face of pressure, threats, and fears of militant or political backlash. In the case of political talk shows competing for TV ratings, these freedoms have been abused. Taliban sympathizers spew viciously on TV against liberal thinkers, writers, politicians, and academics. TV channels have portrayed pro-establishment retired army personnel as saviours of the 'national interest'.

The pressure from the establishment is real. Many senior editors are forced to exercise self-censorship of views considered too liberal or secular in the English-language press. The same censure is applied to analysts who defend democratic freedoms and human rights on TV. In 2015, a senior female editor at *Dawn* newspaper received a telephone call from someone wanting to submit an article 'in the national interest' on how safe the state's new nuclear energy plans for Karachi were—undoubtedly in response to the outcry regarding how unsafe they were. The article's authorship was vague, suspicious, and the editor was not keen to accept. Others in the media group had received the same request. What worried Ayesha more was a phone call from a former armyman in Lahore who expressed serious reservations about her paper's objections to death penalty. He said such opinions were against the tenets of the majority faith, in a tone intending to intimidate. Some days later, the same man called again, this time inquiring after security matters. She surmised he had been charged with monitoring, pursuing, and pressuring certain papers.

In November 2007 President Musharraf declared a state of emergency, suspended the constitution, dissolved the Supreme Court, and suspended the Chief Justice Muhammed Iftikhar Chaudhry, along with other judges. This followed months of attempts to secure Chaudhry's resignation, and a lawyers' movement led by Chaudhry protested vociferously until Chaudhry's reinstatement on 22 March 2009. Continuous press coverage showed an autocratic military ruler clamping down violently on protesting lawyers and the media. At Dawn News, an English language broadcaster, round the clock live reports were followed by an international audience. Musharraf invoked the PEMRA Ordinance of June 2007 and curbed press freedom through decrees that barred publishing or broadcasting 'anything which defames or brings into ridicule the head of state, or members of the armed forces, or executive, legislative or judicial organs of state' (Human Rights Watch, 2008). During the lawyers' movement, the electronic media were instrumental in mobilising public support and became a target of this ordinance. Under the ordinance, the government could take action against TV channels, confiscate their equipment and seal off their premises. Although PEMRA was formed in 2000 as a media regulatory body, instead of assisting in press freedom it has essentially operated like a license issuing office and obstructed such freedoms.

During 2007–9 unprecedented live TV coverage of protests by the lawyers' movement caught the regime off-guard, and police high-handedness at quelling protestors was aired locally and internationally. Broadcasters were given warnings, and court cases issued against them. The CPJ reported that on 16 March 2007, riot police used tear gas and batons as they swept through the Islamabad offices of the Jang Group, which houses Geo TV, Pakistan's leading private TV station, and the newspapers *Daily Jang* and *The News*. The raid came less than a day after the government ordered Geo not to air coverage of street protests against the chief justice's dismissal. Six weeks later, many channels were permitted back on air after they agreed to restrict criticism of the head of state. Many were forced to stop talk shows by journalists unpopular with the regime. Celebrity anchors began hosting their programmes outdoors, drawing attention to the lack of press freedoms, and press censorship in the lead-up to the 2008 elections.

In Karachi, a vibrant camp outside the Jang Group's headquarters protested for weeks; champions of a free press went on hunger strike.

In 2007 the media became the story. They had turned lively, profitable, competitive, but were not unfraught with issues of sensationalism that undermined their credibility. 180 journalists were arrested in November 2007, and many others beaten and tear-gassed outside the Karachi Press Club. I was amongst the hundreds of protestors with banners and black armbands, demanding the reinstatement of press freedoms. We linked arms peacefully, and distributed roses to baton-wielding policemen. An emerging young media had assumed the political role of advocating in favour of democracy, civil rights, and against state pressure to tone down dissent against Musharraf's dictatorship. There was this uneven tug-of-war between Musharraf's 'enlightened moderation' projects and a vocal, triumphant media yelling for a return to civilian rule. Well-turned out anchors were transformed into overnight celebrities and talk show stars. Competitive presenters even came together on television to discuss the state's repression of the media. This illusion of safety to be found in numbers was instant and adreline-charged, but never meant to survive in an industry driven by commercialism. During this period it appeared the Jang Group began dictating the narrative, setting the agenda, and private TV channels with licenses to broadcast lobbied the masses for the restoration of the chief justice and the return of a democratic government (Talat Aslam, private communications).

Pakistan's image plummeted during the 2001 US-led war on Afghanistan, and particularly after 2007 when mounting terror attacks inside the country brought increased global attention. Editorials questioning the state's commitment to fighting terrorism also advised Musharraf to hold elections. Playing both sides of a risky political game, Musharraf was losing allies, and militant groups were turning on their state sponsors and conducting widespread suicide attacks. The situation dramatically escalated in June 2007 when seminary students from the Red Mosque in Islamabad took seven Chinese and two Pakistanis hostages, accusing them of running a brothel, and demanding that a hard-line version of Sharia law be established in Pakistan. The nation was fixed to their television sets as the Red Mosque siege in Islamabad unfolded. A high point came when its head cleric, Abdul Aziz Ghazi, was seen escaping in a burka. Television channels competed for ratings, wanting to be the first to show footage from the besieged compound, and live rounds fired by security forces echoed on screen. Geo

News hosted a live telethon with presenters slotted in for hours all day interviewing experts. I recall presenting a live discussion with public call-ins and emails where political analysts supported the crackdown, but criticised the numbers killed during the siege. During the siege Ghazi was speaking to a government official on TV, and later the media entered the mosque when the siege ended, reporting on the destruction and dead bodies. All out media support to cleanse the mosque of militant fighters swiftly shifted to a weird sympathy for the gun-wielding militants and Ninja-like female seminary students menacingly holding sticks and promising to fight Western secularism.

By 2007 Musharraf's dwindling political will to fight terrorism at home, and the regime's duplicity in harbouring militant groups in Waziristan, were obvious to the US administration. Summits with India were futile during this time. Ambassador Richard Holbrooke, determined to stop the war in Afghanistan, insisted that Pakistan needed economic assistance, and that the US should deepen engagement with a country he assessed as the region's most dangerous incubator of extremism and anti-Americanism. Holbrooke ensured non-military aid was tripled. Washington and Islamabad discussed issues like energy, water, and women's rights. The American administration paid to air news programmes on popular Pakistani channels such as Geo News, Aaj TV and Express News. Voice of America broadcasts aired on private Urdu news channels. Many were accused of being on America's payroll.

In January 2008, *The Economist* ran a cover with a picture of a grenade with 'Pakistan' written on it, and an article entitled 'The world's most dangerous place'. The issue was published in the aftermath of Benazir Bhutto's assassination, and protested that the abolition of press reforms in November 2007 would take years to undo. With two dozen private television channels broadcasting within an eight-year period—news, entertainment, sports, lifestyle, and culture—it paradoxically portrayed the Musharraf regime as a harbinger of change. Whilst its economic reforms had attracted much positive attention, press freedoms endured only as long as news channels took a pro-regime position. When channels aired criticism, and allowed call-ins from the public asking Musharraf to leave, they were ordered off air.

The war on terror changed core press working conditions and alliances with geopolitical stakeholders, and stifled criticism of the military and intelligence services. In 2013, when Sanam Maher began working as a sub-editor for the *The Express Tribune* in Karachi, the newspaper faced pressure from intelligence agencies, political parties, and extremist groups. Additionally, media markets were rapidly changing in response to online audiences. In April 2015, she described to me how political actors, government officials, and intelligence officers regularly attempted to exert control over content through unofficial 'guidance' to newspaper editors and owners, and intervened over the placement of front-page stories, political opinion, terminology, and permissible topics of coverage. The fear of reprisals resulted in strong self-censorship.

The *International New York Times* is published in Pakistan as an insert in *The Express Tribune*, which often leaves gaping white spaces on its pages. On 21 March 2014 a giant space appeared where a story by Carlotta Gall on the Pakistani government's relationship with Al-Qaeda was removed. One can find the missing article or image online which represents a story the editors perceive as too controversial or offensive, for example, stories on Israel, columns about gay rights, Pakistan's blasphemy law, or nudity in art. These spaces recall restrictions during the Zia era. Then, directives were sent to editors that would lead to blank pages being published as a sign of protest. Yet while English-language newspapers and monthly political journals do not have as wide a readership as the Urdu dailies, and cater to a niche middle and elite readership, digital news platforms are accessible globally and impact opinion within and about Pakistan.

During my years at the *Herald* (2010–14) I became a friend of Raza Rumi Ahmed. His stories on architectural landmarks under threat in Lahore for a 2012 special annual issue earned accolades for the *Herald*. Raza wrote excellent literary stories for the *Herald*, authored a book, *Delhi*, is a respected columnist for the *Express Tribune* and co-hosted a talk show on Express News with a moderate cleric. His Twitter feed challenges the blasphemy law, lack of women's rights, violence against minorities, and those who disparage his secular, progressive, pro-democracy, liberal views.

I met Raza in 2013 in Islamabad on the afternoon of the suicide bombing at the All Saints Church in Peshawar which killed seventy-five. He wanted to convince me to move to Islamabad. Raza has also been a regular panellist at the Karachi Literature Festival. We met there in February 2014 and talked about books and authors. That year I heard Raza had been shot at after his weekly television show. He survived the attack which killed his young driver, and left his bodyguard injured. Raza talked to Amnesty International about being named on a Taliban hit-list in March 2014 (BBC News 2012). Previously, in 2011, rumours had circulated of a Taliban list of press clubs. A *fatwa* (or ruling) was re-issued by the Taliban in October 2013 threatening the media. They accused the media of promoting secularism in their coverage of the war on terror, refusing to use the term 'martyr' for the Taliban, and portraying them as terrorists. Journalists were caught in the crossfire, between the government forbidding reporting on banned armed groups and the Taliban demanding coverage. The attack on Raza was the fifth on a journalist from the Express Media Group. Three staffers lost their lives in January 2014. The Taliban claimed responsibility for that attack, due to the group's anti-Taliban propaganda.

Subsequently the Group curbed criticism of Islamic militants. Newspaper editor Kamal Siddiqi warned senior staff in an email that no criticism of any militant organisation and its allies should be published. The Taliban's Mohmand media wing threatened journalists for their coverage of the North Waziristan military operation in October 2014. In an email to various media groups and journalist bodies, with the subject heading 'Global War of Ideologies and the Behavior of Media', a Taliban representative wrote:

> The media thinks it has a legitimate right to…spread false and baseless news, make propaganda against us on behalf of our enemies…call mujahideen bad, disgusting and absurd names; blaspheme [against] Islamic traditions; not listen to our views;…represent Islamic teachings in wrong and misleading ways; and judge us on every matter.

When the government fails to prosecute the killers of media workers, editors cannot be blamed. Sanam Maher revealed she was instructed not to use the word *masjid* (mosque) for an Ahmadi place of worship, or take a harsh editorial line regarding Operation Zarb-e-Azb. Often it is not actual threats that define editorial policy, but fear of threats. After the 2014 murders of the media workers, the Tehreek-e-Taliban Pakistan (TTP) spokesperson Ehsanullah Ehsan phoned into a live discussion programme on Express News, the Urdu-language television channel, to claim responsibility. He complained the group was playing a propagandist role in the state's war against the Taliban. They had ignored his regular complaints to the channel. To the dismay of liberals at the newspaper, Ehsan was assured the station and newspaper would present the TTP's position if its reporters were protected. The TTP also issued warnings to media houses and reporters on social media and attached journalists, including at the BBC after its Urdu-language service aired critical comments about the group's attempt to kill Malala Yusufzai in 2012 (BBC News 2012).

Prior to the May 2013 general election, media houses, their editors and reporters, received threats from militant and sectarian groups demanding they broadcast and print anti-election messages. Prior to voting day, intimidating tactics were reported by staff at *Dawn*, *Daily Jang*, *Mashriq*, Geo News, Express TV, ARY TV, Waqt TV, and smaller media outlets in Karachi, Sindh, Balochistan and the FATA. According to the European Union Election Observation Mission report on the 2013 election, Dawn TV and GEO TV were unavailable in areas around Kharan, Khuzdar, Gwadar, Panjung, and Kech in Balochistan owing to pressures on cable television operators by militant groups. Cable operators were forced to 'move' television channels from the priority list to lists with limited access, curtailing their election reporting. Although airtime was sold to advertisers benefiting mainstream political parties, safety concerns kept reporters away from constituencies where the Pakistani Taliban and their affiliates had threatened voters. The Pakistan People's Party's media pundits complained the election results were manipulated in favour of the PML-N. The ANP, who traditionally refused support to extremist ideologies, were forced to quit the election race in Karachi, to close campaign offices, and ANP candidates were threatened and murdered. Karachi Pashtun reporters faced threats from sectarian groups and political parties. The TTP attacked local ANP leaders and Pakhtun elders, extorted from and threatened residents and businesses, and formed parallel courts to provide rough justice in exchange for support, consolidating its hold over many Pashtun neighbourhoods.

Balochistan in Karachi

In 2014 the prominent Geo News television journalist Hamid Mir sent a taped message to the CPJ, citing elements within Pakistan's

Inter-Services-Intelligence (ISI) agency which had threatened him for broadcasting programmes on enforced disappearances in Balochistan. In February Mir had supported a long protest march from Quetta to Islamabad, led by the seventy-four year old activist Qadeer Baloch and his eleven year old grandson, to protest against enforced disappearances and demand the perpetrators be produced in court. Mir, and Geo News, faced immense pressure not to cover Qadeer's march, including threats of being shut down, but he did so nonetheless. That month the Secretary of Defence told the Supreme Court, which had requested a report, that the number of missing persons in the Baloch insurgency was 1,100. The 'Voice for Baloch Missing Persons', founded by Mama Qadeer Baloch, estimated numbers higher at 19–23,000.

In April 2014, Mir survived being shot at six times outside Karachi airport. Mir rarely travelled to Karachi but this time he came to record a programme on how 100 days without drone attacks had impacted ongoing Taliban peace talks. Mir had informed Amnesty International detailing the threats to his life, and told government officials, his colleagues, and family. He had written an email to the editorial board of his channel stating that if he was attacked and killed, those responsible would include the Director General of the ISI, Lt. General Zaheer-ul-Islam. Earlier, in November 2012, a bomb had been found under his car in Islamabad. Mir had supported Malala Yusufzai after she was shot by the Taliban in Swat. The Taliban later took responsibility for his attempted assassination—ironic because in 2007, President Musharraf banned Mir from appearing on television, accusing him of being pro-Taliban. Mir was one of many who were banned because the channels had reported on the lawyers' movement and showed the regime's heavy-handedness. Geo TV faced threats of closure for suggesting the state's intelligence forces were behind the attack on Mir (BBC News April 2014).

Mir was shot after a CPJ delegation met Prime Minister Nawaz Sharif in March 2014. Sharif agreed to improve media security but did not follow through. Addressing journalists' protection as a negotiating point with the Taliban, the delegation proposed that media safeguards should include forming a media complaints commission, a joint government-journalists' commission, and the appointment of special provincial prosecutors to investigate attacks. The delegation included the journalist Ahmed Rashid, and also the CPJ's Asia Programme Director Bob Dietz. Dietz told me in April 2014 in a telephone interview, after he visited Pakistan to lobby the government to investigate the killing of journalists, that two Indian journalists were given a week's notice in 2014 to leave the country: one had interviewed Qadeer Baloch in Islamabad. Their visas were refused, despite pledges to 'make Pakistan accessible to journalists'.

An investigation did not identify Mir's attackers. Later, two arrest warrants were issued against Mir for anti-army reporting. Geo News faced ongoing challenges. The failure of investigation commissions in the aftermath of attacks and murders of journalists meant media workers were threatened with impunity. When Dietz interviewed Mir on the outcome of the judicial commission to probe the attack, the top management of a media house, who also appeared in front of the commission, confirmed he faced pressures from military and intelligence officials to prevent him from highlighting enforced disappearances, from criticising the security agencies for their involvement in the treason trial of former dictator General Pervez Musharraf, the involvement of powerful intelligence officials in terrorizing the media, and he complained the Karachi police and security agencies had not cooperated with the commissions.

After the attack on Mir, Geo News was subjected to a concerted campaign of defamation by competing TV channels and newspapers. *The News* lost government advertising, and pro-establishment writers stopped writing. The group had to tread a softer line. According to Talat Aslam, although recent years have been kinder to the press, no one in Pakistan—politicians, the establishment or the militants—is yet accustomed to an independent, robust press. The establishment favoured columnists within newspapers, even reporters. Aslam suggested that *Dawn* newspaper is comparatively independent because it has an editor, rather than an owner-editor. This is not the case with *The News* and the younger entrant, *The Express Tribune*. The Jang Group is more vulnerable because Geo has access to the masses, and therefore the establishment wants control over it.

Following its reports on Mir's attack, and Balochistan, the Jang Group was compelled to make compromises. Geo Television was banned in the country's cantonment areas as were the Jang's print publications, after the channel alleged that the ISI was behind the attack on Mir. ARY News was removed from the cable network, and newspaper deliveries disrupted to assert control over the news flow. Whilst the older media empires have learned over the years how to deal with the establishment, younger media conglomerates must yet learn ways of dealing with those groups and political parties that threaten their economic and human survival.

Conclusion

The obstacles to a moment of reckoning for the media, one that might instantiate a refusal to be intimidated, are substantial. Let me illustrate, and end this chapter, with a cup of coffee. In April 2015, I met the political scientist and security expert Dr Ayesha Siddiqa in London for coffee, and we discussed her strong opinions about the intelligence services. 'They control information, power and resources and use different methods for different people,' she told me. 'It is an open secret that journalists who do not heed their warnings are admonished. Some are threatened, others killed. They attack those who work for them, and also those who don't.' Ayesha Siddiqa writes frequently on the military and the ISI. In 2009 she refused to meet the ISI chief General Shuja Pasha when she was summoned to the military headquarters in Rawalpindi. Her request to meet at a neutral venue was refused. In the subsequent two years the army denied her space in the print media, and blocked her appearance on political shows. After the publication of her book *Military Inc.* in 2007, she claimed the army had waged an intellectual war against her, blocking her work and public activities. To add to this, she lived near the headquarters of a Sunni extremist group and had received threats. Despite the risks to herself and her family, she decided to stay.

Siddiqa pointed to a lethal triangle between the intelligence agencies, the Taliban, and the state. I have personally met many journalists caught in this scenario. Some work anonymously, and take steps to protect their lives; others daringly ignore the consequences, or leave the country until the dust settles. Others live and publish in exile. One young reporter living in the US, whom I interviewed in April 2015, suffers from the separation from his family. When he speaks publicly he is called a traitor and abused. In Pakistan he was building a reservoir of young Pakistani reporters for a digital news platform. He described, 'It feels strange living away from Pakistan yet still living in fear. For every article I write, I kill ten others. It's intellectual genocide. Jihadi supporters have all the freedom of expression, even on television. I have respect for human rights, peace, and reconciliation, but I cannot write freely.'

Given they can be detained, threatened and killed with impunity, senior journalists in Pakistan know there is a red line that cannot be crossed. Political parties have long controlled Karachi through violence, with state support. The intelligence services are bolder and more violent. Few feel able to act against state violence when the intelligence services are deeply involved. The press corps knows who kills journalists, and lament that the suppression of information exposes the nation to propaganda. To get ahead, journalists must uncritically follow state narratives. Investigative reportage that exposes fraudulent practices, corruption, money laundering, and tax evasion is rarely encouraged by media bosses, and autonomy is a rare commodity.

Pakistani journalists killed have failed to elicit a collective response from the industry which prioritises corporate interests and professional rivalries. Journalists' killers are rarely prosecuted. The government does not deem the protection of journalists an urgent issue. Yet journalists either refuse or are afraid to protest against the murder of colleagues, and newspaper owners and editors fail to protect them. Amidst such silence, there can be little safety. Perhaps, then, it is time to speak out. Let me end with a famous verse by the Urdu poet Faiz Ahmed Faiz that captures this sentiment. The poem is entitled 'Speak':

> Speak, for your lips are yet free;
> Speak, for your tongue is still your own;
> Your lissom body yours alone;
> Speak, your life is still your own.
> Look into the blacksmith's forge:
> The flame blazes, the iron's red;
> Locks unfasten open-mouthed,
> Every chain's link springing wide.
> Speak, a little time suffices
> Before the tongue, the body die.

Speak, the truth is still alive;
Speak: say what you have to say.[1]

References

'Attacks on the Press 2007: Pakistan', Committee to Protect Journalists, https://cpj.org/2008/02/attacks-on-the-press-2007-pakistan.php, last accessed 1 Jun. 2015.

BBC News, 'Taliban threat worries Pakistani media', 17 October 2012, http://www.bbc.co.uk/news/world-asia-19978021, last accessed 24 Jun. 2015.

————, 'Pakistan's Geo "Should Be Shut" for Hamid Mir attack coverage', 23 April 2014, www.bbc.co.uk/news/world-asia-27125789, last accessed 22 Jun. 2015.

————, 'Karachi MQM leader Altaf Hussain feels heat from the military', 24 March 2015; http://www.bbc.co.uk/news/world-asia-32016734, last accessed 29 Jun. 2015.

Buner, Shaheen, 'Journalists paying high price for covering Pakistan violence', Gandhara, 11 May 2015, http://gandhara.rferl.org/content/pakistan-journalist-threats/26996221.html, last accessed 20 Jun. 2015.

Human Rights Watch, 'Pakistan: Media Restrictions Undermine Election', 17 February 2008, http://www.hrw.org/news/2008/02/15/pakistan-media-restrictions-undermine-election, last accessed 25 Apr. 2015.

Sethna Razeshta, and Zia Ur Rehman, 'Karachi's sectarian backyard', Dawn, 20 January 2014, Karachi.

Rumi, Raza, 'Hundreds of historical buildings across Lahore await attention', Herald. Annual Heritage Issue, 21 August 2012, http://razarumi.com/hundreds-of-decaying-historical-buildings-across-lahore-await-attention/, last accessed 15 May 2015.

Sethi, Najam, 'Editorial', The Friday Times, 28 March 1991, Karachi.

Siddiqua, Ayesha, Military Inc. Inside Pakistan's Military Economy, London: Pluto Press, 2007.

The Economist, 'The World's most dangerous place', 3 January 2008, http://www.economist.com/node/10430237, last accessed 22 Mar. 2015.

---

[1] Translation by Yasmin Hosain, available at http://pakteahouse.net/2007/11/17/speak-for-your-lips-are-yet-free/, last accessed 4 November 2016.

9

FROM THE DEMISE OF COSMOPOLITANISM
TO ITS REVIVAL

TRENDS AND REPERCUSSIONS FOR KARACHI

Arif Hasan

This chapter draws attention to Karachi's cosmopolitan public culture of the post-Independence years. It documents how politically motivated religious zeal, cultural and artistic oppression, and political narratives imposed on the city's geography by the dictatorship of General Zia-ul-Haq (1977–88) led to the effective death of its dance halls, cinemas, cabarets, and arts culture. This history is useful in understanding indications of a cosmopolitan revival. Whilst these changes are encouraging they urge caution, not least because they reproduce many social hierarchies of class and privilege that did not characterise the earlier cosmopolitan era. These reflections here are based on my work since the 1970s in local communities—in various roles as an architect, planner, teacher, social researcher, activist, and writer. Since 1982 I have also worked extensively with the Orangi Pilot Project, a non-governmental organisation set up to provide low-cost housing, sanitation, healthcare, and microfinance to poor communities. In 1989 I founded the Urban Resource Centre to protect the interests of low- and lower-middle-income settlements in the government urban planning process. The rich perspectives afforded me through these different avenues have led me to document, analyse, and advocate around the many changes I witnessed. My personal relationship with the city, dating back to Partition when I arrived at the camps by the main railway station as a refugee, is also significant, as are the changes I have witnessed in the last sixty-five years. In this chapter I set out my belief in the city's ability to reharness its energy at the local level in order to build a more tolerant society than that produced by the destruction during the Zia years, and the violence that followed in their wake.

Before Partition and the creation of Pakistan in 1947 Karachi was a cosmopolitan colonial port. Like many British imperial cities in South Asia, it contained a mixed population of diverse migrant and ethnic communities, its own exclusive enclaves and neighbourhoods, and a local proletariat. More often than not, ethnicity determined people's professional status. For example, the majority of the Gujrati speaking population, Hindu and Muslim, was engaged in business. Goans, by and large, were teachers, office staff, and some were European-style entertainers. Most big businesses were run by Parsis who were active in developing civic life. Foreigners worked in overseas companies that managed port-related imports and exports. The Baloch population formed the city's early proletariat, and their communities concentrated mostly in Lyari.

Like all port cities, Karachi had its bars and cabarets and places for entertainment serving the sailors of visiting ships. In addition, a thriving red light area served both the working and merchant classes. The Europeanised communities arranged May balls and dance parties in their gymkhanas, clubs, and commercial hotels. Women frequenting such events wore dresses and skirts. Most bars, billiard rooms, and associated eating places served a multiclass clientele although some, particularly in Saddar, were reserved exclusively for the city's elite. The religious ceremonies of Karachi's Hindus, Muslims, and Christians provided other social avenues for mixing and sharing. These diverse communities shared a strong urban culture which dominated the social landscape of Karachi's rural areas and coastal villages. The landlords of interior Sindh certainly profited from its fruits for as long as governance rested effectively with colonial British power, few serious ethnic or religious conflicts erupted. However, the rise of nationalist movements and the weakening of colonial power in the 1920s and 1930s saw the beginnings of concerns about the future among those ethnicities and groups that were not dominant.

After the creation of Pakistan, Karachi's urban culture flourished. The city received poets, artists, journalists, writers, painters, and performers from all over India. They became a part of the Karachi melting pot and enriched it. This process of enrichment was supported, first, by the Mohajir intelligentsia, which had strong left-wing roots, and second, by the civil service which governed Karachi in the style of an old and well-established decadent colonial tradition. By 1978, Karachi's downtown Saddar district contained seventeen bars and billiard rooms, four music and dance schools, eighteen bookshops, two clubs for sailors, five discotheques, and thirty-four popular eating places (four featuring Goan music bands); across the city as a whole there were 119 cinemas and numerous cabarets, of which six showcased striptease acts (Hasan 2000). In addition, regular international film festivals played at local district cinemas. The working classes frequented them at regular cinema rates. Students' debates, variety programmes, professional bodies' meetings, and political gatherings were held in the halls and institutional buildings of Saddar. In all such establishments women worked as waitresses, hostesses, and performers. Behind Radio Pakistan on Bunder Road was Fankar *gali*. Here musical instruments were made, repaired and tuned. The neighbourhood was frequented by many would-be radio and stage artists; many of Pakistan's most famous cinema stars and singers were 'spotted' here by producers and directors. This is where, for example, Muhammad Ali, the famous hero of Pakistani films of the 1960s and 1970s, began his career. Wandering musicians and singers also performed in the city's parks and could hope to be picked up by rich Karachiites and taken home to perform for them or their guests.

Nostalgia tends to exaggerate and to treat unkindly processes of change. Therefore, it is important to sympathetically understand the changes that have taken place in the city's social environment. Without such an understanding, the creation of a tolerant city culture for the future (let alone a liberal one) will not be possible. In most of pre-Partition Pakistan, in rural areas especially, possibilities for physical, social, and economic mobility were non-existent. The feudal system exercised almost complete control over the personal and property law of the peasantry and was an integral part of the colonial establishment. In this feudal dominated society Karachi survived culturally, socially, and economically as a relatively autonomous entity—as did Lahore, although to a lesser extent. The changes in the second half of the twentieth century that swept the rural and urban areas of the country, first as a result of large scale migration from India, and secondly the introduction of green revolution technologies, transformed rural subsistence economies into cash economies. This weakened the existing clan-based governance systems and introduced possibilities for socioeconomic and physical mobility to people that made up rural and smaller town populations. Migration from the rural and other urban areas to Karachi ushered in massive transformations. This served to meet the high demands for skilled and unskilled labour required for Karachi's phenomenal growth and development and, in the process, Karachi ceased to be an 'island'.

Meanwhile, with industrialisation and the development of a services sector in trade and commerce, a Mohajir middle class, whose interests were actively promoted by the religious right, evolved. The absence of democracy in the 1960s deprived the city of a process of consensus building. As a result the left-right, centre-province, Urdu-Sindhi divides increased. For the first time, during the movement against Ayub Khan in 1968, alcohol outlets, bars, and music halls were attacked. These attacks did not have long-term serious consequences. However, during the conflict between the Pakistan People's Party (PPP) and the Pakistan National Alliance (PNA) in 1977, the attacks worsened to such a degree that Karachi's night life, bars, and billiard rooms were forced to close down. The city was paralysed. To appease the PNA, the Bhutto government declared Friday in place of Sunday as the weekly holiday, banned alcohol, closed down the discotheques, cabarets, and Karachi's thriving racecourse. The city seemed to change almost overnight. Many people working in those establishments became destitute, and Karachi's multiclass entertainment and recreational spaces were deserted. These premises over time became wholesale markets, marriage halls, and subsequently shopping plazas (Hasan 2000).

It is more than possible that if the democratic process had continued, a new culture that synthesised the values of the political left and right could have evolved. Certainly by July 1977, I found discussions between the operators of the banned entertainment facilities, political opponents of the Bhutto regime, and the Karachi establishment already taking place. However, with Zia-ul-Haq's military coup of July 1977 any compromises became impossible.

Next it is important to examine how the policies of the Zia government, aided by the Afghan War and backed by the US, Saudi Arabia, and the West, have shaped the city of Karachi today. Soon after seizing power, Zia began a process of consolidating the hold of the religious establishment on Pakistani state and society. The majority of Zia's cabinet was composed of members of religious parties who had led the anti-*fahashi* (vulgarity) and anti-*ayashi* (corruption) movement against Bhutto's government. These parties were organised at the grass-roots level in many Karachi neighbourhoods and backed by important mosques and *madrassa*s in the city.

In order to 'Islamise' society and introduce piety, *zuhr* prayers were made compulsory in government institutions, and space provided for them. Many non-government and private organisations adopted the policy too so as to appease the demands of their newly empowered 'religious' employees and members. In addition, *zakat* (charity as a religious duty) and *ushr* (Islamic tax) were made compulsory. This was resisted by the Shia community in whose *fiqh* (jurisprudence) *zakat* is voluntary. A major Shia-Sunni disagreement took place over this issue and finally it was decided that Pakistan's Shia community would not pay compulsory *zakat*. Through obligatory *zuhr* prayers and *zakat*, Pakistanis who worked together soon came to recognise each other, and each other's difference, and to mark each other out as Shia, Sunni, Ahmadi, Christian, or Hindu. This began a process of discrimination and fragmentation. Zia's Hudood Ordinance was also enforced, blasphemy laws were modified and, in both cases, these laws have been used to persecute political opponents of the regime, women, and Muslim and non Muslim religious minorities.

The most serious repercussions of Zia's policies arguably pertained to education. In 1984 extra-curricular activities in public sector high schools, colleges, and universities were banned, as were the students' unions that had produced Pakistan's most radical and democratic leadership, many outstanding journalists, literary figures, sportsmen, and women. As a result, music, drama, film, and political and cultural events vanished from Karachi's educational institutions. Debates were permitted but their subjects had to be approved by the area deputy commissioner, and later the institutional administration. Gradually student debates increasingly focused on issues of Islamic history and theology rather than social and political problems. Many private sector institutions (excepting some elite ones), under pressure from the government and its supporters, also discontinued extra-curricular activities. The school and college curricula were substantially revised. At the high school level, teaching of international history and geography was discontinued. Pakistan Studies and Islamiat courses were considered sufficient for understanding global issues. Many political events leading to the creation of Pakistan and its early history were distorted. Nayyar and Salim found that the new national curriculum was insensitive to Pakistan's religious diversity, incited students to militancy, encouraged bigotry and discrimination towards other nations, women and religious minorities, and glorified war and violence (2004). While this curriculum is still delivered, *madrassa* (religious seminary) education was encouraged and degrees from madrassas made equivalent to normal university degrees (Ibid.). Hence, *madrassa* graduates could be, and were, recruited as functionaries in state institutions.

Budgets for cultural activities and related institutions were drastically curtailed. Important institutions like the PIA Arts Academy, the National Film Development Corporation (NAFDEC, operating 1988–2014) and Lok Versa, an organisation promoting Pakistani folk and cultural heritage, were reduced to the status of nominal organisations. State patronage to the *urs* (celebrations on the birthday of the saint) of Sufi saints and folk heroes (in vogue since pre-British times) was withdrawn; banning music at these festivals was unsuccessfully attempted. Under the new media policy, classical music and dance were banned on radio and television, and folk music discouraged. Suleman Shah, a famous folk singer, was asked to remove the *ghonghroo*s (bells) tied to his wrists when he performed, on the grounds they were not considered appropriate male dress. Downcast, he told this author, 'I have to bear this humiliation simply to feed the demands of my stomach'. Minimum on-screen distances between men and women were specified and covering the head was made compulsory for women compères and newscasters. Debates and quiz programmes on television and radio were permitted as long as the content conformed to the government's 'Islamic' agenda. Meanwhile, a long list of prominent writers and thinkers was compiled by the state. Their appearance on television and radio, along with the poetry and songs of progressive poets and musicians, was banned.

At the neighbourhood level, the system of the *nazim-e-salaat* (prayer official) was introduced. The *nazim* was an individual appointed by the local mosque. He roamed the neighbourhood at dawn informing people through a microphone that it was time for prayers. Those who did not join were contacted politely in the evening and requested to attend. Again, as a result, the *fiqh* of different households was identified, and the social distance between neighbours of different beliefs increased. Political parties could not hand out patronage since the politics of the era was putatively all about the 'restoration of democracy'. Consequently, people turned to their ethnic and clan relationships for patronage. Since power lay with the religious establishment, the clan and ethnic organisations had to seek government support. This resulted in strengthening the religious right in Pakistan's establishment even further.

Thus the religious establishment became the custodian of public morality. In many lower- and lower-middle-income neighbourhoods, and across the city's public space and institutions, the imposition of religious agendas met with little opposition. Schools of music and dance, common before the Zia era, closed down except for a few notable exceptions, such as the Tehreek-i-Niswan. Theatre performances vanished or else only hosted the elite and upper-middle classes in the cultural centres of foreign missions such as the Goethe Institute and Pak American Cultural Centre. The new Islamic public culture created enormous problems for working women (since women's employment was discouraged by neighbourhood mosques), and many disappeared back into the home. The *hijab*, voluntary hitherto in Karachi, became universal in the lower- and lower-middle-income settlements of the city. Amongst Goan and Parsi women, skirts and dresses gave way to the *shalwar-kameez*.

Karachi's red-light area came under attack and its performers relocated to exclusive neighbourhoods to serve the elite. Many brothels had been attacked during anti-Bhutto protests in 1977 and many women working in Karachi's red-light district in Napier Road had refused to move. When Zia took power, he posted police around the district, a moral policy which resulted in a burgeoning extortion racket. Consequently the industry became dispersed across the city. The film industry packed up, unable to survive the new censor code and the suffocating social atmosphere. In a conversation I had with the South Asian film-maker Zia Sarhad, he wondered if the freedom permitted to cheap and vulgar films in the regional languages was granted to keep the 'masses happy'. Heralding the near death of Pakistan's film industry, by 1989 Karachi's 119 cinemas had been reduced to twenty-two.

Pakistan's elite and upper-middle classes are largely 'Westernised' owing to the post-colonial legacy of the British Indian administration. Because of their enmity to Bhutto's 'socialist' populism, they supported Zia's rule. However they could not approve the changes that were occurring in the institutions where their children studied. Consequently, they stopped sending their children to public sector universities and colleges. As a result these institutions ceased to be multi-class. They also stopped participating in public life and visiting museums, zoos and multi-class public spaces. They created elite enclaves separate from the rest of Karachi and became depoliticised. The removal of the elite from the public sphere resulted in a decline in standards of education and in the maintenance and growth of public sector real estate and recreational facilities. In the process Karachi was deprived of the possibility of developing an aware and interested educated elite, which is an enormous asset for an expanding and developing metropolis.

The Zia era coincided with period of urban consolidation for many similar cities in South and South-East Asia. During Zia's era these cities developed effective state institutions that cater to the needs of a young population (living increasingly in a cosmopolitan world), as an alternative to systems of clan- and religion-based patronage. They were able to support the evolution of new social values and freedoms for post-colonial societies that were also struggling to free themselves from feudal influences and backward traditions. In 1977 Karachi was in a similar position. However, owing to Zia's religious populism, this did not happen. Although the old institutions were destroyed, replacements were not created. Emerging social change and values were suppressed, and regressive norms imposed on the city. This effectively destroyed its rich cultural and ethnic diversity, leading to fragmentation, suspicion, and conflict between different religious and ethnic groups. These trends were, and still are, promoted by the religious politics dating back to the Afghan War and the close association of the Pakistani establishment and military with the religious right, and US geopolitical agendas.

By the end of the Zia era, Karachi, like the rest of Pakistan, was a cultural desert. The state was overtly anti-women and anti-change, irrespective of class affiliations. Successive governments, and societal norms, have remained hostage to this institutional state culture. However, the pressures of city life, new global technologies, international migration, satellite television, the internet, and above all, the related social upward mobility and aspirations of the lower middle classes have transformed Karachi society and created new forms of conflict between its aspirations and the legacy of Zia's values. Here it is important to pause and highlight some changes that have taken and are taking place.

The most important statistics in any population census arguably relate to the social indicators of the age group of between fifteen and twenty-four. This age group represents both the present and the future generations and the changes that invariably occur between the two. The Karachi Population Census Report of 1981 reported that 37.54 per cent of women, and 13.14 per cent of men in this age group were married; 66.7 per cent of men and 62.32 per cent of women were literate (Government of Pakistan 1981). If we project the trends established between 1981 and the 1998 Census, then less than 20 per cent of women and 6 per cent of men in this age group are married today. In addition, literacy in this age group is over 84 per cent, with women having a slight edge over men, not only in literacy but also in educational attainment trends. This means that for the first time in Karachi's history, this age group, which we might think of as both Karachi's present and future, consists of an overwhelming majority of unmarried, literate young people. As any sociologist may argue, this in itself is enough to change family structures and gender relations. Statistics, observation, and research, based on lower and lower middle income groups, who constitute 82 per cent of Karachi households, give us some indication of the nature of change and the reasons for it.

According to the Karachi Strategic Development Plan 2020 Survey, 89 per cent of families in Karachi are nuclear. In 1989 the figure was 54 per cent. In many interviews I conducted with the older generation Karachiites, most agree that the break-up of the extended or joint family is the most significant change facing Karachi. They most influential reason they give for the change is economic. Whereas previously one family member earned and the others were dependents, today it is no longer possible to survive on one income. Given that many families now contain a number of earning members, the traditional extended family structure cannot survive. If any member resents sharing their income, s/he may split off and form a smaller autonomous unit.

Working women (now an economic necessity in Karachi) have pressurised extended family structures and ideas about family honour and traditional values: many disputes occur because of women's employment amidst the conservative extended family and/or neighbourhood peer pressure (Asdar Ali 2011). In this scenario, the breakup of the extended family provides greater freedom to working women in many cases (see Hasan 2009). Accompanying the breakup of the clan, and the re-emergence of women in employment, are changing marriage patterns. Marriages are increasingly taking place outside of the clan, the neighbourhood and close community. Young people wishing to marry partners of their own choice face enormous obstacles, as do conservative parents wishing to find 'suitable' marriage partners for their children. Although times have changed, parents are slower to keep up. One older man summed up the situation, saying 'The traditions are gone but we do not discuss these things out of fear' (see Hasan 2009). There is also an enormous increase in applications for court (as opposed to religious) marriages. In 1992, only twelve to fifteen applications were made per day. In 2010, according to an unpublished survey by Riaz Ahmad Khan, the figure varies from 200 to 250.

Most of Karachi's phenomenal population increase was accommodated by the creation of informal settlements and semi-serviced formal plot developments. The majority of these were established in the 1960s and 1970s. Well into the 1980s these were wholly working class settlements. Their leaders, for the most part, were semi-literate middle-aged men who used an archaic feudal vocabulary of terms like *janab* (sir), *hazoor* (respected sir), *sharaf hasil hona* (I am honoured), and *niaz-mand* (grateful) in their conversations and correspondence with officialdom. At that time, there were almost no schools and health facilities in these settlements and very few working women.

I have observed many changes in settlements I worked with from 1971–1978. Today these settlements are not exclusively working class. A sizeable number of the younger generation, men and women, has acquired skills and education. They are teachers, bank managers, IT professionals, and white-collar employees in the formal services sector. Suzuki vans transport women to work in garment and packaging factories. Many women additionally work at home as contract labourers. Many settlements today contain private schools (where over 80 per cent of teachers are women) and health services, as well as beauty parlours, cyber cafes, and marriage halls on the pattern of the city's middle-income areas. Meanwhile, community leadership is young, educated, and has shed the feudal vocabulary of *janab* and *hazoor* in favour of arguably more egalitarian English terms such as 'uncle' and 'aunty' for older people.

The alumni of Karachi's universities and colleges also play an important role in changing societal trends. Today, 68 per cent of all students at the University of Karachi, 87 per cent of all Karachi's medical students, and 92 per cent of all architecture and planning students are women. The number of women students in engineering and business management is increasing. Critics often say that because women traditionally do not work after marriage, their education is a waste. This tradition is changing. Women's education has a profound effect on the value system of children, not only in the nuclear and extended family, but in neighbourhoods and communities. If the professionally educated mother does not work today, her educated daughter most likely will.

These changes have variously played out in the daily lives of Karachiites. Women are highly visible today in public spaces. They move about unimpeded on beaches, in parks and in 'women-friendly' shopping places. Even in working-class and lower-middle-income groups, one sees an increase in the trend of hosting mixed gatherings at marriage ceremonies. Young couples (many with *hijab*s and beards) sit close together, and show affection while travelling on motorbikes. Nobody stops them; the police do not stop them and demand a *nikkahnama* (marriage certificate). All this was unimaginable in Zia's era, and in many 'liberal' eras before him. Something very fundamental has changed. Nonetheless, outside of the settlement or neighbourhood, the religious right is still largely the custodian of public morality, and traditional concepts of family honour still prevail. The trends I have described are weakening these traditions, but the process is slow and painful.

A major reason I hear mooted for violence committed against women (as well as against men) in Pakistan today concerns the emergence of new freedoms and aspirations on the one hand, and resistance by the old clan-based governance systems on the other. The old order gains ground because of regressive laws, weak state institutions, regional conflict, and where opponents of change are seen as having divine sanction. New shared values are needed to bridge this gap between tradition, aspiration, and reality. These can be promoted by the development of suitable curricula for educational institutions. So far, this has not consciously been done. The media can play an important role. However, so far, like many non-governmental organisations, their main focus tends to be to identify victims of injustice, brutal traditions and state violence, and to fight their causes. This is important but it does not promote new societal values. New cultural discourse has to relate to larger process of social change in the country, and for the drivers and processes of that change to be understood sympathetically.

Yet many young people, supported by older mentors, have impacted on Karachi's performing arts culture. The National Association of Performing Arts (NAPA) was established in 2005 in the Hindu Gymkhana to conserve and revive the city's rich cultural heritage in performing arts. Karachi hosts a regular music conference, a Sufi conference and since 2001, the annual international KARA film festival. However, these are not truly *awami* (public) in nature, like the film festivals of the 1960s and 1970s, even though a sizeable number of lower-middle-class participants attend. Security concerns also make them difficult to arrange and manage. Although pop concerts are more *awami*, apart from the Behria Auditorium there are few safe venues. There are more plays being performed in Karachi today than in its entire history. Even so, in almost all cases they are performed at locations not accessible to the vast majority of Karachiites—for example, at the Alliance Francoise, the Goethe Institute, Pak-American Cultural Centre, and the Arts Council. There is a lack of democratic egalitarian public space for the performing arts. However, *mushairas* (Urdu poetry symposia) are one exception and do draw large crowds—except when they have been forced to close because of security concerns.

For a tolerant, let alone a liberal Karachi to emerge, physical and institutional space needs to be developed. All Karachi localities contain musicians, singers, poets, and traditional story tellers, both men and women. Yet there is virtually no public space for them to gather, dialogue or perform. Religious figures in local neighbourhoods often prevent such performances. In addition, although many groups that promote libraries, clubs and sports facilities exist, they face problems concerning space and finance. Next, whilst a very rich folk culture surrounds Karachi's shrines, events here are badly organised and the venues that host them cannot cater to large audiences. Moreover, these events are perceived as 'unfashionable' and not patronised by Karachi's 'liberal' elite, or 'intelligentsia'. Similarly, city parks do not cater to hawkers and performers who entertain the general public. Often, their activities are disallowed and officially persecuted. Last, the city does not have a city museum that can inform its citizens of its rich history and evolution.

This essay leaves us with two important questions. One, how can we develop new societal values that can reflect Karachi's changing sociology and demography, and make our transition to a more humane society less painful? Two, what can we do to bring about the necessary changes in governance to provide institutional and physical space required for the expression of a progressive culture? Both these questions are closely related to the development of a vision for the city which can be shared by the vast majority of its citizens, and protected by the political establishment. This vision, to be workable, has to be rooted in the social and physical reality of the city.

References

Asdar Ali, Kamran, 'Women, Work and Public Spaces: Conflict and Coexistence in Karachi's Poor Neighbourhoods', *International Journal of Urban and Regional Research*, 36, May (2012), pp. 585–605.

Government of Pakistan, *Karachi Population Census Report*, 1981.

City District Government Karachi, *Karachi Strategic Development Plan*, 2020.

Hasan, Arif, 'Demographic Change and its Social Repercussions: The Case of Karachi', *International Development Planning Review*, 31, August (2009).

Hasan, Arif, *Understanding Karachi*, Karachi: City Press, 2000.

Nayyar, Abdul Hameed, and Salim Ahmad, *The Subtle Subversion*, Islamabad: SDPI Publications, 2004.

10

FOUR 'ORDINARY' DEATHS

Kausar S. Khan

This account is shaped, first, by my professional work focused on community-based initiatives for empowering marginalised sections of Karachi society, especially women, and second, by my voluntary activism for women's rights, human rights, and equality for Karachi's citizens. The first strand is university-based; the second is largely focused around participation in the Women's Action Forum (WAF), a nongovernmental organisation based in Karachi. The chapter is also a tribute to four Karachiites, two women and two men, who died brutal deaths in 2013 within a few months of each other. I knew them in different capacities, as friends, colleagues, and fellow activists; they did not know each other. This is also a humble salute to many others who have died violent deaths whom I did not know personally. Death unites victims, paid killers, even their mothers perhaps. Common suffering also forges unity through deaths. Importantly, let not this chapter's small diversion into an account of painful losses dilute the broader political projects of justice and peace. It is my hope that working

187

through to disentangle our reactions to violent deaths may bring about stronger connections.

Whilst these four individuals died violently in the first half of 2013, many other killings occurred in the same period. Thus, far from being extraordinary these deaths were quite 'ordinary'. My reflection on these four, as well as on this particular year, is likewise arbitrary and contingent. Nonetheless, on each occasion, my mind span, my heart sank into deep sorrow. In this chapter I query a collage of ways in which personal and public responses become stitched together in death. Whilst individual pain, anger, and a deep incomprehension accompany brutal killings, they also crystallise and sharpen desires to create properly meaningful and transformative civil society responses. Out of deep despair I have struggled for 'good' to prevail. Many similar battles with grief shape Karachiites' search for existential meaning in a society and polity in crisis. I write as an insider. Personally, collective action represents for me a struggle for resilience over dejection, for death over life. Politics is profoundly emotional and, to cite the old adage, personal. This chapter also raises the paradox of how political talk is sharpened by killing, whilst its unforgiving reality seems strangely at odds with the unfathomable emotions it produces—emotions which, like the sea bordering Karachi's shores, stir with the rhythm of waves—bouncing, crashing, rising, and sinking.

Getting started, with sadness and love

For unfamiliar readers, WAF was formed as a lobby-cum-pressure group in 1980. The group emerged when Shirkat Gah, a Karachi-based women's resource centre, mobilised diverse non-governmental women's organisations to protest against a couple being sentenced to flogging under General Zia-ul-Haq's newly decreed Hudood Ordinances. WAF secured support from a leading lawyer. Since then, WAF has lobbied for women's rights. WAF is non-hierarchical, autonomous, and non-partisan, and accepts no funds from international or national donors, or the government (Mumtaz and Shaheed 1987). Its origins in protest against Zia's deeply punitive and misogynistic laws are reflected in the following member statement by WAF members Anis Haroon, Maria Rashid Nausheen Ahmed, Quratulain Bakhtiari, Uzma Nurani (reproduced with permission):

'My' politics raises a collective voice against any injustice that violates the basic rights of an individual or community…to destabilise the political or the social…that I speak up each time and take a principled stand on all matters. 'My' politics does not end at the polls. It means taking a principled stand even if it results in temporary setback. It always pays in the longer run to create new professionals and challenge power structures that oppress me, and others around me.

Despite the normalisation of brutality, extreme violence inevitably administers a harsh shock when it occurs to a close friend. An intimacy with grief became deeply politically formative for me when a close friend was raped. Together with my WAF colleagues, we began counting and mapping out comparisons with other women who had been raped. Sometimes grief-stricken, other times more controlled, we painstakingly learned to forge a way to publicly articulate our rage, and denounce a society where rapes are routine and go unpunished. In the case of my friend our protests seemed ineffectual, camouflaged in generalities; words felt inadequate and I ached with helplessness. Even after years of protesting against violent deaths in Karachi, having friends killed violently, or even hearing about the killing of someone I knew only by name, or had exchanged pleasantries with, death is a blow. I am intrigued by ways reactions to death and grief vary, even while they establish a common understanding and shared loss. Given that such killings are reported by the media, in politics, and discussed at length amongst communities and individuals, perhaps in these realms rumours, whispers, anger, and grief may coalesce into a force for good. At the same time, if activism means taking a principled stand in the face of a hopelessless struggle, it also means accepting with clarity the possibility we may also die, one by one.

On her way home

Let me turn first to the killing of Perween Rehman on 3 March 2013. Perween Rehman was an internationally renowned architect, planner, social scientist, development worker, and civil society activist, and an icon for community based development workers. In 1982 she joined a sanitation project in a squatter settlement of Karachi. Thus began her career in the Orangi Pilot Project (OPP), established in the 1980s by the prominent South Asian social scientist Dr Akhtar Hameed Khan. In 1983 she became the OPP's Joint Technical Director. In 1985 she studied at the Institute of Housing Studies in Rotterdam and in 1988 assumed the post of Director of OPP-Research and Training Institute (OPP-RTI). In 1989 Perween Rehman helped found the Urban Resource Centre with Arif Hasan. When I began working in Karachi's squatter settlements (*katchi abadis*) in the early 1980s, the best known *katchi abadi* projects were the OPP, and the Baldia Water and Sanitation Project. I meet Perween when I joined the Department of Community Health Sciences at Aga Khan University. My department initiated a health programme in Orangi's *katchis abadis*. Here Perween became an invaluable resource. Feeding her fieldwork into teaching, she also instructed undergraduate medical students about the city's health needs. Fast becoming one of Karachi's most prominent social activists, Perween worked to empower local communities around health, housing and infrastructure development; she also protested and meticulously gathered data on land grabbing, political violence, corruption surrounding water tankers, and water supplies to the poor.

On 3 March, Perween Rehman was killed by four gunmen in Western Orangi. Her car was slowly rolling over the speed breaker on the main thoroughfare; it was dusk, and she had just left a women's meeting. After the shooting her driver called her colleague ahead. He quickly turned his car and together they drove Perween to Abbassi Shaheed hospital. During the half hour journey there, the news spread through text messages, emails, phonecalls, and as breaking news headlines on television. The following day, Perween's death was front-page news in all Karachi's leading newspapers.

WAF members reacted. Some joined the crowd of public mourners outside her home. Others waited silently for WAF to chisel out a collective response. Perween's sister, the author Aquila Ismail, took comfort with WAF members. No group claimed responsibility for Perween's killing. Rumours took on a life of their own, circulating like wildfire. Many attributed general blame to the shifting of the Taliban conflict from FATA to Karachi. This had seen increased bigotry, anti-Shia, anti-Ahmadi, anti-Christian, ethnic, criminal, and anti-minority violence, and renewed support for the blasphemy law. WAF members presented a tribute for Perween to her sister. (The tribute was collectively composed by WAF members Zubaida Mustapha, Anis Haroon, Hilda Saeed, Uzma Noorani, and Kausar S. Khan. It is edited by myself and reproduced here, in part, with permission.)

WAF's tribute to Perween Rehman

Perween's death struck us like lightning, dimming our hopes of change. As activists let us not be cowed by fear, but rather transform this tragedy into courage and renewed commitment. Perween's determination saw the OPP develop into an active, forward-looking entity. In essence, this is also the role of the women's movement: to make women aware of their rights, enable them to stand autonomously, with dignity. Perween, who achieved all that, is dear to WAF. She was courageous, principled, committed to the marginalised, to women, and fought terror and gunfire with dialogue and words. While WAF stands for the empowerment of all women, Pakistan's vast societal and class divisions mean the women's movement is far from a homogeneous whole. Some concentrate on advocacy and creating awareness. Others work with women in poverty who lack the education and resources to undertake a wider advocacy, and whose energies are completely subsumed in everyday survival. Perween worked devotedly to cross these boundaries. Privileged and internationally educated, she worked with a small budget and contributed to raise awareness of *all* women's struggles. Her gift to Pakistan's women, in life and so poignantly in her death, was in bridging connections between women and women's movements.

> She was strong in her gentleness!
> Perween, you our icon.
> We are proud of you
> You will always be with us

Murky waters

I turn next to the case of Abdul Waheed Khan, whom I knew for only two short months after Perween Rehman's assassination. Waheed was a prominent figure at the first public conference for Perween, jointly organised by WAF and the PMA (Pakistan Medical Association). A Pashtun from northern Pakistan, and the son of a migrant labourer,

Waheed originally joined the Orangi Pilot Project to study development under Akhter Hameed Khan. Two months following Perween's death, on 13 May 2013 Waheed was gunned down in front of his home. A tall broad-shouldered man with a commanding presence, he had been sitting with his daughter on his lap.

Waheed had been instrumental in assisting WAF members to visit Orangi to pay condolences to Perween's colleagues in the OPP. Here, eerily, the ghostly presence of Akhtar Hamid Khan hovered. He had mentored both Waheed and Perween. Informally, Waheed recalled happy moments with Perween and also confided that several colleagues had begun taking medication. This phenomenon is not new in Karachi. Prescription drugs are being increasingly abused by an embattled populace. Now, people sank into solitude as they came to terms with their pain. After Waheed's death they sank even deeper. Markedly, no collective intervention was organised. There was little enthusiasm even when WAF professionals offered therapeutic intervention.

Nonetheless, Waheed offered to help plant two trees (gul-mohor) in memory of Perween. WAF wanted to plant the trees next to the spot where Perween died. The road was a thoroughfare, and the hardened ground next to it, a makeshift footpath which also housed some makeshift looking shops, seemed appropriate. The speed breaker was a hard swell on the road; the gunman must have stood and stared at the ground where the trees were to be planted. Few workers were willing to travel to Orangi to plant the trees. When he learned of this, Waheed offered to prepare the ground and bring labourers himself. As WAF waited for arrangements for Perween's memorial to take form, we were again shocked by news of Waheed's murder.

An outcry followed. A group deliberating legal action for Perween considered including Waheed's murder in its litigation efforts. Matters, however, began closing in as Waheed's family were pressurised to withdraw the case they had registered against 'unknown assailants'. As more complexities surfaced, the legal case faltered. Rumours surfaced that his brother had withdrawn a large amount of money after his death, and ransacked his home. WAF members visited his home in order to support his wife, but their efforts were blocked. People whispered. Waheed knew his killers, indeed had received threats. The key suspect, a Taliban commander, had supporters in Waheed's neighbourhood. He had publicly expressed disapproval of Waheed's support of mainstream state education and local polio immunisation programmes. Waheed had additionally challenged *madrassa* teachers about their curriculum. The police dared not enter the neighbourhood.

Questions of ways whispers, rumours, stories, and distortions circulate and create or follow the lethal conditions for the circulation of hate have also troubled the anthropologist Veena Das in her book *Life and Words* (2007). Writing about violence in Delhi neighbourhoods, Das shows how rumours occupy a region of language with the potential to make us experience events by producing them in the very act of telling. Rumours, she argues, capture the simultaneity of events occurring at the level of phenomenal time which are far apart in physical time: these make the whole of the past simultaneously available for deployment as a lethal component in the phenomenology of violence (97). Yet, and I ask this rhetorically, might we take the circulation of rumours and whispered stories that accompany killings as a site for rethinking the political, in terms of potential for a more positive, 'vital' form of dynamic change? One that may also 'spread like wildfire', beyond the sluggish and reluctant tempo of governments, bureaucracy and institutions, assume a more critical function, and engender peace rather than violence in intimate connections with communities, and the state?

A doorstep execution: Zahra Shahid Hussain

On 11 May 2013 general elections were held in Pakistan. They followed the five years of civilian rule following the ousting of General Musharraf, who had been president for over ten years. The PPP, who entered into government in 2008, had gained strength after the assassination in 2007 of Benazir Bhutto, PPP leader and former prime minister of Pakistan, which many attributed to Pakistan's security forces. Yet five years of PPP rule had soured its popular support. The party was expected to fail in the 2013 elections. The two main national contenders were Nawaz Sharif of the Pakistan Muslim League (PML), and Imran Khan, leader of the Pakistan Tehreek-e-Insaf (PTI). These elections occurred amidst a resilient insurgency by the Pakistan Taliban (TTP) in Karachi and persistent violence, bombings, attacks, killings—between the TTP, PPP, MQM, ANP and other groups. Yet, there was widespread support for the PTI amongst Karachi's youth and middle and upper-middle classes, who saw in the party the real possibility of a viable challenge to the MQM. That is, vociferous support in PTI neighbourhoods signalled a rejection of the MQM's militant politics and its stranglehold on Karachi society.

Widespread reports of irregularities led Jamaat e Islami to boycott the 11 May polls in Karachi and Hyderabad. These reports led the Pakistan Election Commission to announce a repoll in forty-two stations in Karachi's NA-250 constituency. Criticising the handling of the voting across the constituency overall, MQM boycotted the repoll that was scheduled for 19 May. The elections were plagued by violence and accounts of 'historic rigging'. The secretary of the Election Commission in Karachi was forced to resign. Finally, the results returned the PTI candidate Arif Alavi the winner in NA-250, followed by the MQM, and Nawaz Sharif became prime minister.

One day before the scheduled repoll on the night of Saturday 18 May, Zahra Shahid Hussain, a senior member of Imran Khan's PTI was shot outside her home. She had joined Pakistan Tehreek-e-Insaf in 1997 and was president of the party's women's wing. She belonged to NA-250, a constituency that had openly challenged the MQM. Imran Khan accused the MQM leader Altaf Hussain of ordering her murder, and the UK government of harbouring him in exile. She belonged to Karachi's elite, had a Masters degree from Karachi University, supported human rights and women's initiatives in Pakistan and development initiatives for the marginalised. Nonetheless she was a familiar figure at WAF events. 'It's a pattern,' said one who had seen over fifty friends killed in the last three years. 'They shoot in the head and in the neck...just two bullets, they are well trained...boom, boom...the person is gone.' Zahra was killed according to the same pattern. A young man followed her as she got out of her car and went through the gate into her house. In an attempt at self-protection, she offered him her bag which he took before he fired directly at her face. Then he turned and fired at the back of her head. These targeted killings deliberately seek to spread widespread terror (*dahshat*), and as their details circulate across the city, they do so with a chilling frequency.

The result was that her family did not want to pursue the case legally. Some WAF members balked at this decision, which seemed a remarkable concession to her killers, but they respected the family's decision and the grief and fear which underpinned it. Others argued strongly for the party to pursue a public litigation case on her behalf, but their voices were drowned out by party officials wary of acting without the family's permission. Or perhaps they were just wary of acting. Other women's activist groups sought to pursue this option, but subsequently discovered how complicated Pakistan's judicial system and processes are in regard to public litigation, and were unable to continue. Zahra's death soon became enshrouded in stillness and the silence that seems to descend after every death, immobilising frustration, fear, and despair.

If the purpose of Zahra's execution was to terrorise, then how still she lies in her resting place. The purpose in killing her, it seemed, was to terrorise the supporters of PTI so that they would stay silent and away from the re-polling. The suspect militant party disrupted the polls, and was unhappy they were rescheduled in some stations. This fearsome act did not deter PTI supporters. Zahra would be proud.

'Irfan the lion'

I first met Irfan Khudi Ali at a meeting of the *Ammanittehad* (Solidarity for Peace) group in Karachi. Young, with a bounce in his stride, his words to me were 'Remember me as Irfan the lion'. Neither of us imagined I would take him at his word. Irfan was basically a human rights defender, and focused on the youth of Balochistan in particular, and Pakistan in general. He founded the organisation Human Rights Commission for Social Justice and Peace, in Balochistan. He was also a member of the Civil Society Advisory Group for UN Women, Pakistan. He belonged to the Hazara community, which is a Shia community, and under constant attack by the extremist Sunni groups (of the larger sect of Islam in Pakistan). Whenever his community was attacked, he would be there to help, support, and provide relief. After our first meeting, we would communicate directly, and run into each other at human rights meetings. He was one of those young men of Pakistan one would be proud to know.

On 10 January in Quetta, Balochistan, two blasts ripped through the neighbourhood of a Hazara community that had been living in Balochistan for over a century. They were integral to the communal diversity of Balochistan where many people easily spoke three languages or more.

The blast killed Irfan Ali, the energetic human rights and peace activist, my friend and comrade. Not one of the missing, or of the 120 people injured, he was one of the ninety victims who were killed. After the first blast he hurried to tend to those wounded, and was killed in the second explosion. Irfan believed in peace, that God's justice would prevail eventually. He must surely have the highest station with God, for violence has no place in God's realm. 'Your soul is one with peace, my friend,' I murmured to myself when I heard of his death. Feeling totally at loss, I sent the following text to his mobile phone: 'I am Kausar. Irfan's friend. My deepest condolences to all Irfan's family and friends.'

I imagined Irfan at the moment he felt the fateful blast. I imagined him dashing out to provide first aid to the injured. He was someone who could be depended on in times of crisis. Violence saddened him immensely. 'I feel tired of carrying dead bodies,' he once texted to my phone. 'What has happened to my city?' I cannot bear to imagine the details of the second blast. A mutual friend wrote to me afterwards: 'When I heard about the first blast that evening, I contacted all of Irfan's friends. A short while after a second blast came. It shook our home. I telephoned Irfan but his cell was switched off. I kept calling but there was no response. Later I discovered he had been providing first aid to those injured in the first blast, together with his younger brother and brother in law. His younger brother was also injured, and his brother-in-law was missing. When the details became clear, I discovered that they both also lost their lives in the second blast.'

Imaginations can be cruel. My mind was awash with awful images. I imagined Irfan's mobile phone lying indifferently on the ground, surrounded by smouldering bodies. I wondered if a rescuer had picked it up and read my message. I imagined Irfan walking, talking, bending forward then back in a chair, laughing, thoughtful, his head bent down brooding, him shaking his head sadly. Now, he must be lying motionless, his body in pieces, lying quietly in a long line of friends and dear ones, laid out with the dead. Hazara community leaders prepared the bodies and body parts for burial but refused to conduct the burial unless the government assured them of security. Wrapped in his white burial cloth (*qaffin*), Irfan became part of a gruesome protest of corpses. I wonder if he smiled at his part in this final outcry for justice to be done. On 16 February the Hazara community were again attacked, and sustained almost one hundred deaths. Yet again, community leaders and family members sat with the bodies of their lost loved ones, demanding security and for the Pakistan army to secure their safety of their community. This time Irfan was not there to help them.

* * *

This chapter has concerned my struggles to make emotional sense of some deaths that have touched me. These four ordinary deaths are part of an acceleration in Karachi's violence that analysts, activists, and commentators have also sought to unravel. Whilst sophisticated theories and explanations inform efforts to contain and to stop violence, they do not capture the utter weariness many people feel at their apparent failure to bear down on formidable organisations of violence that once seemed sporadic. At the same time, citizens tirelessly resolve to fight back, to not abandon peace as a right. This struggle unites rich and poor. It is this struggle that enfolds my commitment to activism and efforts for peace, alongside my academic work. To cite a popular WAF slogan, *'jaddo jehad jari hai'* ('the struggle continues'). Thus so it is that by setting out on our way, the way will appear. If we cannot see a clear solution to end violence, we hope that along our journey against violence the way will appear.

I once heard the Pakistani peace and human rights activist Ibn Abdur Rehman say in a presentation that the words *aman* (peace) and *bey-aman* (conflict, the opposite of peace) are inextricably related. Remove *bey-* and *aman* will come. These are simple and wise words. In the mayhem that constitutes everyday life in Pakistan, it is difficult to say what constitutes peace. *Bey-aman* is more easily identifiable. Targeted killings, extortion, corruption, the diversion of security to guard government officials, the abandonment of ordinary citizens to the mercy of bigots and killers all comprise *bey-aman*. Like good and evil, the one is the face of the other. Therefore, as violence flourishes, so do women's groups and efforts by many activists in Karachi to end suffering on the grounds of class, sex, religion, ethnicity, or poverty. Therefore I do not consider it trite to propose that this short commemoration of four deaths be considered, not in terms of an obituary, but a call to action.

To conclude, I will re-emphasise how grief, academia, and activism are inextricably tied for me, and briefly turn to my community health research at the Aga Khan University. Since my work in Orangi in the 1980s in *katchi abadi*s, I have studied the effects of structural, gendered, and political violence on health, particularly women's health. The term 'structural violence' was coined first by Johan Galtung in 1969 to correspond with systematic ways social structures or institutions kill people slowly by preventing them from meeting their basic needs. Institutionalised classism, racism, discrimation, and nationalism are examples of structural violence. This may sound extreme until one considers that lifespans are reduced when people are socially dominated, politically oppressed, or economically exploited. Structural violence and direct violence are highly interdependent—structural violence frequently produces direct violence, including family violence, racial violence, hate crimes, terrorism, and conflict. Violence occurs at Karachi's tertiary hospitals with regularity. Healthcare providers are threatened by militants for saving those they tried to kill; violence is perpetrated by patient attendants, party supporters when the injured person has political affiliations, or after a major accident as crowds enter hospitals. Doctors and polio vaccination workers are routinely targeted by extremist groups. At the time of writing I am conducting a study on people's experiences of seeking healthcare during armed conflict in Lyari, a volatile area with around a million inhabitants (see Kirmani, this volume). One objective is to involve respondents in developing strategies for violence reduction that can challenge structural and political violence simultaneously. Yet whilst violence reduction is a global agenda of the World Health Organisation, that unites research consortia from public health institutes across the world, Karachi's public health institutes have yet to adequately integrate violence and health agendas into their educational or research programmes. Likewise, domestic violence against women and children must yet be systematically addressed in public healthcare systems, as part of the social determinants of health. It is in working on these matters that means academic research is for me inseparable from public engagement and activist agendas.

References

Das, Veena, *Life and Words*, Berkeley: University of California Press, 2007.
Mumtaz, Khawar and Farida Shaheed, *Women of Pakistan. Two Steps Forward, One Step Back*, London: Zed Books, 1987.

AFTERWORD I

Farzana Shaikh

For a city plagued by decades of appalling violence, Karachi can be forgiven for not looking its best. And when insult is added to ignominy by condemning it as 'the most dangerous city in the world', looking good can be harder still. The deadly brew of kidnappings, bombings, and extortion, encapsulated in references to the 'routinisation, of violence', has now come both to define and consume this erstwhile 'city of lights'. Yet Karachi—the city of my birth and of much of my education—is and always has been as much about the light as the dark, about living as about dying. In the midst of untold horrors of ethnic, religious, and criminal violence, millions of its inhabitants have found ways, as they still do, to co-exist—sometimes uneasily but often in harmony. 'What,' asks Laura Ring in her account of the creative tensions involved in securing peace in strife-torn Karachi, 'do we make of this?' (2006, 83).

This collection of essays takes up that challenge. Uniting them is the premise that any understanding of violence in Karachi requires us not only to acknowledge its 'ugly reality', but also its daily conquest through repeated acts of negotiation and ever-insistent strategies of pacification. The temper of rival ethnicities, competing sects, and polarised classes that animate Pakistan's most notorious megalopolis, we are told, is as prone to hardness as to elasticity. But these essays go much further than that. By inviting us to partake in the conversation with the help of multiple approaches they lay bare the objective conditions that determine the structure of violence in Karachi and subject to close scrutiny many untested assumptions that continue to inform our understanding of that violence.

In doing so, these critical voices navigate a complex terrain that is at once local, national, and global. Indeed, one recurrent question is whether so-called 'local' narratives of violence (more commonly described as 'local turf wars') that have engulfed Karachi in recent decades can be read as representative of a larger 'national' narrative of violence that is sustained by the language of Pakistan's militarised state. For there would be good grounds to argue that Karachi's violence is an echo of the foundational violence of Pakistan's creation in 1947 and no more than just a reflection of the resistance to state power resting on the claims of an over-arching discourse of 'Islam' to regulate the language of ethnic, linguistic, and religious diversity. This interpretation is not devoid of some irony. For while a city whose rich cultural diversity was once held up as a microcosm and desirable 'local' version of a multi-cultural Pakistan, Karachi finds itself today to be emblematic of the very fault-lines of ethnic, linguistic, and religious difference that are judged to threaten the 'national' edifice of which it is a part. Yet, what these essays suggest is that just as tensions stemming from the fragmentation of state and society at the national level have been constitutive of a certain collective life—however fragile—Karachi's violent transition is no less involved in the negotiation of tensions that, however acute, may yet redefine received ideas about conflict and its relationship to the construction of community. By doing so, we are offered ways not only to imagine exiting the apparent circularity of Karachi's violence but, more importantly, to explore possibilities for change.

These essays also lend themselves to other readings, which lead us beyond the vagaries of local and national developments to encompass global trends. Thus while the scale and intensity of Karachi's local violence can be seen to mirror the specific distortions of a national hinterland, we are constantly reminded that they are also symptomatic of today's global mega-city or megalopolis. Resulting from the demographic explosion triggered by rapid mass migrations that far exceeded most calculations (see Hasan 2010, 145–69), Karachi's transformation from a sleepy coastal town into a vast metropolitan area bears all the hallmarks of the quintessential 'instant city' (Inskeep 2011). Here homelessness, the scramble for scarce resources, crime and environmental degradation have all emerged as sites of interaction, where relations between disparate ethnic, religious, and class configurations act as combustible fuel for social and political conflict. Yet even here in Karachi, as many of the essays demonstrate, far from being necessarily corrosive or an index of anarchy, violence has come to stand for a framework—a kind of 'ordered disorder' (Gayer, 2014)—for the negotiation of difference binding individuals to the larger social and political community.

It is precisely this binding of people, in this case the people of Karachi, and their attachment to the larger national community that interest me. Questions of collective identity and belonging—what they express and how they are imagined—have formed a large part of my own work on the troubled relationship between Islam and what is sometimes referred to as the 'national imaginary' in Pakistan (Shaikh, 2009). Katherine Pratt Ewing develops interesting discussions on the relationship between the act of *qabza* (the illegal seizure of, and contestation over, specific sites ranging from property to politics) and the national imaginary (2010, 531–40). While the collective and often conflicted attachment to the nation continues to centre on the contestation over the remit of Islam to define Pakistan's national identity, Karachi's violent present suggests that what may arguably be at greatest stake is the challenge of deepening a collective commitment to pluralism, if not plural expressions of Islam, as the foundation of a nationally shared cultural and political citizenship.

Many of the essays point to the urgency of securing just such a commitment to pluralism. Zia ur Rahman calls on us re-imagine Karachi as a *mohajir* (migrant) city. But rather than understanding the term *mohajir* to designate the city's Urdu-speaking migrants with whom it has come to be virtually synonymous, he makes a plea for it to stand for all migrants with an equal claim to Karachi. Rahman focuses on the Pashtuns, one of the earliest groups to migrate to Karachi which over the decades has withstood the violence of the city's internecine politics, endured political discrimination, and survived the vagaries of regional power politics that have led the Pashtuns to emerge as Karachi's second largest ethnic group after the Urdu-speaking minority. Today the Pashtuns lay claim to Karachi and seek recognition from the city as one of its own. Yet, as Rahman demonstrates, the Pashtun's marginal status as 'outsider' persists. And with mounting hostility to the influx of ever larger numbers of Pashtun militants from the conflict-ridden regions of north-western Pakistan, that status as 'alien' to Karachi has been reinforced by allegations of Pashtun complicity in eroding Karachi's 'secular' landscape through a process of so-called 'Talibanisation'.

It is Rahman's discussion of the appropriation of the term '*mohajir*' by a single group that echoes larger anxieties about the terms of collective attachment and belonging. Who is the 'authentic' migrant that 'really belongs' to Karachi? What are his desired attributes and how are they to be settled? At the national level these questions have long resonated in the chronic uncertainty over the 'authentic' Pakistani subject and his relationship to a national imaginary informed by the terms of Islam—an uncertainty rehearsed daily by violence, as in Karachi, against religious 'others' to settle the question of what it means to belong 'really' to Pakistan.

Was it always thus (and always thus will it be)? Not if we go by Arif Hasan's arresting portrait of the early years of Karachi and his prescriptions for the revival of the city's once 'progressive culture'. While Karachi's modern-day incarnation as a city scarred by communal hostility and violent tensions leaves little, if any, room to imagine it as the cradle of a 'cosmopolitan public culture' that was once openly embraced across different classes and communities, Hasan's representation is consistent with fast-fading portraits of Karachi as a quintessentially 'post-colonial' rather than an Islamic city that hardly conformed to expectations as the erstwhile capital of the world's first self-consciously created Islamic republic. As Michel Boivin has observed elsewhere, even today, after the influx of millions of Muslim refugees from India, the physical contours of Karachi's cultural space remain impervious to any exclusively Islamic appeal: no mosque serves as an organising pole for the city, nor is any religious symbol evoked to recall the glories of the Muslim past. Instead, Karachi city's vast geography has come to stand as a potent reminder of its rich multi-cultural heritage.

That heritage owes much to the significant presence of a once thriving community of mercantile Hindus who, along with Sikhs, constituted just over a majority of the city's population at independence, as well as to a class of affluent Parsis (Zoroastrians), who dominated the business sector. No less important in shaping this heritage was the role of educated local Christian families of mixed Portuguese-Indian descent with roots in the western Indian port of Goa. While the mass exodus of Hindus following Partition transformed the face of Karachi into a city where Muslims now represented 95 per cent of its population (a trend that threatens to repeat itself with the steady flight of Christians and Parsis, who now fear persecution from violent Islamist groups in Karachi or harassment resulting from the application of discriminatory legislation against non-Muslims), the memory of Karachi's mixed colonial cultural heritage continues to resonate in the imagination of its residents and to fuel what some regard as 'the modernist myth' of the city's unshakeable 'secular' credentials (Gayer 2014, 165).

However, Karachi's reputation as a melting pot of diverse ethnic and religious communities was not the only feature that marked it out from other cities in Pakistan. As significant was the fact that, notwithstanding its absorption of millions of refugees, Karachi emerged relatively unscathed by the sustained and widespread Partition-related violence that convulsed urban centres elsewhere in Pakistan, notably in parts of Punjab and Bengal. The riots which erupted in Karachi in early 1948, while causing the flight of thousands of Hindu and Sikh families, were judged at the time to be unusual for a region known for its 'communal harmony' (Zamindar 2010, 169–95). The memory of a city where different communities had long since learned to live together in pursuit of a common urban culture that rested on a broad popular appreciation of pluralism is a strong thread running through Hasan's essay. Yet, Hasan is careful to eschew any suggestion of nostalgia that could dilute the power of explanation. In so doing he makes a strong case for 'sympathetic' attention to changes that made Karachi more receptive to a democratic culture even while making the city more vulnerable to a violent transition. Like many, Hasan also locates the roots of Karachi's violence in the breakdown of social hierarchies, often legitimised by the 'vocabulary' of 'feudal culture', which weakened in the wake of the rapid industrialisation of the 1970s and the spread of a populist discourse favoured by the Pakistan People's Party under its founder, Zulfiqar Ali Bhutto. But this burgeoning 'culture of consensus', which

Hasan argues drew on a rich vein of public entertainment whose cosmopolitan and inclusive complexion spoke directly to Karachi's newly emerging classes and social formations, rapidly came under assault. Right-wing religious parties, aided and abetted by the Islamising zeal of Pakistan's military ruler, General Zia-ul-Haq, who seized power in 1977, led the charge, ushering in an 'Islamic public culture' that was both violent and divisive. The 'cultural wasteland' it produced was hard to reverse and the violence it spawned soon deeply entrenched.

Yet it was from within Karachi's besieged and much eroded 'cosmopolitan culture' that the language of protest resurfaced and where the possibilities of pacifism as a counter-movement were arguably most creatively explored. Long established spaces of sociability provided the context for these strategies of pacification. Such spaces of social life had, of course, long been a feature of Karachi as the city that would successfully consolidate its status as Pakistan's most important commercial metropolis and key centre of modern administration. Here the worlds of advanced bureaucracy, high finance, and industry learned to co-exist with a ubiquitous *bazaari* presence that in turn rubbed shoulders with a thriving port culture organised around established coastal fishing communities, which predated the creation of the state. Other social spaces structured around Karachi's many *dargah*s, *imambara*s, *jamaat khana*s, *mandir*s, *girjaa*s, and *gurdwara*s, which reinforced the city's reputation as host to a mélange of religious groups, also served to underscore Karachi's sociability and to act as a brake against the process of cultural cleansing dictated by Zia's unitary vision of Islamization. Spaces of gang warfare and ethnic confrontation rooted in Karachi's more volatile neighbourhoods, such as Lyari, held tenaciously to their own forms of sociability organised around the *mohalla*. Here, as Nida Kirmani so vividly demonstrates, sociability came to be informed by the idea of 'humanitarian service' that was seen to transcend the violent divisions of caste, creed, and ethnicity.

But nowhere did Karachi's sociability and the politics of protest appear to intersect more boldly than in the 'secular' spaces occupied by the *sharabi* (alcoholic). The so-called 'Zia years' revealed the potential of these spaces as sites for the articulation of a powerful counter-cultural movement. Nadeem Paracha, an active participant, gives us an insight into these spaces by showing how the drinking of alcohol became as much an act of insubordination aimed at the social and political controls imposed by a militarised state as a challenge to emerging narratives of belonging that sought to re-cast the Pakistani subject within a moral discourse resting on the idea of Pakistan as a 'bastion of Islam'. For the young Paracha and his peers, drinking alcohol represented much more than youthful rebellion: 'drinking', he tells us, 'became an act of defiance' against Zia's military regime, but also against its promotion of an exclusionary, national discourse based on Islam, which sought to revise the conditions of cultural and political citizenship in Pakistan.

The milieu of Karachi's student politics emerged as a key site to settle this often violent struggle. While pro-Zia student organisations, notably the Islami Jamiat-i-Tulaba (IJT), co-operated actively with the military regime to impose the standards of 'proper' Islam expected of the new Pakistani 'subject', Paracha and his fellow students from the National Students Federation (NSF) invoked a more inclusive sociability that called into question the idea of Pakistan as a single 'nation of Muslims'. What began as acts of protest and rebellion played out on the stage of Karachi's local student politics now echoed a wider contestation over the terms of national belonging. Those terms had been called into question by the crisis that had followed the separation of East Pakistan (now Bangladesh) in 1971, which exposed the fragility of a national imaginary resting on 'Islam' and deepened uncertainty about Pakistan's national identity. Many turned for an explanation of the crisis to the moral decline of the nation and to the spread of so-called 'secular' values, whose most potent symbol was judged to lie in the consumption of alcohol. The polarising discourse it generated in the late 1970s was captured in an apocryphal account of a confrontation between the PPP leader, Zulfiqar Ali Bhutto, and his pro-Zia Islamist critics, who questioned Bhutto's Muslim credentials by accusing him of drinking alcohol, to which Bhutto is said to have responded: 'Yes, I drink *sharab* but at least I don't drink the blood of our people'.

It is no wonder then that Karachi, with its hardened reputation as Pakistan's 'secular centre' (Gayer 2014, 201) and its growing notoriety as the purveyor of *laissez-faire* codes of morality revolving around the city's bars, clubs and casinos, found itself in the eye of this storm. Indeed the mood of violent vigilantism against so-called 'traders of public immorality', which gained ground in Pakistan in the decade following the military coup that ousted Bhutto in 1977, was most profoundly felt in Karachi. However, the perception of Karachi as the established hub of a 'secular' cosmopolitan culture under siege has not been without its critics. They point to the elitist bias inherent in most representations of Karachi as 'secular' and critical of the 'historicist' disregard of the Islamist discourse promoted by religious parties, such as the Jamaat-i-Islami, which strongly opposed the city's 'liberal' and 'secular' aspirations (Ibid., p.163).

There is some truth to these objections. For while the forces of Islamic radicalism spawned by Pakistan's involvement in the Afghan civil war of the 1980s and the inroads made by Taliban groups in Karachi since 2001 were decisive in shrinking the space for secular possibilities, the language of political Islam was by no means new to Karachi. For at least three decades after independence Karachi served as a bastion of support for Pakistan's Islamist organisations, such as the Jamaat-i-Islami, with much of that support rooted in the Urdu-speaking refugee population, sections of which later espoused the cause of secularism. They were also at the forefront of Karachi's sectarian campaigns in the 1950s, which were directed against the minority Ahmadiyya community. *Ulama* parties were no less popular in Karachi. For much of the 1960s and 1970s the city played host to the strident discourse of Deobandi *ulama*, who had migrated in large numbers after Partition, and responded enthusiastically to the not always benign influence of *ulama* parties representing the majority Sunni Barelvi sect, which held sway over many parts Karachi as elsewhere in Pakistan.

The concerns of sceptics who question accounts of Karachi as 'historically' secular ought not, therefore, to be lightly dismissed. Descriptions of Karachi's 'golden age' rife with bars, bands, and billiard rooms, which flourished from the 1950s until the introduction of prohibition in the late1970s, have indeed tended to equate the preferences of an affluent, Westernised class with assumptions about Karachi's 'liberal' disposition. (For a representative sample see Mooraj 2010, 313–45, in Khuhro and Mooraj 2010; also see Shaikh 2015, 419–39). Yet it is worth noting that, even if access to Karachi's elite 'secular' culture remained restricted to the few, the climate favoured by that culture significantly widened social, economic, and artistic opportunities for women across social classes and instilled unprecedented expectations about the role of religious minorities as equal participants in the creation of common cultural spaces.

The democratic interregnum of the 1990s exposed the real extent of the damage wrought by the Zia years on the shared spaces encouraged by this cultural climate. While there were some attempts to roll back the worst excesses of the Zia era, their results were often too feeble or uneven. It took the return of military rule in 1999 under General Pervez Musharraf to introduce the facade of a more liberal dispensation and, with it, claims to favour a fresh appreciation of Karachi's social and religious diversity. It marked the onset of a new style of military patronage that sought to compensate for the lack of political freedoms by offering its captive audience what came to be known as 'life-style liberalism'. It spoke directly to Pakistan's burgeoning middle classes who were now exposed to the pull of global technologies, the lure of international migration, and the relentless pressures of upward social mobility.

All presented new triggers of conflict, whose effects were particularly acute in Karachi, where the erosion of cultural solidarities and the steady pace of social, political and spatial fragmentation since the 1990s had resulted in a process resembling what Appadurai (2000) has described as 'decosmopolitanisation', a term applied by Gayer to Karachi (2014, 41). It pointed to the irretrievable loss of a multi-class and multi-religious popular culture that had rested on the aspiration, if not the experience, of a shared cultural citizenship. In its place there emerged a segregated culture scarred by the Zia years in which a privileged and moneyed elite, long habituated to pursuing its illicit leisure activities behind closed doors, now shunned participation in the common spaces of public recreation that had had once proliferated in Karachi—its cinemas, open-air theatres, and parks. It was left to others, often less fortunate, to begin the arduous process of reclaiming a common culture and framing a new language of collective belonging.

In recent years their initiatives have led to some remarkable ventures, including the National Association of Performing Arts, the annual Karachi Literature Festival, the Kara Film Festival and the artistic forum, Peace Niche. All have sought to break down the barriers of Karachi's segregated culture but they too have faced charges of elitism.

Despite this, they herald an important and novel development. For they aim not only to restore Karachi's 'lost' cosmopolitan heritage and affirm the values of a plural society but to use these emerging cultural spaces to produce strategies of pacification that can serve as meaningful antidotes to stem the cycle of ethnic and religious violence that has gripped Karachi. Not surprisingly, many of these initiatives have looked to Karachi's much discussed—and now disputed—'secular' past for inspiration. They are intended to revive the ethos of a city that many still imagine was grounded in a 'liberal' culture of tolerance, whose foundations were weakened by a divisive rhetoric and the promotion of sectarian ideologies favoured by the Islamisation programme of the 1980s. However, this historical (re)construction of Karachi has come under pressure as much from sceptical observers (as seen above) as from the internal dynamics of Karachi's volatile ethnic politics that threaten to expose the idea of a 'secular' Karachi as a 'myth' created by self-appointed 'liberals'. At issue are the interests of the city's Urdu-speaking classes, who are said to have burnished Karachi's secular image by equating it with the mandate of the dominant dominant Mohajir Qaumi Mahaz (MQM) in an effort to weaken its main political rival, the Awami National Party (ANP), whose largely Pashtun constituency has been frequently charged with 'Talibanising' Karachi.

If so, the invention of a 'secular' Karachi hardly exhausts the city's repertoire of urban myths upon which to pitch its claim to be representative of an inclusive plural culture dedicated to peaceful co existence. In recent years Karachi has come to share with other parts of urban Pakistan a new-found and pronounced interest in the cult of Sufi saints, whose spiritual appeal has recently received the close attention of the Pakistani state (and its foreign sponsors) as a potentially winning 'home-grown' narrative against political Islam and its programme of violence (Shaikh 2012). State sponsorship of Sufism as an antidote to Islamist violence reached its apogee under General Musharraf, whose military regime took a keen interest in promoting Sufi festivals across Pakistan. One of the most important of these, the Sufi International Festival, was held in Karachi in 2007. Though scarcely known for its promotion of spiritual pursuits, Karachi rose to the occasion by invoking its own patron-saint, Shah Abdullah Ghazi, an obscure eighth-century Sufi, who lies buried on a hilltop in the affluent suburb of Clifton.

His cult has long attracted devotees from Karachi's working classes representing diverse ethnic and sectarian groups, but it is only in recent years that sections of Karachi's local media have taken to referring to the saint's shrine as the city's 'axis mundi' and a marker of Karachi's spiritual identity (*Dawn*, 6 October 2015)—in emulation, it seems, of Lahore and its ties to the cult of its acknowledged patron-saint, Data Ganj Bakhsh Ali Hujweri.

This novel development appears to point to a more concerted effort to mine the sources of an indigenous tradition rooted in Karachi's Sufi past by those in support of strengthening the city's image as a model of 'secular' co-existence. The habit of tapping into 'neglected aspects of popular religiousity' to sustain urban-based political projects would by no means be new to Karachi. In his discussion of the Dawat-i-Islami, a Sufi-informed proselytising religious movement, Oskar Verkaaik shows how its strong accent on religious piety and the promotion of mystical practices associated with Sufi rituals, such as *zikr*, found favour among urban followers of the MQM in Karachi in the 1990s. And while choosing between the transcendent language of Sufi-informed piety and the partisan discourse of ethnic politics has not been without its problems for those seeking to reconcile the two, Verkaaik argues that this structural tension was often defused by resorting to 'mild mutual teasing' between rival enthusiasts. But what is arguably most striking about Verkaaik's account is the challenge it poses to many received ideas about the relationship between 'modern Muslimness' (a trope as common to Karachi's *mohajir* as to its non-*mohahjir* population) and 'popular' religion of the kind associated with the cult of local Sufi saints. It suggests, on the contrary, that the 'secular' and 'modern' Muslim—here typified by his membership of the MQM in Karachi—in his turn away from the constraining influence of politics is liable to adopt the language and practices of 'multiple religiosities', including those commonly regarded as 'popular'. And while Verkaaik's conclusions are aimed primarily to challenge what he calls 'the ethnicisation of Islam', which ascribes to Mohajir religiousity a preference for 'textual' over 'lived' Islam, they are no less significant as keys to understanding the creation of common spaces that seek to transcend the polarised realm of politics. If the Dawat-i-Islami would come later to be implicated in one of the most egregious acts of violence after one of its members shot dead the Governor of Punjab, Salman Taseer, in Lahore in 2011 for recommending the reform of Pakistan's blasphemy laws, its appeal in the 1990s as the site of an alternative religiosity based on 'popular' Islam still serves as an instructive guide to the enduring power of spiritual motifs to address urban anxieties stemming from political strife and ethnic violence in Karachi.

It is worth noting that even today most of the devotees who flock to the shrine of Abdullah Shah Ghazi in Karachi continue to be drawn from the city's Urdu-speaking *mohajir* population, with much the same working and lower middle-class backgrounds at ease with both the 'modern' discourse of the MQM and the more 'popular' language of religious piety they once associated with the Dawat-i-Islami. But the shrine also serves as a magnet for Karachi's non-Muslim communities, who include Christians and Hindus. Their participation has been strongly encouraged since 2005 when the MQM-led local government oversaw an extensive programme to renovate the shrine complex. Although judged by some critics to be a deplorable example of garish 'modernisation', Karachi's shrine-by-the-sea stands for many followers of Shah Abdullah Ghazi as an alternative 'communal' space, where spiritual sustenance can be set against the menace of violence and the contestations of every-day life in the city. According to the cultural critic Nadeem Paracha, poor attendance at the shrine by local Sindhis is said to stem from Sindhi perceptions of Shah Ghazi as a man of war who stands outside the pantheon of 'peace-loving' Sindhi saints, led by Shah Abdul Latif and Lal Shahbaz Qalandar (Paracha, 2014). It is precisely this setting of an ever robust language of peace against the spectacle of daily violence that could eventually define Karachi.

Their uneasy co existence is brought sharply to focus by Kausar Khan, whose poignant discussion suggests that the greatest challenge facing those who must live daily with violence in Karachi may be to recall what peace actually looks like. Indeed her graphic account of the 'ordinary' deaths of four 'extraordinary' Karachi-ites, in confirming the habitual state of violence to which Karachi has fallen prey, raises questions about whether the act itself of remembering peace has been permanently compromised: 'If we cannot see a clear solution to end violence,' she writes, 'we hope that along our journey against violence the way will appear'. Yet, there is no doubt about Khan's passionate

commitment to carve out spaces of public engagement from which to
claw back 'peace as a right'. To do so she is prepared to accept that the
exigencies of peace in Karachi may have changed forever, requiring the
application of instruments—'whispers, rumours, stories, and distortions'—that while once reserved for the circulation of hate could now
be moulded to serve the ends of a 'more positive "vital" form of dynamic
change'. A more self-aware public, a combative media, and increasingly
discriminating civil society groups all promise to serve as the new sites
for the circulation of 'whispered stories' about Karachi that narrate
tales which speak more urgently of reconciliation rather than recrimi-
nation, of living rather than dying.

In so doing, they would echo the voice of Azra Abbas, the Karachi-
based poetess whose lack of sentimentality in confronting the violence
of urban life is justly celebrated by Asif Farrukhi. With her 'gritty distinct style' Abbas captures the embeddedness of violence in the 'everyday' order of life without compromising a vision of the future as open
to the power of human negotiation. Her poem, 'When You Want to
Write a Story', charts the ambiguous and contingent course of violence that every *Karachi-wallah* will recognise: a story written about
living people:

> Who are all round you,
> Going about,
> Running here and there,
> Who leave their bed early in the morning
> And go home at the end of the day
> When their wives, mothers, sisters, children
> Wait for them,
> Or when they quarrel with each other
> In the neighbourhood,
> or on the road,
> Over some petty matter,
> Or happily
> embrace each other.[1]

---

[1] Taken from Asif Farrukhi's contribution to this volume.

References

Appadurai, Arjun, 'Spectral Housing and Urban Cleansing: Notes on Millenial Mumbai', *Public Culture*, 12, Fall (2000), pp. 627–51.

Anwer, Mooraj, 'Being Young in the Fifties', in Hamida, Khuhro, and Anwer Mooraj (eds), *Karachi: Megacity of Our Time*, second edition, Karachi: Oxford University Press, 2010, pp. 337–47.

———, 'Karachi before Prohibition', in Hamida, Khuhro, and Anwer Mooraj (eds), *Karachi: Megacity of Our Time*, second edition, Karachi: Oxford University Press, 2010, pp. 313–45.

Boivin, Michel, 'Karachi et ses territoires en conflit: pour une relecture de la question communautaire', *Herodote*, (2001/2002), pp. 180–200.

Ewing, Katherine Pratt, 'Anthropology and the Pakistani National Imaginary', in Naveeda Khan, *Beyond Crisis. Re-evaluating Pakistan*, London: Routledge, 2010, pp. 531–40.

Gayer, Laurent, *Karachi. Ordered Disorder and the Struggle for the City*, London and New York: Hurst & Co., 2014.

Hasan, Arif. 'The Growth of a Metropolis', in Hamida Khuhro and Anwer Mooraj (eds), *Karachi: Megacity of Our Time*, second edition, Karachi: Oxford University Press, 2010.

Inskeep, Steve, *Instant City. Life and Death in Karachi*, New York: Penguin, 2011, pp. 171–95.

Paracha, Nadeem, Farooq, 'Abdullah Shah Ghazi: the saviour saint', *Dawn*, 23 November 2014, http://www.dawn.com/news/1145799, last accessed 27 Sept. 2015.

Ring, Laura, *Zenana. Everyday Peace in a Karachi Apartment Building*, Bloomington: Indiana University Press, 2006.

Shaikh, Farzana, *Making Sense of Pakistan*, London: Hurst & Co., 2009.

———, 'Will Sufi Islam Save Pakistan?', in Bashir Shahzad and Robert Crews (eds), *Under the Drones. Modern Lives in Afghanistan and Pakistan*, Cambridge: Harvard University Press, 2012, pp. 174–91.

———, 'Pakistan and the Languages of Islam', in Michel Wieviorka, Laurent Levi Strauss and Gwenaelle Lieppe (eds), *Penser Global: Internationalisation et Globalisation Des Sciences Humaines et Sociales*, Paris: Editions de la Maison des Sciences de l'Homme, 2015, pp. 419–39.

Zamindar, Vazira, '1947: Recovering Displaced Histories of Karachi', in Michel Boivin, and Matthew Cook (eds), *Interpreting the Sindhi World*, Karachi: Oxford University Press, 2010, pp. 169–95.

AFTERWORD II

Kamran Asdar Ali

The following poem '*Aik Din*' (One Day) is by the late Zeeshan Sahil.
Sahil emerged as an important Urdu poetic voice in the late 1980s.
Despite his early death, he left behind several published volumes of work.

Every day in the city
Everyone is fearful to roam around
Of the incoming bullet that could kill us
Those who are shot either die or their wounded bodies wait for their
turn in the hospital
Everyday news of death
Everyday a heap of burnt cars
Newspaper
Like a sparkler (*phool-jhadi*)
From day break to sunset
Keeps on flickering in our hand

Seeing people die
Does not make us cry anymore
Our hearts have smoke instead of pain
Running away from the gun fire from the cars
We trample everything
Nothing concerns us

213

Even when we hear the cries of women who take refuge in the shops
We do not run to help them
Rather seeing the police mobiles and armoured cars approaching
We change directions
Hearing the sirens of the fire brigade or ambulances
We do not say a word
We just clench our teeth and try to swallow our sleeping pills
We put the pillow on our face
And sleep until another similar day dawns.

(Sahil, tr. Ali, 1995)

Written in the 1990s, Sahil's verse reminds us of Azra Abbas' poem 'Eye Witness' that Asif Farrukhi translates in his contribution to this volume. Both poems are about Karachi's violence. Both register the indifference that has made us immune to the horrific scenes of killing and death. These episodes have either become good dinnertime stories—as in Abbas' poem, 'Hot and Fresh for Tonight's Dinner'—or we turn our backs on them and sleep. The act of story-telling itself can become a pathological way of relishing someone else's pain. Perhaps as new stories emerge they substitute those urban legends of violence and ghost stories that we grew up with in Karachi, for example 'the woman at Cheel Kothi' or 'the Hathora murders'. Likewise, taking tranquilizers to sleep and shutting out noise with a pillow on our faces hints at the damage to our collective psyche. Both sensitive and creative voices, Abbas and Sahil lead us into a world of conflict and contradiction, ambiguity and doubt, that many sociological or journalistic renderings may not able to completely capture.

Like the poets, this volume informs us how after the 1980s Karachi gradually became an unsafe place filled with ethnic, sectarian, religious, and social tension. The chapters narrate different periods of this violence, and they collectively search for an incipient moment when 'all this started'. The seminal moments in such narratives include the early Zia era, the rise of the ethno-nationalist Mohajir Qaumi Movement (now Muttahida Qaumi Movement), the schoolgirl Bushra Zaidi's death in a bus related accident in 1985, and the 1986 Sohrab Goth incident and its aftermath in Orangi. This narrative arc then leads to the anti-MQM action in the early 1990s, the violence perpetuated by the MQM and its splinter groups, the subsequent violence by sectarian and other Islamic groups, and the state violence of the security services. Yet there could be other narrative timelines for the same period. The 1980s, always remembered as the dreaded Zia era, is also the decade when the Orangi Pilot Project was initiated in Karachi, when left-wing activists started theatre groups such as *Dastak*, when the women's movement Tehreek-e-Niswan and the Women's Action Forum organised activities in the city, and the centenary of Karl Marx's death was celebrated at the Karachi Press Club. Such renditions are also valid histories. Assembling them and other histories creates the narrative mosaic that helps us understand the multiple social continuities and ruptures that remain with us until now.

This is what the volume seeks to accomplish, by bringing together different genres of writing (academic, literary, journalistic) drawn from an experiential knowledge of the city. Further, echoing the sensitivity of those poets discussed above, several contributions to this volume provide an understanding of how we have become immune to the violence in Karachi. Through the use of life histories, autobiographies, and media stories they help us to literally navigate Karachi's alleyways to bring the city alive—ironically in an atmosphere that is permeated with death—in multiple ways. For example, in Nichola Khan's contribution to the volume, separate from her introduction, we find ourselves immersed in stories that take us into the lanes of Lalu Khet (Liaqatabad). She shares with us some everyday, mundane, and also absurd aspects of violence (such as the burying of guns on the Lyari River banks, comprising a cache that might be discovered when construction is completed for a highway designed to run along it). Khan guides us through the lives of some who lived and died in this area during the state-sponsored violence against the MQM in the early 1990s. Her chapter traces the history of young men who conducted violence for the ethno-nationalist party, and it highlights their ambivalence towards their actions. While the violence perpetuated by these men numbs them, it has a transformative effect on the ethnographer. Like the protagonists in the poems above, Khan's chapter and others attend to the psychological cost that all of us pay.

The self-reflexivity that Khan shares is important to underscore here because it represents a methodological shift that enables the reader to view the position of the narrator, and that opens up the text to a range of readings. This lack of closure is also present in Laurent Gayer's essay. He too uses life histories to show how an assortment of motivations can be simultaneously at play in the formation of a violent foot soldier in the service of a political group—and his use of Danny Hoffman's and Janet Roitman's work on West and Central Africa adds useful comparative resonance. Both Khan and Gayer use the biographical mode to track the ways in which violence seeps into lives of ordinary young men in Karachi. These histories may not necessarily be generalised and they do not give us a complete picture of the social and psychological reasons why these men perpetuate the most heinous forms of violence without remorse or justification. However, they do give us a glimpse into the emotional landscape, in a given time-frame, that compels some young men in Karachi to choose this path. Of course these lives must be analysed in terms of ways they are also linked to political agendas and to leaders who use young men to selectively spread fear, terrorise the populace, and create the politics of silencing and censorship. These shifting modes of state, media, and institutional violence are compellingly and quite terrifyingly described in Razeshta Sethna's chapter.

On one hand, the ethnographic focus by authors like Khan and Gayer allow us entry into intersections of individual lives with the production of violence. On the other, Arif Hasan cogently reminds us about the city's other pasts, and perhaps futures. His chapter emphasises changes in Karachi's cosmopolitan character that are sometimes lost in our focus on 'killing fields' and 'deaths'. Hasan, as Khan does in her introductory chapter, reminds us that historically social violence and class hierarchies have always been woven into Karachi's very fabric, as indeed in any large city. Yet he compels us to look at, as well as beyond, the more visible forms of violence in order to identify and attend to those social phenomena that are present in the margins, do not get relayed, and remain inaudible. We can sense this in the first part of Khan's chapter: in her descriptions of life in the alleyways, the *paan* shops, the kite-flying, and the local bakery selling *naan khatai*. Certainly, in a volume on violence, one should expect the essays to be on violence in the city. This is not to critique the excellent work by each contributor here. But as I have been given the task of writing a commentary on the topic, I seek to humbly push the envelope to see if there are other ways to narrate the city we call Karachi.

Expanding the evolving mosaic of representations offered in this volume, let me offer some examples from my own earlier work. My approach to violence in Karachi is shaped particularly through the registers of women's experience, labour struggles, and movements. An anthropologist by training, I am well aware of representations of Karachi in social science literatures. In recent years these have primarily focused on the rise of ethnic and sectarian violence, its topographical distribution across Karachi's neighbourhoods, the ascendance of the Muttahida Qaumi Movement, work on housing and infrastructure, and conflicts over resource distribution. Although the essays here contribute to filling this gap, the literature has sometimes ignored how violence filters through to the public, domestic, mundane, and everyday experiences of urban women. Thinking about these lives can add some necessary additional perspectives on female experiences and on other marginal voices in the urban milieu.

Women and the city

We are all aware that social changes over past decades in Pakistan have forced large numbers of women from all classes to work in the traditional and non-formal sectors of the economy. Owing to economic pressures and the dissolution of extended families in urban areas many more women are engaging in wage labour. Women are leaving domestic spaces to work in the expanding service sector as bank clerks, schoolteachers, office workers, and more. All this is profoundly affecting marriage patterns and household formations, as Arif Hasan's essay illustrates. Of course, in urban areas the poorest women have always left their homes to work as midwives, domestic servants, urban labourers, sweepers, or maids. Many poor urban women also remain at home and sell manufactured goods to middlemen for compensation. The proliferation of global media, the expanding nature of consumerist desires, and the addition of women to the labour force, particularly at the bottom rungs, have produced many conflicting and contradictory ideas about women's place in Karachi society. While working women challenge many historical conservative and religious ideas, the proliferation of conservative dress codes may reflect strategies women employ to negotiate Karachi's hyper-masculinised public spaces, and the punitive effects these discourses have in their daily lives. Indeed feminist scholars and activists such as Kausar S. Khan have been at the forefront of documenting these changes, and the interplay of gendered, sexual, domestic, and institutional forms of violence they provoke. Karachi's working-class women use urban space for mobility and trans-gression, and for different pleasures, in the process of 'negotiating' their way through the everyday. In a social and cultural landscape of potential harassment, women regulate their movements according to the imminent threats to their bodies and emotions.

We should reflect on the uses of other representational, including literary, forms for rendering meaningful the range of women's social experience in Karachi. Thus, we might turn to women's voices from informal archives such as diaries, biographies, memoirs, poetry, and fiction—indeed, to wherever we find women speaking in non-public spaces. Here one recalls the poet and author Azra Abbas' short book, *Mera Bachpan* (My Childhood), discussed by Asif Farrukhi in this vol-ume. This text depicts a window onto Karachi's not so distant past, and onto Abbas' early life. Published in 1997, it draws us in with images of small rebellious acts by a young girl growing up in the city in the late 1950s, while she is trying to understand the world around her with all its ironies and contradictions. Told in short passages and paragraphs with dream-like sequences, mirroring the way memory works when recalled many years later, *Bachpan* shows us a world through a girl's eyes and emotions. A distinctive aspect of this memoir is the changing face of the city and the place of girls in it. Abbas fondly remembers the dusty unpaved street in front of her house where she, along with other boys and girls from her neighbourhood, would play marbles, fly kites, go to the cycle shop, rent a bike and ride it for hours. In today's con-servative climate the reader is surprised to find that in Karachi in the late 1950s and early 1960s young girls could ride bikes, even in the city's lower middle-class neighbourhoods. In the story, Abbas employs a striking motif between light, darkness, and fading light. As Abbas grows older the city outside changes, and the unpaved streets become lit with streetlights. At the same time her own life darkens with the increasing restriction of her movements to the house, and the end of her days of playing outside in the dusty road.

Abbas' remembrances echo those of the journalist and author Zeenat Hassam's memory of her childhood in the early 1960s, described in the essay '*Guzre Din, Guzarte Din*' (Past Days, Passing Days) (1996). Hassam describes how, in the middle of the afternoon, her mother would take her to meet her mother's friend and daughter. They would be ready when the pair arrived. All four would then walk over to the nearby cinema to catch the *matinée* show of the latest Indian movie—indeed, just like my own relatives did. Hassam's text, published alongside a series of essays on Karachi in the journal *Aaj*, explores her childhood in the newly developing middle-class neighbourhoods of greater Karachi (known as PECHS, after the Pakistan Employees Cooperative Housing Society). As children she, her siblings and cousins played all afternoon near and farther away from their homes in the subdivision's undeveloped plots without fear or hesitation. Hassam's nostalgia for Karachi appears through memories of a city of peace and tranquillity, with fluttering butterflies, blossoming bougainvilleas, and fruit-bearing almond and tamarind trees.

There is a poignancy in these voices and the sense of freedom lacking in generalised discussions about women's contemporary experiences in public spaces. These memories of childhoods across Karachi were ironically published and read in the mid-1990s, when the city was ridden with ethnic violence, police action, kidnappings, burglaries, and car snatchings. In their continuity into present discussions of women in the public sphere, the narratives demarcate a more serious differentiation. Women today face constant struggles to maintain their safety in Karachi's public spaces, and must also battle the sense of threat and foreboding that all the essays in this volume have captured in various ways. These earlier prose poems may form a social nostalgia which is 'peaceful' only to people from certain classes and ethnic backgrounds. Like anywhere, Pakistani women of different strata and economic class have varied histories and variegated abilities to negotiate state-imposed and social restrictions. The public harassment and domestic surveillance of working women serve classed forms of state, religious, and patriarchal control over female desires for specific freedoms. Where men easily present themselves as 'bathing in the crowds of the city' the mobility of women, particularly working women, is constrained by moral discussions about sexuality, domestic responsibility, and the corruption of public space by their presence. These are complex urban stories of violence that require more attention. We also need many more depictions of women's lives—in all their unruly, contradictory, and angry aspects—in order to more fully bring women out of the space of discursive and representational invisibility. Many similarities exist between women's experiences of violence and those of labourers in Karachi's working classes. Requesting to indulge in the reader's patience, I turn to these next.

Workers and their struggles

At Independence in 1947 Pakistan inherited only 9 per cent of the total industrial establishment of British India. The lack of industrial capital characterised the weakness of organised industrial labour (Shaheed 1983, 270–90). The first phase of private industrialisation occurred in the early 1950s, when the profits gained by Pakistani traders were channelled into industrial investment. The state also relied heavily on agricultural exports, specifically East Pakistani jute, to subsidise industrial development in West Pakistan (Papaneck, 1967). Special areas were developed in Karachi, the Sindh Industrial Trading Estate (SITE), and Landhi-Korangi industrial area. Land was sold to construct factories at generous rates. With the state's role in setting up industries, the state bureaucracy became intrinsically involved in controlling industrial expansion. Between 1947–1955, 774 new industries were established in Karachi, representing almost 50 per cent of all Pakistan's industrialisation (Salar 1986). Sowing the seeds of structural inequality instituted by the state and private sectors working together, state agencies directly financed the industrial concerns, or else participated in passing laws to favour growth. On one hand, the collusion of the bureaucracy and industrialists facilitated the flow of finance for the expansion of industrial groups that were controlled by different families (for example, Adamjee, Dawood, Saigol, Isphahani, Valika). On the other hand, the alliance kept wage rates down and ensured the suppression of the working class. State-sponsored repressive measures increased, alongside worker unrest. The deteriorating social and economic conditions of the working classes, and the disparity in income levels in the 1950s, resulted in several labour strikes. In autumn 1951 in Karachi, left-wing trade unions oversaw organised strikes by the employees of Hotel Metropole, one of the poshest hotels in the city, as well as the Transport

Workers Union, the Pakistan Tobacco Company, and the oil companies Burmah Shell, Standard Vacuum and Caltex. Between 1954 and 1957 more than 250 strikes in Karachi involved more than 200,000 workers (Salar 1986).

General Ayub Khan's military takeover in 1958 intensified forms of violent repression against labourers. The next decade saw bureaucrats and ex-army officers directly running major industrial units. This was an era of unprecedented growth in the wealth and holdings of Pakistan's major industrial houses. As industrialists moved into banking and insurance they acquired the funds for further expansion. Pakistan's growth was heralded by economists from the United States as a model for the rest of the Third World, and a premier example of 'free enterprise'. Throughout the 1960s retrenchment and dismissals were common tools for disciplining workers. Workers' frustrations finally erupted in the March 1963 demonstration in the Sind Industrial Trading Estate (SITE) area, led by the Mazdoor Rabita Committee (Workers Coordinating Committee) (Naqvi 2003). The police fired on demonstrating labourers, and killed several workers. This incident led to the increased radicalisation of organised workers, and to mass arrests of their leadership. The industrialists were encouraged by the state response, and continued with their policy of dismissals and retrenchment. The trade union leaders who lived through this and subsequent labour struggles witnessed first-hand how the state bureaucracy used the labour courts, industrialists used their jobbers, and masters paid strong-arm men and the police to violently suppress the labour movement. This early coalition of violence established between the state and private business continued workers' repression.

Pakistan's reliance on foreign capital for industrialisation faced a major setback when World Bank funds were cut off after the 1965 war with India and then resumed at much lower levels. As the industrialisation process was largely built on the inflow of foreign capital, growth began to sputter. Bad harvests in 1965 and 1966, and the demand of the East Pakistani middle classes for a more equitable share of the spoils of development, intensified political turmoil (Alavi, 1983). In 1968–9, Ayub Khan's much heralded 'decade of development' ended abruptly when students, intellectuals, the urban poor, and the working classes all participated in a massive civil disobedience movement. Spearheaded by the

Pakistan People's Party (PPP) in the West and the Awami League in the Eastern province, the movement opposed the political bankruptcy of the Ayub regime, deteriorating economic conditions, and increasing inequalities in wealth distribution. By the end of the 1960s the concentration of wealth in Pakistan resided with twenty-two families who controlled 87 per cent of the banking and insurance and 66 per cent of the industrial wealth of the country (Ali 1970; Burki 1988).

Consequently a new military regime assumed power, promising social and political reform. One of its first tasks was to call a tripartite labour conference and work on a new labour ordinance. The registration of unions was made easier, and where there was more than one union in an industry an electoral system was devised to choose collective bargaining agents. While the ordinance criticised earlier labour laws and industrialists who used extra-legal means to curtail trade unionism's growth, in practice the regime remained committed to preventing strikes that were undermining production (Ahmed, 1970). Legal proceedings in military courts and the arrests of labour leaders, workers and other pro-democracy activists persisted unabated. The military regime also gave industrialists virtual freedom in hiring and firing decisions. In Karachi alone almost 45,000 workers were retrenched between 1969 and 1971 (Shaheed 1983, 270–90).

At the same time, after decades of state repression the ordinance also brought new energy into the labour movement. Taking advantage of the clauses for registration and constituting collective bargaining agents, moribund and underground unions began reviving. New alliances were made as communist groups and student activists assisted the working-class leadership in reorganising their trade unions. Before long, in response to the sustained repression of its leaders, an alternative trade union leadership took root. These workers started to demand bonuses, better working conditions, back pay, and they protested against unfair dismissals. I document elsewhere the nascent labour movement in Karachi in the early 1970s, and its brutal suppression by the elected government of Zulfiqar Ali Bhutto in 1972 (Ali, 2005). Re-reading this earlier work I see hints at the changes in social and historical processes that subsequently led to the substantive decline of labour and class-based politics, alongside the emergence of a different politics of publicking and counterpublicking increasingly shaped by issues of ethnic, religious, and sectarian difference.

This said, some voices enable us to penetrate the life and times of that period and they also help us to remember the kind of violence that the state perpetuated against its own working classes. Towards this end let me share an extract from an extended interview I conducted in 1998 with an activist and labour leader of the era, Aziz ul Hasan. Hasan was one of the main labour leaders during the mobilisation of labourers in October 1972 in Landhi-Korangi in Karachi:

> My parents came from Ghazipur, India. They died when I was young. I completed my matriculation in 1968. I needed to work, I heard they were recruiting at Dawood Textile Mills. Many prospective workers had gathered at the mill entrance and were waiting to be selected by the labour officer. It was customary for the officers to come out of the factory gate and select people from the assembled crowd. I was wearing my kurta pyjama, and standing with a very sad, forlorn expression. Perhaps seeing this expression the labour officer gestured towards me, and I got the job that day. Soon after I started work, some of my brother's friends who were close to an underground Maoist group, approached me to organize the workers in Dawood Mill. I had already been politicized due to my brother's involvement in union work. In those days there was no labour policy, the management had its own union through which it controlled the workers. These were called pocket unions. I started to work with other comrades to create a union of our own. Noticing my activities, the management gave me harsh duty hours. So I worked as an operator in the nylon department, and they put me with four others so they could keep an eye on me. It was a time of much labour oppression. People were harassed and beaten up by goons who worked for the company if they raised a voice against the management.
>
> In the early 1970s we created a charter of demands for the workers in our factory. Once when we were demonstrating, possibly April 1970 for back pay and the reinstatement of dismissed labourers, the police charged on us with batons. There were arrests; some arrestees were taken to the factory owner's personal office, stripped naked, and beaten with canes. We were told the owner himself would pay the police a sum of money for each lash. I too was picked up and taken to the police station. They took my clothes off and beat me severely. I still recall the names of my torturers. This continued for almost three weeks. The person in charge had a foul mouth, used the most abusive language, and constantly asked me the names of the party members I was working for. They taunted me of being a communist involved in creating a Red Guard, and accused me of being part of a bloody revolution plotted by my seniors. After days of torture I could barely lie on my back, or walk properly.

We were then put in a lock-up and charged with several cases under martial law regulations. We were presented in a martial law summary court in front of military judges. They convicted us all in all cases. When my colleague Shahnawaz objected that he was not Raji Mohammad, under whose name his case was registered, and proceeded to give his and his father's name, the presiding judge calmly changed the names and upheld the conviction. I spent fourteen months in Karachi Central Jail. I was released on bail around the time Bhutto came into power.

I admit I could not have survived those days without my comrades; they cared for me in all respects. At times I would lose hope and give up trade union work, but people would come and encourage me, give me sustenance, and help me back into active politics.

Such life histories are important in many respects. They also allow us to reflect on generational shifts amongst young men from working- or lower-middle-class backgrounds who choose different media to express their politics. The life histories by Khan, Gayer, Kirmani, and Paracha in this volume show how young men from the margins of society (similarly to the labour activist above) joined ethnic outfits, whether these were student organisations or political groups. Perhaps in an earlier era these same men may have entered working class and union politics based more inclusively around class. The life-story is valuable in untangling the shifts between and within political generations—and in the counterpoint they provide to analyses at the level of ethnicity or class.

Looking ahead

In her PhD dissertation, Saikat Maitra analyses the rapidly proliferating spaces of consumption such as shopping malls, upscale cafes, and gated communities in Kolkata. Underclass bodies that labour in Kolkata's service sector embody certain codes of cosmopolitanism that bring success at work by attracting upper-class consumers with spoken English and modern comportment. At the same time, workers themselves are prohibited from the 'good life' they aspire to and see around them. While they work in the 'dream-worlds' of luxurious commodities and branded lifestyles, the reality of de-industrialisation linked to low wages, worsening job security, and the lack of state protection make precarious living. Maitra highlights how these inherent contradictions in workers' lives create boredom, rage, and exhaustion. This response differs from the violent capital-labour antagonisms and radical socialist politics of Kolkata's past involving the Communist government and Naxalite struggles of the early 1970s. Rather, it is the recalcitrant workers' bodily capacities that remain an ever-present hindrance to value extraction and efficient productivity. This marks for Maitra the contested nature of contemporary capitalism in the Indian urban context.

Maitra's argument about Kolkata's 'dreamlike' present may have relevance for Karachi. Karachi too witnessed the suppression of labour movements in the seventies by a popularly elected government. The proliferation of malls, elite cafés, and gated communities which exclude underclass labourers from the good life is also clearly recognisable. In cities like Kolkata and Karachi we can hence see, in addition to violent deaths, ways in which the violence of contemporary capitalism manifests in contradictory registers of hope and despair, constitutionalism (democracy) and deregulation, controlled markets and speculative exuberance, anti-modern nostalgia and progressive narratives. No wonder then that uncertainty and fear are constitutive cultural, political, and affective responses to these processes.

In Karachi changes in labour patterns, diminished long-term industrial jobs and a proliferation of service sector and informal sector employment are happening alongside severe levels of ethnic, sectarian, religious, criminal, political, and state-sponsored violence. According to the Human Rights Commission of Pakistan these claimed around 3,200 deaths in 2013 alone, one of the worst years of such deaths in the city's history. The intimate toll on academics and activists, families, and communities is compellingly described by Kausar S. Khan in her chapter. As Kirmani also shows, the yearly accumulation of deaths also sustains a pervasive fear. This is the fear of poverty, unemployment, workplace abuse, the random eruption of ethnic and sectarian conflict that may engulf livelihoods and loved ones, and the fear of domestic and sexual violence. These experiences need placing within Karachi's particular urban vocabularies of fear and risk, occurring as they do within a heightened sense of social vulnerability about the present and the future.

In response to these real and imagined forms of fear and violence, the state invariably reacts to what it terms 'popular pressure' by increasing violent surveillance and security measures of its own. Police and paramilitary actions have periodically continued since the 1990s, frequently with the approval of the middle classes. These include deaths in military operations, police encounters, and torture in custody. Roadblocks, searches, unauthorised arrests, and general harassment by the law enforcement agencies, particularly of the urban poor, create other anxieties. Hence, alongside the violence perpetuated by religious and political groups and criminal gangs, state violence creates the double binds of structural violence and employment uncertainty, and the terror of violence that is unexplained and un-redressed.

The question for me, and this book, becomes how the city heals and recuperates after long decades of violence? How might we imagine a (therapeutic) process of social, economic, and cultural healing? Following the cultural geographer Nigel Thrift, cities like Karachi do bounce back from periodic crises, and while people's mundane everyday lives are transformed by violent events they also continue in meaningful and creative ways (2005, 133–50). Thrift argues, albeit for Western cities, that despite the vulnerability of cities to epidemics, natural disasters, terrorist attacks, and violent conflict, cities continually undergo processes of social repair and maintenance. He suggests that by focusing on everyday practices of people themselves, a different register of understanding cities and their future politics may emerge. This politics is not always dependent on an analysis of conflict and friction. Rather it is grounded in living with disagreements and in creating consensus.

I find this formulation theoretically productive for understanding ways that people in Karachi, despite the endemic interpersonal, social, and political violence that affects working-class neighbourhoods, do co-exist, share resources and work together. One way to follow this argument might be to focus on the everyday experiences of working-class men and women who enter the public space as they set off to perform various kinds of labour (domestic, service sector, industrial) across the city. Their experiences might enable us to explore the contours and possibilities for a future politics for Karachi based on the challenges and compromises of co existence. Rather than blind optimism this implies the need for more detailed public understandings of people's intimate lives. This might nudge us towards imagining a different political space where in a spirit of co-living, disagreements can be managed in a general gesture of kindness and tacit agreements with others about how to get by (Thrift, 2005).

Karachi's poor neighbourhoods reveal distinct possibilities. People do fall in love with the 'wrong' ethnicity. Arif Hasan reminds us that in earlier times Karachi's public universities allowed much more for the mingling of different classes. A boy from Nazimabad could marry a girl from Clifton or Defence, as in my own case. Perhaps because of previous intermarriages, a couple might share a heritage more similar than it initially appears. I do not mean to undermine the reality of social conflict and ethnic violence in Karachi's neighbourhoods, but rather I emphasise ways that women and men do recombine contingent relationships, as well as bodies, spaces, signs and infrastructures, in order to connect with varied modes of living in their different communities.

Finally, in addition to our discussions on fear, violence and ethnic conflict, we need to continue to seek analytical rigour and empirical insight in making and imagining possibilities of co-operation between people from different backgrounds and persuasions. Perhaps this might also comprise a kind of class solidarity, or a new form of 'publicking'. In surprising ways, people's shared lives in Karachi's multi-ethnic and potentially violent poor neighbourhoods reveal spaces of civic agreement, shared rules, and reciprocal obligations. These hint at an underexploited counter public, or perhaps a new public politics of co existing with difference. Understanding these processes and building on them may be some first steps towards a political sense of repair—one that can allow for a more enduring peace.

References

Abbas, Azra, *Mera Bachpan*, Karachi: Aaj Publications, 1997.

Ahmed, Mohammed, 'The New Labour Policy', *Dawn*, Karachi, 13 December 1970.

Alavi, Hamza, 'Class and state', in Hassan Gardezi and Jamil Rashid (eds), *Pakistan: The Roots of Dictatorship. The Political Economy of a Praetorian State*, London and Delhi: Zed Press, Oxford University Pess, 1983, pp. 40–93.

Ali, Kamran Asdar, 'Strength of the State Meets the Strength of the Street: The 1972 Labor Struggle in Karachi', *International Journal of Middle East Studies*, February (2005), pp. 83–107.

Ali, Tariq, *Pakistan: Military Rule or People's Power*, New York: W. Morrow, 1970.

Burki, Shahid Javed, *Pakistan under Bhutto*, London: Macmillan Press, 1988.

Hassam, Zeenat, '*Guzre Din, Guzarte Din*' in *Karachi Ki Kahani*, compiled by Ajmal Kamal, *Aaj*, Winter (1996), pp. 151–85, Karachi.

Human Rights Commission of Pakistan, 'State of Human Rights in 2013', Human Rights Commission of Pakistan, March 2014; http://www.hrcp-web.org/hrcpweb/report14/AR2013.pdf, last accessed 22 Feb. 2016.

Maitra, Saikat, *Laboring to Create Magic: The New Worker in the Emerging Retail Industries of Kolkata*, PhD dissertation (Anthropology), Austin: University of Texas, 2014.

Naqvi, Nayab, *Yakam March 1963 Ki Mazdoor Tehreek. Aik Pas Manzar*, Karachi: PILER and Pakistan Study Centre, University of Karachi, 2003.

Papaneck, Gustav, *Pakistan's Development*, Cambridge, Harvard University Press, 1967.

Sahil Zeeshan, 'Aik Din'. In *Karachi Aur Doosri Nazmain*, (trans.) Kamran Asdar Ali, Karachi, Aaj, 1995.

Shaheed, Zafar, 'Role of the Government in the Development of the Labour Movement,' in Hassan Gardezi and Jamil Rashid (eds), *Pakistan: The Roots of Dictatorship. The Political Economy of a Praetorian State* London: Zed Books, 1983, pp. 270–90.

Thrift, Nigel, 'But Malice Aforethought: Cities and the Natural History of Hatred', *Transnational Institute of British Geography*, 30, 2, 2005, pp. 133–50.

SELECT BIBLIOGRAPHY

(scholarly works cited, and further relevant works)

Abbas, Azra, *Neend Ki Musafatain*, Karachi: Jadeed Classic Publishers, 1981.

———, *Maiz Par Rakhay Haath*, Karachi: Jadeed Classic Publishers, 1988.

———, *Mera Bachpan*, Karachi: Aaj Ki Kitabain, 1995.

———, *Main Linain Khenchti Hoon*, Karachi: Jadeed Classic Publishers, 1996.

———, *Mera Bachpan*, Karachi: Aaj Publications, 1997.

———, *Kicking Up Dust*, Lahore: ASR Publications, 1996 (1981), trans. Samina Rahman.

———, *Voyages of Sleep*, Karachi: Pakistan Association for Women's Studies, 1998 (1981), trans. Yasmeen Hameed.

———, *Raastay Mujhay Bulatay Hain*, Karachi: Scheherzade, 2001.

———, *Hairat Kay Us Paar*, Karachi: Scheherzade, 2006.

———, 'Seven Poems from the Far Side of Wonder', *Annual of Urdu Studies* 22, 2007, pp. 271–274, trans. Muhammed Umar.

Ahmad, Tania, 'Bystander Tactics: Life on Turf in Karachi', *South Asia Multidisciplinary Academic Journal* (SAMAJ), 5, 2011, http://samaj.revues.org/3537, last accessed 21 Mar. 2016.

——— 'Socialities of indignation: denouncing party politics in Pakistan', *Cultural Anthropology*, 29, 2, May (2014), pp. 411–32.

Ahmed, Feroz, *Ethnicity and Politics in Pakistan*, Karachi: Oxford University Press, 1999.

Akhtar, Saleem, *Pakistani Shairaat: Takhleeqi Khado-o-Khal*, Lahore: Sang e Meel Publications, 2008.

Alavi, Hamza, 'The State in Post-Colonial Societies: Pakistan and Bangladesh', *New Left Review*, 74, July–August (1972), pp. 59–81.

———, 'Class and State', in Hassan Gardezi and Jamil Rashid (eds), *Pakistan: The Roots of Dictatorship. The Political Economy of a Praetorian State*, London and Delhi: Zed Press, Oxford University Pess, 1983, pp. 40–93.

————, 'Nationhood and Communal Violence in Pakistan', *Journal of Contemporary Asia*, 21 (2), 1991, pp. 152–78.

Albinia, Alice, *Empires of the Indus*, London: John Murray, 2009.

Ali, Kamran, Asdar, 'Strength of the State meets the Strength of the Street: The 1972 Labor Struggle in Karachi', *International Journal of Middle East Studies*, (February) 2005, pp. 83–107.

————, 'Men and Their 'Problems': Notes on Contemporary Karachi', in Asdar Ali, Kamran and Martina Rieker, *Comparing Cities: The Middle East and South Asia*. Oxford University Press, 2009, pp. 49–64.

————, 'Women, Work and Public Spaces: Conflict and Coexistence in Karachi's poor neighbourhoods', *International Journal of Urban and Regional Research*, 36, May (2012), pp. 585–605.

Ali, Tariq, *Pakistan Military Rule or People's Power*, New York: W. Morrow, 1970.

Anderson, Benedict, *Imagined Communities*, London: Verso, 1995.

Ansari, Sarah, *Life After Partition. Migration, Community and Strife in Sindh, 1947–1962*, Oxford University Press, 2005.

Anwer, Mooraj, 'Being Young in the Fifties', in Hamida, Khuhro, and Anwer Mooraj (eds.), *Karachi: Megacity of Our Time*, second edition, Karachi: Oxford University Press, 2010, pp. 337–47.

————, 'Karachi before Prohibition', in Khuhro Hamida and Anwer Mooraj (eds.), *Karachi: Megacity of Our Time*, second edition, Karachi: Oxford University Press, 2010, pp. 313–45.

Appadurai, Arjun, 'Spectral Housing and Urban Cleansing: Notes on Millenial Mumbai', *Public Culture*, 12, Fall (2000), pp. 627–51.

Aretxaga, Begoña, *States of Terror: Begoña Aretxaga's Essays*, in Joseba Zulaika (ed.), Reno, Nevada: Center for Basque Studies, 2006.

Aretxaga, Begoña, 'Madness and the Politically Real: Reflections on Violence in Postdictatorial Spain', in Mary-Jo DelVecchio Good (ed.), *Postcolonial Disorders*, Berkeley: University of California Press, 2008, pp. 43–61.

Baig, Noman, God and Greed. Money and Meditation in Karachi's Marketplace, PhD dissertation (Anthropology), Austin: University of Texas, 2014.

Baillie, Alexander, *Kurrachee, Past, Present and Future*, Rarebooksclub.com, 2013 (1839).

Bakhtin, Mikhail, *Speech Genres and Other Late Essays*, Austin: University of Texas Press, 1986, trans. Vern McGee.

Banerjee, Mukulika, *The Pathan Unarmed*, Karachi: Oxford University Press, 2000.

Benjamin, Walter, 'Theses on the Philosophy of History', in *Illuminations*, trans. Harry Kohn. New York, Schocken Books, 1968 (1937), pp. 253–64.

Bhabha, Homi, *The Location of Culture*, New York: Routledge, 1994.

Biehl, João, *Vita: Life in a Zone of Social Abandonment*, Berkeley: University of California Press, 2005.

Blok, Anton, 'The Peasant and the Brigand: Social Banditry Reconsidered', *Comparative Studies in Society and History*, 14, September (1972), pp. 494–503.

Blom Hansen, Thomas, *Violence in Urban India. Identity Politics, 'Mumbai' and the Postcolonial City*, Delhi: Permanent Black, 2005 (2001).

———, *Wages of Violence. Naming and Identity in Postcolonial Bombay*, Princeton University Press, 2004.

Blom Hansen, Thomas and Fenn Stepputat, 'Introduction', in *Sovereign Bodies: Citizens, Migrants and States in the Postcolonial World*, Princeton: Princeton University Press, 2005, pp. 1–36.

Boivin, Michel, 'Karachi et ses territoires en conflit: pour une relecture de al question communautaire', *Herodote*, (2001/2002), pp. 180–200.

Bollas, Christopher, *Cracking Up*, New York: Hill & Wang, 1995.

———, *Free Association*, Birmingham: Ikon Books, 2002.

Bourdieu, Pierre, *Outline of a Theory of Practice*, Cambridge University Press, 1977.

Brass, Paul, *The Production of Hindu-Muslim Violence in Contemporary India*, University of Washington Press, 2003.

Burki, Shahid Javed, *Pakistan under Bhutto*, London: Macmillan Press, 1988.

Butalia, Urvashi, *The Other Side of Silence. Voices from the Partition of India*, London: Hurst & Co, 2000.

Chatterjee, Partha, *The Nation and its Fragments. Colonial and Postcolonial Histories*, Princeton University Press, 1993.

Chaudhry, Lubna, Nazir, 'Reconstituting Selves in the Karachi Conflict', *Cultural Dynamics*, 16, October (2004) pp. 259–90.

Collins, Randall, *Violence. A Micro-sociological Theory*, Princeton: Princeton University Press, 2008.

Comaroff, Jean and John L. Comarof (eds.), *Law and Disorder in the Postcolony*, University of Chicago Press, 2006.

Das, Veena, *Life and Words. Violence and the Descent into the Ordinary*, Berkeley: University of California Press, 2007.

———, *Affliction*, New York: Fordham University Press, 2015.

———, 'Adjacent Thinking: A Postscript', in Roma Chatterji (ed.), *Wording the World. Veena Das and Scenes of Inheritance*, New York: Fordham University Press, 2015, pp. 372–99.

Das, Veena, Arthur Kleinman, Margaret Lock, Mamphela Ramphele, and Pamela Reynolds (eds), *Remaking a World. Violence, Social Suffering and Recovery*, Berkeley: University of California Press, 2001.

Davis, Mike, *City of Quartz*, London: Verso, 1990.

———, *Planet of Slums*, London: Verso, 2003.

Deleuze, Gilles and Félix Guattari, *Capitalism and Schizophrenia, vol. 2. Anti-Oedipus*, New York: Penguin, 2009 (1972), trans. Robert Hurley.

SELECT BIBLIOGRAPHY

DelVecchio Good, Mary-Jo, Sarah Hyde, Sarah Pinto, and Byron Good (eds), *Postcolonial Disorders*, Berkeley: University of California Press.

Ewing, Katherine Pratt, 'Anthropology and the Pakistani National Imaginary', in Naveeda Khan, *Beyond Crisis. Re-evaluating Pakistan*, London: Routledge, 2010, pp. 531–40.

Farmer, Paul, *Pathologies of Power*, Berkeley: University of California Press, 2005.

Farrukhi, Asif, *Look At The City From Here. Karachi Writings*, Karachi: Oxford University Press, 2010.

Farrukhi, Asif and Frances Pritchett, *An Evening of Caged Beasts. Seven Postmodernist Urdu Poets*, Karachi: Oxford University Press, 1999.

Fassin, Didier, 'Why Ethnography Matters. On Anthropology and its Publics', *Cultural Anthropology*, 28, 4, November (2013), pp. 621–46.

Feldman, Allen, 'Violence and vision: the prosthetics and aesthetics of terror', *Public Culture*, 10, 1, Fall (1997), pp. 24–60.

Freud, Sigmund, *The Neuropsychoses of Defence*, 'Project', Standard edition, Vol 3, London: Hogarth Press, 1966 (1894).

Gayer, Laurent, 'Guns, Slums, and "Yellow Devils": A Genealogy of Urban Conflicts in Karachi, Pakistan', *Modern Asian Studies*, 41, May (2007), pp. 515–44.

————, *Karachi: Ordered Disorder and the Struggle for the City*, London and New York: Hurst & Co., 2014.

Gazdar, Haris, 'Karachi battles', *Economic & Political Weekly*, 17 September 2011, pp. 19–21.

Gilsenan, Michael, *Lords of the Lebanese Marches: Violence and Narrative in an Arab Society*, London: I.B. Tauris, 1996.

Goffman, Erving, *Asylum. Essays on the Social Situation of Patients and Other Inmates*, New York: Anchor Books/Doubleday, 1961.

Good, Byron, 'Theorizing the "Subject" of Medical and Psychiatric Anthropology', *Journal of the Royal Anthropological Institute*, 18, August (2012), pp. 515–535.

Green, Linda, 'Fear as a Way of Life', *Cultural Anthropology*, 9, 2, May (1994), pp. 227–56.

Gul Khattak, Saba, 'Violence and the centrality of home: women's experiences of insecurity in the Karachi Conflict', Working Paper series *73, Islamabad: Sustainable Development Policy Institute, 2002.

Haider, Waseem and M. Aslam Chaudhry, 'Prevalence of Alcoholism in the Punjab, Pakistan', *Biomedica*, 24, July (2008), pp. 80–84.

Hameed, Yasmeen, *Pakistani Urdu Verse. An Anthology*, Karachi: Oxford University Press, 2010.

Hamid, Omar Shahid, *The Prisoner*, New York: Arcade Publishing, 2015.

Hasan, Arif, *Understanding Karachi. Planning and Reform for the Future*, Karachi: City Press, 2000.

————, 'The Political and Institutional Blockages to Good Governance: The case of the Lyari Expressway in Karachi', *Environment and Urbanisation*, 2, 2005, pp. 127–41.

————, 'Demographic Change and its Social Repercussions: The Case of Karachi', *International Development Planning Review*, 31, August (2009), p. 229.

————. 'The Growth of a Metropolis', in Hamida, Khuhro, and Anwer Mooraj (eds), *Karachi: Megacity of Our Time*, second edition, Karachi: Oxford University Press, 2010, pp. 171–95.

————, *Karachi: The Land Issue*, Karachi: Oxford University Press, 2015.

Hassam, Zeenat, '*Guzre Din, Guzarte Din*' in *Karachi Ki Kahani*, compiled by Ajmal Kamal, *Aaj*, Winter (1996), pp. 151–85, Karachi.

Hobsbawm, Eric, *Primitive Rebels. Studies in Archaic Forms of Social Movement in the 19th and 20th Centuries*, New York and London: W. W. Norton and Co. 1959.

Hoffman, Danny, *The War Machines. Young Men and Violence in Sierra Leone and Liberia*, Durham: Duke University Press, 2011.

Hoodbhoy, Nafisa, *Abroad the Democracy Train*, Delhi and New York: Anthem Press, 2011.

Howell, Elizabeth, *The Dissociative Mind*, New York and Hove: Routledge, 2005.

Hughes, Everett, Cherrington, *The Sociological Eye. Selected Papers*, New Brunswick/London: Transaction Books, 2009 (1951).

Hussain, Akmal, 'The Karachi riots of December 1986: Crisis of State and Civil Society in Pakistan', in Veena Das (ed.), *Mirrors of Violence. Communities, Riots and Survivors in South Asia*, New Delhi, Oxford University Press, 1990, pp. 185–93.

Hussein, Aamer, *Hoops of Fire: Fifty Years of Fiction by Pakistani Women*, London: Saqi Books, 1999.

Imtiaz, Huma, 'Kingdom of fear', *The Express Tribune*, 18 July 2010, http://tribune.com.pk/story/27844/kingdom-of-fear/, last accessed 15 Feb. 2014.

Inskeep, Steve, *Instant City. Life and Death in Karachi*, New York: Penguin, 2011.

Jackson, Michael, 'Custom and Conflict in Sierra Leone: An Essay on Anarchy', in *Existential Anthropology. Events, Exigencies and Effects*, New York: Berghahn Books, 2005, pp. 53–74.

Jalal, Ayesha, *The Sole Spokesman. Jinnah, the Muslim League and the Demand for Pakistan*, Cambridge University Press, 1998.

————, *Democracy and Authoritarianism in South Asia. A Comparative and Historical Perspective*, Cambridge University Press, 1995.

————, *The Pity of Partition. Manto's Life, Times, and Work across the India-Pakistan Divide*, Princeton University Press, 2013.

Jalil, Rakhshanda, *New Writings from India and Pakistan*, New Delhi: Tranquebar, 2013.

Jaspers, Karl, *General Psychopathology, vols. 1 & 2*, Baltimore and London: Johns Hopkins University Press, 1997 (1913), trans. J. Hoenig and Marian W. Hamilton.

Kaker, Sobia, 'Enclaves, Insecurity and Violence in Karachi', *South Asian History and Culture*, 5, December (2013), pp. 93–107.

Kapferer, Bruce, 'How Anthropologists Think: Configurations of the Exotic', *Journal of the Royal Anthropological Institute*, 19, November (2013), pp. 813–37.

Kaur, Raminder (ed.), *Religion, Violence and Political Mobilisation in South Asia*. New Delhi: Sage, 2005.

Khan, Naveeda (ed.), *Beyond Crisis. Re-evaluating Pakistan*, London, New York, Delhi: Routledge, 2012.

Khan, Nichola, *Mohajir Militancy in Pakistan. Violence and Practices of Transformation in the Karachi Conflict*, London and New York: Routledge, 2010.

———, '*Naturalising Politics; Politicising Nature: Ethnicity, Violence and the Indus in Sindh*'. Keynote Address, 22nd Annual Conference of World Sindhi Congress, London, 28 August, 2010.

———, 'Violence, anti-/convention and desires for transformation amongst Pakistan's Mohajirs in Karachi', *Cultural Dynamics*, 22, November (2010), pp. 225–46.

———, 'The Poetics of Violence', Book Review of *Karachi: Ordered Disorder and the Struggle for the City* by Laurent Gayer (Hurst and Co.). *The Herald*, November (2014), pp. 87–9.

Kirmani, Nida, *Questioning 'The Muslim Woman': Identity and Insecurity in an Urban Indian Locality*, New Delhi: Routledge, 2013.

Kleinman, Arthur, Veena Das, Margaret Lock (eds), *Social Suffering*, Berkeley: University of California Press, 1997.

Laing, Ronald. D., *The Divided Self*, London: Penguin, 1960 (2010).

Lambek, Michael, *Ordinary Ethics. Anthropology, Language, and Action*, New York: Fordham University Press, 2010.

Lari, Yasmin and Mihail Lari, *The Dual City. Karachi During the Raj*, Karachi: Oxford University Press, 1996.

Leader, Darian, *What is Madness?*, London: Penguin, 2012.

Mahmoud, Saba, *Politics of Piety. The Islamic Revival and the Feminist Subject*, Princeton University Press, 2005.

Maitra, Saikat, Laboring to Create Magic: The New Worker in the Emerging Retail Industries of Kolkata, PhD dissertation (Anthropology), Austin: University of Texas, 2014.

Malik, Iftikhar, *Religious Minorities in Pakistan*, London: Minority Rights Group International, 2002.

————, *State and Civil Society in Pakistan*, London: Macmillan, 1997.

Michalak, Laurence and Karen Trocki, *Alcohol and Islam*, New York: William S. Hein & Co., 2006.

Moghadam, Valentine, 'Patriarchy and the Politics of Gender in Modernising Societies: Iran, Pakistan and Afghanistan', *International Sociology*, 7, 1, March (1992), pp. 35–53.

Mumtaz, Khawar and Farida Shaheed, *Women of Pakistan. Two Steps Forward, One Step Back*, London: Zed Books, 1987.

Nadeem, Azhar, Hassan, *Pakistan. The Political Economy of Lawlessness*, Karachi: Oxford University Press, 2002.

Naqvi, Nayab, *Yakam March 1963 Ki Mazdoor Tehreek: Aik Pas Manzar*, Karachi: PILER and Pakistan Study Centre, University of Karachi, 2003.

Nasr, Seyyed, Vali, Reza, *The Vanguard of the Islamic Revolution*, Berkeley: University of California Press, 1994.

————, *Islamic Leviathan. Islam and the Making of State Power*, New York: Oxford University Press, 2001.

Nayyar, Abdul Hameed, and Salim Ahmad, *The Subtle Subversion*, Islamabad: SDPI Publications, 2004.

Orangi Pilot Project, *Katchi Abadis of Karachi. Volume One: The First Hundred Katchi Abadis Surveyed*, Karachi: Orangi Pilot Project, 2002.

Papaneck, Gustav, *Pakistan's Development*, Cambridge, Harvard University Press, 1967.

Piliavsky, Anastasia and Tommaso Sbriccoli, 'The Virtue in Efficacy: Goonda Raj (Rule of Strongmen) and Political Authorisation in Northern India', *Democratic Cultures* conference, King's College, Cambridge University, 5 September 2014.

Rahman, Tariq, *Language and Politics in Pakistan*, Karachi: Oxford University Press, 1996.

Rashid, Ahmed, *Taliban. Militant Islam, Oil and Fundamentalism in Central Asia*, New Haven: Yale University Press, 2001.

Rehman, Zia Ur, *Karachi in Turmoil*, Islamabad: Narratives, 2013.

Ring, Laura, *Zenana: Everyday Peace in a Karachi Apartment Building*, Bloomington: Indiana University Press, 2006.

Roitman, Janet, *Fiscal Disobedience. An Anthropology of Economic Regulation in Central Africa*, Princeton University Press, 2005.

Sahil Zeeshan, 'Aik Din'. In *Karachi Aur Doosri Nazmain*, Karachi: Aaj, 1995, (trans.) Kamran Asdar Ali.

Sami, Abdus, *Urdu Mein Nasri Nazm*, New Delhi: Idara Tehqeeq, 2014.

Schafer, Jessica, 'Guerrillas and Violence in the War in Mozambique: De-Socialization of Resocialization', *African Affairs*, 100, April (2001), pp. 215–37.

Scheper-Hughes, Nancy and Phillipe Bourgois, (eds.), *Violence in War and Peace. An Anthology*, Oxford: Blackwell Publishing, 2004.

Shaheed, Farida, 'The Pashtun-Muhajir Conflicts 1985–6: a national perspective', in Veena Das (ed.), *Mirrors of Violence: Communities, Riots and Survivors*, New Delhi: Oxford University Press, 1990, pp. 194–214.

Shaheed, Zafar, 'Role of the Government in the Development of the Labour Movement,' in Hassan Gardezi, and Jamil Rashid (eds), *Pakistan: The Roots of Dictatorship*, London: Zed Books, 1983, pp. 270–90.

Shaikh, Farzana, *Making Sense of Pakistan*, London: Hurst & Co., 2009.

———, 'Will Sufi Islam save Pakistan?', in Bashir Shahzad and Robert Crews (eds.), *Under the Drones: Modern Lives in Afghanistan and Pakistan*, Cambridge: Harvard University Press, 2012, pp. 174–191.

———, 'Pakistan and the Languages of Islam', in Michel, Wieviorka, Laurent Levi Strauss, and Gwenaelle Lieppe (eds), *Penser global: internationalisation et globalisation des sciences humaines et sociales*, Paris: Editions de la Maison des Sciences de l'Homme, 2015, pp. 419–39.

Siddiqa, Ayesha, *Military Inc. Inside Pakistan's Military Economy*, London: Pluto Press, 2007.

Singh, Brighupati, *Poverty and the Quest for Life. Spiritual and Material Striving in Rural India,* University of Chicago Press, 2015.

Slimbach, Richard, 'Ethnic Binds and Pedagogies of Resistance. Baloch Nationalism and Educational Innovation in Karachi', in Paul Titus (ed.), *Marginality and Modernity: Ethnicity and Change in Post-Colonial Balochistan*, Karachi: Oxford University Press, 1996, pp. 138–67.

Strauss, Anselm, Leonard, *Social Organization of Medical Work*, New Brunswick: Transaction Publishers, 1997.

Syed, Ghulam Murtaza, *Sindhu Desh: A Study in its Separate Identity Through the Ages*, Karachi: G. M. Syed Academy, 1990.

Taussig, Mick, 'Terror as Usual: Walter Benjamin's Theory of History as a State of Siege', *Social Text*, 23, Autumn-Winter (1989), pp. 3–20.

———, *The Nervous System*, New York: Routledge, 1992.

———, *The Magic of the State*, New York: Routledge, 1997.

———, *Shamanism, Colonialism and the Wild Man. A Study in Terror and Healing*, University of Chicago Press, 2001.

Tambiah, Stanley, *Leveling Crowds. Ethnonationalist Conflicts and Collective Violence in South Asia*, Berkeley: University of California Press, 1996.

Tanweer, Bilal, *The Scatter Here is Too Great*, New York: HarperCollins, 2014.

Thrift, Nigel, 'But Malice Aforethought: Cities and the Natural History of Hatred', *Transnational Institute of British Geography*, 30, 2, 2005, pp. 133–50.

Verkaaik, Oskar, 'At Home in Karachi: Quasi-Domesticity as a Way to Know the city', *Critique of Anthropology*, 29, March (2009), pp. 65–80.

———, 'Fun and Violence. Ethnocide and the Effervescence of Collective Aggression', *Social Anthropology*, 11, 1, February (2003), pp. 3–22.

———, *Migrants and Militants. 'Fun' and Urban Violence in Pakistan*, Princeton University Press, 2004.

SELECT BIBLIOGRAPHY

Warner, Michael, *Publics and Counterpublics*, New York: Zed Books, 2002.

Weiss, Anita and Gilani, S. Zulfiqar, (eds), *Power and Civil Society in Pakistan*, Karachi: Oxford University Press, 2001.

Wilkinson, Iain and Arthur Kleinman, *A Passion for Society. How We Think about Human Suffering*, Berkeley: University of California Press, 2016.

Yusuf, Huma, *Conflict Dynamics in Karachi*, Washington: United States Institute for Peace, 2012.

————, 'The Convergence of Old and New Media During the Pakistan Emergency', in McLagan, Meg, and Yates McKee (eds.), *Sensible Politics. The Visual Culture of Nongovernmental Activism*, New York: Zone Books, 2012, pp. 183–211.

Zaidi, Akbar S., 'Politics, institutions, poverty: the case of Karachi', *Economic & Political Weekly*, 20, December (1997), pp. 3282–93.

Zamindar, Vazira, '1947: Recovering Displaced Histories of Karachi', in Michel Boivin, and Matthew Cook (eds.), *Interpreting the Sindhi World*, Karachi: Oxford University Press, 2010, pp. 169–95.

Zulaika, Joseba and William Douglass, *Terror and Taboo. The Follies, Fables and Faces of Terrorism*, New York: Routledge, 1996.

237

INDEX

INDEX

Kunwari Colony, 78; Landhi Industrial Area, 65; Landhi-Korangi, 223; Liaquatabad, 18, 41–3, 45, 49–51, 54, 215; Lucky Star, 138, 142; Lyari, 70, 103–9, 111, 113, 115, 117–18; Manora Island, 1; Metrovel, 78; Mingophir, 78; Muslim (Mohajir) population of, 1–2, 41–3, 66, 69–70, 82–3, 121–2, 125, 129–30, 137, 175, 210; National Highway, 97–8; Nazimabad, 12, 49, 69, 145, 227; night life in, 175–7; Orangi, 12, 21, 173, 190, 192, 197–8, 214; Paradise Point, 1; Parsi population of, 174; Pashtun Abad, 78; Pashtun population of, 41, 45, 63, 65–6, 68, 71–3, 82, 106, 112, 125, 202; performing arts culture of, 184–5; PIB Colony, 45, 48, 51; Pipri, 65, 78; Pirabad, 78–9; political landscape of, 10; Qasba Colony, 78; Saddar, 138, 175; Sandspit, 1; Seaview, 1; Shah Latif Town, 78; Sherpao Colony, 78; Sindh Industrial Trade Estate (SITE), 65, 112, 220; Sindhi Hotel, 45, 49–50; Sindhi population of, 63–4, 66; Sohrab Goth, 65, 150, 214; Sultanabad, 65; Taliban presence in, 156; Tariq Road, 145; TTP presence in, 77–9; violence in, 2, 4–5, 9–11, 17, 43, 49–50, 52–3, 105, 153–4, 158–9

Karachi Literature Festival: 11, 165–6, 207

Karachi Municipal Corporation: 90

Karachi Population Census Report (1981): findings of, 181

Karachi Port Trust (KPT): 69

Karachi Press Club: 215; arrests outside (2007), 163

Karachi Strategic Development Plan 2020 Survey: findings of, 182

Karachi Water and Sewerage Board (KWSB): 69

Khan, Abdul Waheed: background of, 191–2; murder of (2013), 191–3

Khan, Ayub: 109, 125; opposition to, 221–2; regime of, 128, 147, 221; rise to power (1958), 221

Khan, Imran: leader of PTI, 193

Khan, Kausar S.: 191

Khan, Liaquat Ali: 45

Khan, Naveeda: 4, 14

Khan, Nichola: *Mohajir Militancy in Pakistan* (2010): xiii, xxiv, 23, 61, 100, 119

Khan, Riaz Ahmad: 182

Khan, Sher: murder of, 77–8

Khan, Tariq: leader of *jirga*, 70

Khan, Wali: 70, 76

Khatta, Amin: opposition to *jirga*, 70

Khattak, Sadiq Zaman: murder of, 80

Khilafat Movement: 108

Kleinman, Arthur: 16

Kurin, Richard: observations of public image of Mohajirs, 126

Kutchi Rabta Committee: conflict with PAC supporters, 113

Kutchis (ethnic group): 108; political representation of, 113; territory inhabited by, 105

Laing, Ronald: view of psychosis, 53

Latif, Shah Abdul: 210

Leader, Darian: view of psychosis, 53

Mustapha, Zubaida: 191
Muttahida Majlis-e-Amal (MMA): members of, 74; supporters of, 71
Muttahida Organising Committee: as PPOC, 74
Muttahida Qaumi Movement (MQM): 9, 18, 47–8, 52, 68–9, 75–6, 88–92, 95–9, 107, 111–12, 121–4, 132–4, 140, 156, 159, 193, 208, 214, 217; burning of newspaper offices, 157; coalition with Islami Jamhoori Ittehad (1990–2), 157; conflict with ANP, 72, 74–5, 83, 159; conflict with PPP, 110–11, 150; Coordination Committee, 75; electoral performance of (2008), 72; formation of (1984), 41; ideology of, 88, 128–9; media coverage focusing in, 156–60; members of, 19, 54, 58, 75–6, 85, 126–7, 130, 194; militants, 18, 21, 49–51, 92–3, 194; military operations targeting, 47; Nine Zero raids (2015), 59, 157; offices of, 110; political rhetoric of, 54–6; supporters of, 42, 121, 132–3, 158, 209; targeting of Lyari, 103, 115–16; Union Council, 91–2

National Arts Council: 11
National Association of Performing Arts (NAPA): 207; establishment of (2005), 184
National Film Development Corporation (NADDEC): 178
National Students Federation (NSF): 146, 148
nationalism: 73; Baloch, 115; Basque, 57; ethno-, 66, 214;

Hindu, 128; Islamic, 125; Pakistani, 127; radical, 57; Sindhi, 97; state, 3, 136, 145
Nawaiwaqt: suicide attack on offices of (2000), 10
Naz, Saniya: 104; first female MPA, 104
NED University of Engineering: APMSO-PSF conflict at, 149–50
neo-Marxism: 2, 43
Netherlands: Rotterdam, 190
News, The: 169; editorial staff of, 160; offices of, 162
Newsline: editorial staff of, 158
Noorani, Uzma: 191
North Atlantic Treaty Organization (NATO): presence in Afghanistan, 68
Northern Alliance: 81
Nurani, Uzma: 188

oil price crisis (1973): 136
Omar, Mullah: 81; death of, 82
Operation Clean-Up (1992): 47; political impact of, 158
Operation *Rah-e-Nijat* (Path to Salvation)(2009–12): 67
Operation Zarb-e-Azb (2015): 157; media coverage of, 166
OPP-Research and Training Institute (OPP-RTI): 190
Orangi Pilot Project (OPP): 97, 173–4, 191; establishment of (1980), 189–90, 215; personnel of, 189–90, 192

Pak American Cultural Centre: 179, 185
Pakhtunkhwa Milli Awami Party (PkMAP): 71, 74
Pakistan: 1, 3, 6, 14, 19, 27, 42, 47, 54, 58, 67, 85, 99–100,

125, 127, 133, 136, 153, 161,
170–1, 178, 184, 191, 204;
Bajaur, 65, 67, 76; Bannu, 68;
Constitution of (1973), 69; Dir,
76; economy of, 1–2; Federally
Administered Tribal Areas
(FATA), 64–5, 68–9, 71, 76, 83,
154, 190; film industry of, 180;
government of 66, 165; IDPs
in, 66; Independence of (1947),
2, 26, 43, 48, 174–6, 200,
220; Islamabad, 162–4, 168–9;
Khyber Pakhtunkhwa, 64–7,
69–70, 73, 76, 79, 83; Kohat,
68; Lahore, 137, 150, 161, 176,
210; Lakki Marwat, 68; military
of, 3, 83, 94–5; Mohmand, 76;
Muree, 138; National Assembly,
138; North Waziristan, 68,
78, 166; North West Frontier
Province (NWFP), 64, 66, 71,
125; Peshawar, 63, 67–8, 147,
165; Provincial Assembly, 138;
Punjab, 138–9; Quetta, 63, 82,
168, 195–6; Rawalpindi, 138;
Saddar, 148; Sindh, 71–2, 106,
121, 139–40, 150, 158; Sorabh
Goth, 76; South Waziristan,
65–6, 76–7; Supreme Court,
162; Swat, 66, 67, 76–8, 80, 168
Pakistan Electronic Media
Broadcasting Authority
(PEMRA): formation of (2000),
162; Ordinance (2007), 162;
threats of issuing notices to TV
channels, 160
Pakistan Employees Cooperative
Housing Society (PECHS): 219
Pakistan Institute of Labour
Education: 'I am Karachi'
(2014), 63
Pakistan Medical Association
(PMA): 191

Pakistan Music Conference: 11
Pakistan Muslim League (PML):
members of, 193
Pakistan Muslim League-Nawaz
(PML-N): 69–71, 116; supporters of, 167
Pakistan National Alliance (PNA):
136, 138, 143; conflict with PPP,
176; members of, 136
Pakistan People's Party (PPP): 20,
69, 71, 115, 140, 193, 203–4,
221–2; conflict with MQM,
110–11, 150; conflict with PNA,
176; electoral performance
of (1970), 136, 146; electoral
performance of (1977), 137–8,
146; electoral performance of
(2008), 72; electoral victory of
(2008), 193; founding of (1967),
135; ideology of, 125; Karachi
division of, 108; media pundits
of, 167; members of, 70, 72,
74, 83, 108, 112–13, 204–5;
Peoples Students Federation
(PSF), 146–9; political alliances
of, 72; presence in Lyari, 108–9;
purging of, 136; supporters of,
74, 88, 93, 108
Pakistan Tehreek-e-Insaf (PTI):
194; founding of (1996), 69;
members of, 80, 193–4; supporters of, 159, 194–5
Pakistan Tobacco Company: 221
Pappu, Arshad; family of, 109; killing of Faiz Mohammad (2003),
110
Paracha, Nadeem: 210
Parsis (ethnic group): employment
of, 174, 203; women's fashion,
179
Pasha, General Shuja: 170
Pashto (language): 63, 65